THE
AS IT HAPPENS
FILES

THE
AS IT HAPPENS
FILES

For Eric –
A loyal listener –

MARY LOU FINLAY

Thanks
Mary Lou Finlay

ALFRED A. KNOPF CANADA

For David

PUBLISHED BY ALFRED A. KNOPF CANADA

Copyright © 2008 Mary Lou Finlay

All rights reserved under International and Pan-American Copyright Conventions.
No part of this book may be reproduced in any form or by any electronic or
mechanical means, including information storage and retrieval systems, without
permission in writing from the publisher, except by a reviewer, who may quote
brief passages in a review. Published in 2008 by Alfred A. Knopf Canada, a division
of Random House of Canada Limited. Distributed by
Random House of Canada Limited, Toronto.

Knopf Canada and colophon are trademarks.
www.randomhouse.ca

LIBRARY AND ARCHIVES CANADA CATALOGUING IN PUBLICATION

Finlay, Mary Lou
The As it happens files : radio that may contain nuts / Mary Lou Finlay.
ISBN 978-0-307-39662-4

1. As it happens (Radio program). 2. Interviews—Canada. 3. Radio
journalism—Canada. I. Title.

PN1991.77.A8F55 2008   791.44'72   C2008-903176-8

Text design: Leah Springate

First Edition

Printed and bound in the United States of America

2 4 6 8 9 7 5 3 1

CONTENTS

INTRODUCTION

A few months after taking my leave of the CBC and my job hosting *As It Happens,* I tuned in one night to hear this listener's phone call:

> *The sale of a 36-year-old ham-and-cheese sandwich half-eaten by Richard Nixon: this is why I listen to the CBC. This is why I love* As It Happens.

The caller was expressing what thousands of people from across Canada and around the world have told us for years: however good we may be at covering the Big Story, it's the half-eaten-by-Richard-Nixon-ham-and-cheese sandwiches that really stick in their minds.

As It Happens is the Canadian Broadcasting Corporation's second-longest-running current affairs show (*Ideas* is the longest), and on good days it still sounds younger and brighter than almost anything else on the dial. I can say this because I don't claim credit for it; I think the credit is due mainly to the format devised in the early years by Mark Starowicz and exploited so brilliantly by a succession of producers and hosts, including Barbara Frum and Al Maitland. Basically, it's a phone-out show that daily chases down the stories the producers find most beguiling and delivers up people for one of the hosts to talk to. On any given day, the topics may range from war in Chechnya to a nettle-eating contest in Yorkshire and anything in between. Sprinkled among the interviews are bits of music and readings and recorded speeches and humour that add colour and texture.

The show has been drawing fans to CBC Radio from around the world for 40 years. When I left, over one hundred U.S. stations were broadcasting *As It Happens,* and we were breaking new ground at home; the ratings at that time put AIH in first place in its time period in the very competitive Toronto and Vancouver markets. Not that markets are a prime concern since CBC Radio is commercial free, deriving its financial support from a government-mandated annual taxpayer subsidy.

Perhaps it's because CBC Radio doesn't have to worry about advertising sales that it's developed into such a different animal than its TV cousin, or maybe it's because radio as a medium is so different. In any case, CBC's radio arm has been more successful at creating an identity that sets it apart from its competitors at the same time as it unites Canadians across the country. What people say they like about *As It Happens,* in particular, are its breadth and depth, its fairness, its sense of humour and its ability to take them immediately to the heart of unfolding events, be they regattas, riots or bank robberies.

But above all, listeners seem to cherish the show's devotion to the odd and the eccentric. During our 30th and 35th anniversary years, when we invited the audience to tell us what they would like us to dredge up from our archives, the most common request was for Barbara Frum's Big Cabbage story, otherwise known as the Goddamn Cabbage Story (see Chapter 3).

Now, as the show celebrates its 40th birthday, it seems like a good time to remember some of the weird and wonderful people I met while hosting AIH—people like the Canadian inventor of the bear suit, the guy who walks naked across the U.K., and Mike the Headless Chicken from Fruta, California (not, strictly speaking, a person).

I couldn't write about these exotics, though, without also remembering a few of the seekers, adventurers and heroes whose tales have thrilled and moved me over the years. Their names include Ignacio Siberio, the man who wouldn't drown; Canadian astronauts Roberta Bondar and Julie Payette; and Mike Stevens, who brought music and hope to a remote village where both were in short supply.

Sometimes the people make the story, and sometimes it's the story that brings forth the people. It was 9/11 that introduced us to Kathie Scobee Fulgham. As the daughter of the man who was in command of the space shuttle *Challenger* when it exploded in 1986, Kathie Fulgham knows what it's like to watch your father die over and over and over again on TV. The Air India crash, recounted in Chapter 15, brought us Anant Anantaraman, who planted flowers among the ashes of his life. And the war in Iraq led us to Salam Pax, the Baghdad blogger who provided a rare insider's view of the conflict.

Combining these themes—the silly and odd, the brave and pioneering, the big news events—will result, I hope, in a kind of print version of the radio show. Of course, I've omitted more than I could include. To mention all the men and women, boys and girls, fish, pigs, turkeys and uncooperative parrots who informed and delighted me over the years would be to embark on a never-ending journey. I hope all the people who are not mentioned will forgive me. To all of them, from the bottom of my heart, a big thank you for being part of our great conversation.

To CBC Radio, too, I owe a huge debt of gratitude for having provided the opportunity, in *As It Happens,* to air this conversation and for allowing me to burrow about in the archives to retrieve material for the book.

Above all, I am beholden to my former colleagues at *As It Happens*. It's partly to honour them that I've written this, for without their dedication, patience, brains and perseverance, the show would not have lived up to the lofty standards set by its creators, and it wouldn't have been such a joy to host. I salute them and thank them. I hope I haven't misremembered too much.

ONE

The Man Who Wouldn't Drown

Radio to buoy you up

〜

In December 2004, Ignacio Siberio, a Miami lawyer, was spearfishing alongside his small power boat when a stiff wind came up and took the boat away. For about an hour and a half, he did his best to catch up to it, but in the end he had to concede defeat. Ignacio figured he was going to die. He couldn't swim to shore, because the wind was against him; he would only use up all his energy trying. No one would miss him for hours, and by the time a search was organized, it would be dark and the wind would have blown him even farther out to sea.

Then he spotted a buoy bobbing nearby. Clinging to it might just give him a slight chance of surviving. Ignacio knew that the forecast was for the wind to swing around to the north during the night. If he could get through the night alive, he could try swimming to shore when it got light. But how to stay alive until then without falling asleep and succumbing to hypothermia?

He devised a plan. First he would review the cases he was working on—go over them in every detail. He figured each case would take about two hours. When that was done, he started reviewing his life. It was amazing what he learned about himself during that exercise.

In the meantime, the wind had shifted to the north and his muscles were now rigid with cold. He knew he had to keep them from knotting or he wouldn't be able to swim when the sun rose. "Try to relax your right hand," he told himself. When that was done, he moved on to the whole arm, then to his left hand and so on until, to his surprise, he actually managed to get his whole body relaxed in the frigid water.

Still, he realized that, for all his efforts, he was probably not going to make it through. He thought how sad that would make his family and friends, and just before Christmas, too. He thought he wouldn't like to make them sad. He thought, *But I have it in my power to turn tragedy into happiness if I just don't die.* And so he made up his mind not to.

Around 10:30 the next morning, 20 hours after he'd gone into the water, Ignacio was fished out of the waves and delivered to shore. He was swimming for shore at the time.

Oh yes—and at the time, he was 80 years old.

Ignacio Siberio told us this story in the most matter-of fact tones on December 14th, the day after his rescue. He was well enough when he was pulled out of the water to be taken directly to his office—back to all those cases he was working on. I asked him if he thought an angel had been looking out for him, and he replied, "Something was. That buoy that popped up out of nowhere? It had no business being there. It was an abandoned buoy. And do you know, it had my birthdate on it! I was born on July 31; the number on the buoy was 7–31.

A magazine show like *As It Happens* is a blend of many elements—interviews, readings, music, commentary, debate— but at the heart of the programme are the stories and the often amazing people who live them. Ignacio Siberio's adventure was pure gold, of course. It was the kind of story that would put a smile on your face for the whole day, even a

Monday just before Christmas. The season of good fellow-ship and cheer was always hell around the office. The desire to give everyone a bit of extra family time in the week between Christmas and the New Year means you have to do a certain amount of prepackaging in the weeks before Christmas, which also happen to be the weeks of maximum shopping and maximum partying and cooking and visits from relatives. The result is maximum stress for everyone. By the time you bid everyone adieu on Christmas Eve and make way for Alan Maitland's reading of *The Shepherd*, you're whacked. You spend your extra time off recovering from the effort it took to get the extra time off.

This is also the season when everyone else is partying or shopping or ducking work; sometimes news is scarce, and often it's gloomy. The show that featured Ignacio Siberio included an interview with Paul Martin about his first year as Canadian Prime Minister, but there was also a story about Viktor Yushchenko, the Ukrainian leader whose face had been ravaged by dioxin poisoning; a poignant tale about a Lethbridge, Alberta, man who was about to be reunited with the four brothers and sisters he'd lost when they were all sent to different foster homes as children; and a rather scary account of personal financial information from a Canadian law office winding up in a California jail cell. It was good to have Ignacio Siberio to remind us that amid all the misery and meanness and the pure, unadulterated evil that abound in the world, there are people who refuse to die because of the unhappiness it might bring to *others*. What god in his heaven would not be stirred to pluck him from the jaws of death and restore him safely to his family (and his clients)?

More often than not, it is the suicide bombers, the assas-sins, the cheats and tyrants of the world who make headlines, along with the train derailments, ice storms, hurricanes, tsunamis, earthquakes and floods. Small wonder that people in the news business tend to have a rather gloomy view of fate and human nature. On *As It Happens,* we've told those stories, too. "We bring you the world in your radio," we tell people. It's history-in-the-making told by the people making it: the lawyers and crooks, the teachers and bums, the doctors, victims, bankers, prime ministers, presidents, movie stars, singers, scientists and Nobel Prize winners.

It's fun to have the movers and shakers at the other end of a phone line, and I know I'm lucky to have had the opportunity to chew the fat with Margaret Atwood and Judi Dench and Chubby Checker. But after eight years and more than ten thousand interviews, I find it's the Ignacio Siberios who stick in my mind even more than the big names; ordinary people more than celebrities—ordinary people who surprised us, and maybe themselves, with their escapades or their extraordinary efforts in the service of a particular goal.

I'm thinking of Donald Flickinger of Toledo, Ohio, for instance, who took 75 years to complete his university degree; he was 96 when he got his first degree—an associate degree from the University of Toledo. The ceremony was awesome, he said, but he wasn't happy that it took him so long to get it.

"Why *did* it take so much time?" I asked him.

Well, he'd started in 1928. Then came the Depression; he didn't have the five dollars per credit hour he needed to pay for his courses. Then there was the war, and after that he got married, and he travelled a lot, programming computers. There was no time to attend class regularly. For a few years, he and his wife *did* attend classes together, but then he retired and they did more travelling together until she died. Now that he did have a degree of sorts, though, he felt he should get serious about his education and get himself a *real* degree, a Bachelor of Science maybe, or a B.A. *Maybe even a new romance,* I mused.

Or how about Doug Stead, who spent over $120,000 fighting a $117 speeding ticket in British Columbia, because the ticket was based on photo radar, which he thought violated the principle of "innocent until proven guilty"? It was a principle that took precedence over more money apparently. The same perceived aversion to injustice and bullying led senior citizen Betty Hyde to crash a Royal Bank meeting in Ottawa so she could tell the President in person how outraged she was over the bank's decision to close her local branch in New Edinburgh.

"There were bankers to the left of us and bankers to the right," she said, making it sound like the Battle of Queenston Heights.

But Betty Hyde was not cowed, and shortly afterwards bank officials announced that the branch would remain open. The day we got Mrs. Hyde on the phone to tell us about her victory was her 80th birthday, and the Royal had sent her birthday greetings and a bouquet of flowers. My Ottawa spies tell me, however, that Betty Hyde is now deceased and the Royal Bank has indeed closed its doors on the people of New Edinburgh. I don't know if there was a connection.

You can't predict what will push people to the edge—and over. David and Nicola Hunt sold their house, gave up their jobs and moved 480 kilometres from Manchester to Hessenford, England, to look for a dog that had gone missing on a visit to Hessenford some weeks earlier. Now David and Nicola have gone missing; at least, I can't find them. If anyone knows where they are now, or whether Holly has been found, please let me know.

Of course, when you're talking about pets, you're entering a new dimension. We've interviewed people who've had brain surgery performed on their goldfish (What's that you say? You didn't know goldfish had brains?) and people who've given them mouth-to-mouth resuscitation. Sometimes it's the animals themselves that are bent on overcoming the odds, like the pet-store dog who was in the habit of unlatching his cage at night and then liberating all his doggie friends from *their* cages so they could come out and revel the night away.

Some of these people (and their four-footed friends) could be considered slightly eccentric perhaps. As every loyal listener knows, British eccentrics are a category unto themselves on *As It Happens,* but the breed has also been spotted elsewhere. You might want to put Jess Yeager of North Platte, Nebraska, into this group. Mr. Yeager washes his horse—actually, all his horses—at the local car wash, or at least he did until the day the police told him it was illegal. They said if he did it again, he'd be fined.

I asked him if the horses liked being run through the car wash.

"You soap the horse down, spray her off . . . they like it a lot," he said. He didn't see why it was suddenly a problem.

"I've been living here for 30 years and doing it the whole time."

Mr. Yeager said if the police couldn't show him the law that said it was illegal to wash your horse at the car wash, he'd just keep right on doing it.

Or how about the man in Grande Prairie, Alberta, who insisted on riding his horse to town and *parking* him? Apparently, this is also in contravention of the local municipal code. Would you call him eccentric? Would you say the same of the man in North Bay, Ontario, who's spent half a lifetime trying to produce the perfect bear-proof suit?

And who could forget the screaming Finns? This is a group of strong-lunged men who, for some reason that escapes me now but must have made perfect sense at the time, decided one day to start shouting clauses from the Maastricht Treaty (the European Constitution as it then was) to an audience. We were entertained by the shouting and the conversation, and when they came to Toronto, they gave a live performance in the atrium of the CBC building and popped into our studio to shout "O Canada!"

Here's a strange thing about Finland: I don't know why, but *As It Happens* has a devoted following there. Fans have written to tell us that they get up at 5:30 in the morning to listen to CBC Radio. I guess it's so dark there in the winter that five in the morning isn't too different from noon, but it has always struck me as odd that we should have forged this special link with the Finns. Perhaps it's just because *they* are odd or because Finns and Canadians are odd in the same way.

There's no limit to the weird stuff people get up to, which brings me back to the indomitable Ignacio Siberio. Two years after our conversation, I called his office in Miami to see how he was doing and whether there had been any lasting fall-out from his fishing mishap. I have to confess that I was a bit apprehensive about phoning; he was no spring chicken, after all. What if Ignacio were not among us anymore? A preposterous notion, as it turned out. He answered the phone, and we resumed our conversation as if we'd spoken the day before. I asked him first if he'd had any further adventures since we'd last talked.

"Oh yes," he said. "It happened again the next week."

"What happened the next week? You lost your boat again the next week?"

"Yes, exactly. I had lost my anchor, you see, and it was a very expens—"

"Just a second, Mr. Siberio. You lost your boat *again?* Was it the same boat? Did you recover your boat?"

"Oh yes, I got it back. It was 80 miles away when we found it."

"So you went out and you lost your anchor . . ."

"Yes. I went fishing again a few days later, and a pin came out of the anchor and I lost it. It was a very expensive anchor, so I went back to where I'd lost it and I let the boat drift to where I thought it might be and I got out to look for it. My attention was on the ocean floor and the wind shifted, and while I was swimming one way, the boat started drifting in the opposite direction. But I got it this time. It was about four blocks away when I looked up.

"You have more lives than a cat," I told him.

"More than 20," he agreed. "I've been close to death probably more than 20 times. There was the time I was hanging from a building six floors up, in my underwear, trying to get into my apartment . . ."

Here's the story: Ignacio was living in a sixth-floor penthouse at the time. It was a hot summer day, and a couple of children came to the door to ask him if he could help them get their parakeet back; the bird had somehow got tangled up in the TV aerial on the roof. Ignacio wasn't dressed, but he stepped just outside his door, to an exterior walkway, to see if he could spot the bird—and the wind blew the door shut behind him.

When the kids saw what had happened, they ran away.

"I was a young guy then," Ignacio told me. "I thought, *I won't go in this fashion to the manager.* Society was more prudish then. Today I wouldn't mind going in my underwear anywhere."

Ignacio decided that if he went up onto the roof, he might be able to lower himself to his balcony and get back into his apartment from the other side, but he miscalculated. He let himself down partway, clinging to a piece of ironwork, but he couldn't reach the balcony, and now it seemed he couldn't get back up either. His hands were sweating in the heat, and he thought, *This is it for me. Now I'm going to die.*

What was worse, he had an audience. The children had run to the vacant lot next door and, seeing his predicament, had begun to make a lot of noise, which had drawn a substantial crowd of interested onlookers.

Somehow he scrambled back to the roof and lived to tell that tale, too. I forgot to ask about the parakeet. When I finish this book, I may move to Miami and write about the further adventures of Ignacio Siberio—but first, some more tales from Radioland.

TWO

The Princess of Love

Radio fit for a king

〜

The day before I started hosting *As It Happens,* Princess Diana was killed in a car crash in a Paris tunnel. I remember turning on the radio that Sunday morning to hear the news from Michael Enright:

> *And now, just to recap: Diana, the Princess of Wales, is dead. She was killed early this morning, along with her friend, Dodi Fayed . . .*

My first reaction was shock, the way we are always shocked by sudden and untimely deaths. How could this be? She was so young, so beautiful, so . . . *alive.* And I felt sad. Sad for her, sad for her two young boys, sad even for Charles. I was sad on my own behalf, too. Diana seemed flaky at times, her marriage was a bust, and maybe she hadn't been prepared for the unique demands that marriage to a royal heir would make on her, but she was beautiful—and glamorous, too. I know this may sound ridiculous, but I think for many girls and women, Diana the Princess Bride reminded us of a time when we were very small and could imagine ourselves in the role of fairy princess dreaming of knights on white chargers.

Diana's life, though, wasn't a fairy tale, and it wasn't to be lived happily ever after. After her marriage fell apart, she pulled herself up by her Valentino straps and went back to work. She campaigned for a ban on land mines, she visited hospitals, she reached out to children dying of AIDS. She doted on Harry and William, of course, and when she learned to laugh again, her smile lit up the world. She also gave television interviews in which she revealed far too much about her private life, but that seems to be the way of a modern celebrity, royal or not.

But as we all know, bad news is good news for people who work in news—hence my second reaction, which was along the lines of "What a great story to kick off with!" As I continued hearing about Diana on that last day of August 1997, I was busy putting wine and beer on ice and setting out food for a little garden party I was throwing, a sort of getting-to-know-you affair for me and the *As It Happens* crew. Naturally, we had planned to talk about what might be put on the air the next day, which was Labour Day in Canada and the U.S. Holidays can be a problem when it comes to finding stories and people to talk about them, but there was no mystery about what the story would be this Labour Day; the only question was, who would we find to talk to?

An event like Diana's death—a Big Event—is both easier and harder than less earth-shaking stories to cover. It's easier because it's a story everyone's interested in. Easier, too, because almost everyone you can think of to call will be happy to talk to you about it on the radio, provided they're not fully booked doing other radio and television shows.

It's harder because, with all the media in the world focused on the same topic, it's a challenge to find an angle that isn't already being covered. We comforted ourselves with the thought that if people were listening to *our* programme, we could assume they weren't taking in all the other shows as well. In any case we wanted to give them the best possible coverage. I don't remember whether we had any eureka ideas that afternoon in my back garden, but early the next day, our chase producers hit the phones, and by air time we had a pretty good roster. Dame Barbara Cartland, Diana's step-grandmother, was first up:

ML: Dame Barbara, let me start by offering you, on behalf of myself and Canadians, our deepest sympathy for the loss of your granddaughter.

BC: Well, it was a terrible shock and I loved her so much for so long and she'd always been very sweet, very helpful, and cared for other people. I called her "the princess of love." She really loved people.

ML: When was the last time you saw her?

BC: I had lunch with her a fortnight ago. Also, I had a very sweet letter from her just before I left England to go up to Scotland.

She gave people her love and then people loved her simply because they felt it pulling them. You see, it's difficult to explain, but people have too little love now in this country; people feel sorry for people, they like them, but they don't actually love them. What she gave people was real love.

ML: Some people think that Princess Diana did not receive enough love in her life. What do you think?

BC: Well, she went through a very difficult time, as you know. She did have a very, very sad time, and she was very lonely at times. She was very much alone.

ML: What about the boys? You've talked about the close relationship they had. How do you think they'll cope with this?

BC: It's awful for them, and I'm so worried about them—that they'll have the right people to look after them. Of course, they go to school now, that's something. But you see, the boys—she adored the boys. When my first son went out shooting one day with the eldest one and I wrote to her that he not only shot well, he was terribly nice to all the older men, she was so pleased, so thrilled, she was almost dancing with joy that her son was such a success.

ML: She tried to protect them, I think, from some of the pressures of royalty. Who will be their guardian now?

BC: Well, I don't know. That's what I'm worrying about. Who will look after them, who will be with them, who'll understand them when they're pretty miserable and unhappy?

ML: Dame Barbara, Diana was, as I think you've pointed out before, a fairy-tale princess to millions.

BC: Oh, I've known an awful lot of people in my life, but I've never known anyone quite so sweet as she was, who minded so much about other people. She wanted to make them better, and she did, you see! If there were people in hospital— The other night, she got up at 12 o'clock, late at night, took the car herself, drove to the hospital, cheered up a man who was dying . . . and then drove back alone. And I did say to her, "You mustn't do that now in England, because things are very dangerous; they might have kidnapped you or they might have smashed you out of the car and taken the car away." She wasn't properly looked after. Of course, young girls are rather inclined to be brave about things; you and I would think twice about going out in the middle of the night alone . . . and of course, she ought to have had ladies-in-waiting with her or somebody to talk to, you see.

ML: Will you have a favourite memory of her that you will keep in your mind? A picture?

BC: I don't know anybody who was as good as she was or so sweet to other people. She was the princess of love. She really gave out love, she felt love for people. We'd have to look very, very hard to find anybody whose heart is given to love the same way.

After Dame Barbara came Lord William Deedes, former Member of Parliament and an editor with the *Daily Telegraph,* who recounted a recent trip he'd taken with Diana to Bosnia to campaign against land mines. She listened to the most gruesome stories without flinching, he said, and she never hurried people. When the day's work was done and she could relax a little, she'd tease him by pretending to offer him a G-and-T and then flourish a bottle of Evian water in front of his nose.

Diana's brother Charles Spencer said later that the Press had blood on their hands in the matter of Diana's death, but Lord Deedes said Diana had not been purely the victim of a pack of braying jackals; it was more complicated than that. She had friends among the paparazzi and the writers, and she knew how to use the media to further her own causes. A lot of people blamed the media for Diana's death, Lord Deedes said, but it was the people themselves who made the market for pictures of Diana. Later in the show, Alan Rusbridger, editor of the *Guardian,* echoed Lord Deedes's observations.

In that first programme, we also reviewed how the world Press were covering Diana's death. We talked to two military men about the desirability and possibility of banning land mines, to an Egyptian writer about the potential fall-out from the Dodi Fayed connection and to Canadian philosopher Mark Kingwell about Diana as a cultural icon. It felt like a good day's work.

Needless to say, the Diana story didn't disappear overnight. Indeed, like John F. Kennedy's assassination, Diana's tragic end will probably live on forever in conspiracy chat rooms. It will also stay in the mind of Dodi's father, Mohammed al-Fayed, who cannot seem to accept that an employee of his, the chauffeur who'd been drinking that night, may have been responsible for the deaths of the Princess of Wales and his own son.

The weeks following Diana's death were also the weeks when I was trying to shuck off the training wheels, so to speak. Getting used to the show, getting to know my co-host, Barbara Budd, and the rest. This wasn't my first crack at hosting *As It Happens*. I'd filled in for my predecessor, Michael Enright, a few times and also for Barbara Frum in the 1970s. But in those days, I had just been dropping in for a brief spot of hosting; now I was in it for the long run—or so I hoped. How would I cope?

Alex Frame, the radio Vice-President who'd appointed me, had a good deal of experience in programming. He was the producer who made Peter Gzowski a star on the radio show *This Country in the Morning*. He then accompanied Peter to the TV talk show *Ninety Minutes Live,* which didn't fare so well. It was a mistake to take radio Peter—sweet, smart, witty, folksy, funny, *rumpled* Peter—and put him into a button-down collar, Armani suit and hair gel and force him to banter with late-night TV guests who were not, by and large, the types of people who had populated his radio show. People who loved Peter on the radio watched with dismay as the debacle unfolded. The highlight of the year was when the eminent Canadian author Pierre Berton shared an appearance with a food blender and nearly chopped off the end of his finger. And then there was the night the American writer Hunter S. Thompson, well soaked in scotch or rum and god-knows-what-other drugs, launched into a profane tirade about some corporate villain whose sins were about to be exposed on the CBC's *fifth estate*.

The question for me was, was I going to be one of Frame's success stories?

"Have fun," he told me. "Make the show yours."

But what did that *mean*? And how was I to do that and still preserve the qualities that had attracted such a devoted following to the show over the years? Michael Enright has talked about how terrified he was the first time he was asked to fill in for Barbara Frum—and now I was set to follow Frum *and* Enright? What was I thinking?

At the same time, I felt that *As It Happens* didn't really belong to me or them or to any one host; it belonged to all of us and also to the army of loyal listeners whose radios came on every evening to the music of Moe Koffman's "Curried Soul." So, yes, I would try to make the show mine, but I would also try very hard not to break it. On odd days, that's what I worried about. On even days, I worried that I'd be too exhausted to make it through the week. But I sensed right from the start that this was going to be the best job I'd ever had. Over the next few months, I talked to Archbishop Desmond Tutu in South Africa about his Truth and Reconciliation Commission and to Max Sisulu, whose father had been in prison with Nelson Mandela, about Mandela's retiring as Prime Minister. I spoke with American civil rights activist Jesse Jackson and scientist Richard Leakey about politics in Kenya and with Colombian President Ernesto Samper about his country's struggle with drug lords and terrorists. We talked about the plight of women in Afghanistan and about U.N. arms inspectors getting kicked out of Iraq.

It's interesting to recall that in 1997 Bill Clinton threatened to bomb Iraq if Saddam didn't start to cooperate with the arms inspectors.

This was also the time of ethnic killings in Kosovo and school killings in Jonesboro, Arkansas, and then—Clinton and Monica Lewinsky. When I'm feeling smug, I remind myself of the day in early 1998 that a producer first raised the subject of another possible Clinton sex scandal at the morning story meeting.

"Just more unproven allegations," I sniffed, or something of the like. "Not a story."

A few days later, Monica's taped phone conversations became public. President Clinton looked into a TV lens and declared, "I have never had sexual relations with that woman," and the impeachment train pulled out of the station. To this day, I wonder why he didn't look into the lens and say, "This is none of your damn business." Would the story have gone away?

In the event, it didn't go away, and we spent many hours over the next few years following the twists and turns of the "non-story" that made Bill Clinton the second president in U.S. history to be impeached. This is what we in the media were doing while the storm clouds of 9/11 were gathering; no wonder we didn't see them coming.

In Canada in early 1998, we were also preoccupied with the ice storm that had toppled power lines and left millions of people freezing in the dark; with the Krever Report on Canada's tainted blood supply; with the Somalia Inquiry into the treatment of Somalis by Canadian soldiers; with Robert Latimer, imprisoned for euthanizing his severely disabled daughter; with teachers' strikes, land mines and global warming.

(Yes, we'd heard of it even before Al Gore made the movie.) At an APEC conference in Vancouver, the RCMP fended off protesters with pepper spray and Prime Minister Jean Chrétien made jokes about it.

All this material was leavened with the usual assortment of strange animals, big vegetables, eccentrics and music. Producers George Jamieson, Bob Coates and Brooke Forbes, in particular, were always on the alert for an opportunity to play some jazz, blues or gospel music—often at the passing of some lesser-known guitarist or drummer or singer or arranger. Barbara Budd liked to add her own accompaniment, but she wouldn't let me sing along, claiming—somewhat cruelly, I thought—that my singing voice was unlistenable and I couldn't carry a tune. But after being instructed in the art of using exploding paper bags for cannon crashes, we did both play along with Erich Kunzel and the Cincinnati Symphony Orchestra one night as they performed Tchaikovsky's *1812 Overture*. It wasn't my fault that my bag didn't go off at the right moment; it was a defective bag.

The only time I ever got to sing on *As It Happens* was one Hallowe'en night when Barbara was away and we decided to mark the occasion—Hallowe'en, not Barbara's absence—by playing the 1962 hit "Monster Mash" and talking to the artist, Bobby "Boris" Pickett. When he agreed to perform live on the radio and invited me to join in . . . well, it would have been rude to refuse, wouldn't it? Oddly enough, the world did not come to an end.

Goldfish were very popular in my first season at *As It Happens*, especially the Old Goldfish, aged 42, and Sharky the Goldfish, the one who underwent an operation to have a brain tumour removed. Dr. Charles Coleman of Richmond, Washington, told us that when he first saw Sharky, the tumour had grown so big that the fish was swimming upside down. For the surgery he knocked him out by putting anaesthetic in the water and probing him and monitoring his breathing until he was sure the fish was unconscious. Then he cut out the tumour, cauterized the exposed tissue and—Bob's your uncle—Sharky was saved. There wasn't any post-op infection either; maybe our people hospitals could take some pointers from the vet.

The most amazing part of the story was that Dr. Coleman's bill was only one hundred dollars. He was grateful to have had the experience, he said. But the PR didn't hurt, I guess. When I talked to him again for this book, he told me that his practice was going great guns and he was in the midst of a major expansion, moving into new quarters in Richmond. He also said he was now heavily into holistic medicine for animals: acupuncture, herbs, homeopathy, animal chiropractic. Changing his diet had saved his own life, he claimed, and he was very keen to promote good nutrition for animals.

I asked Dr. Colson if he'd done any more fish surgery. He said there'd been six more after Sharky, including an angel fish with a tumour.

Sharky himself is no longer with us, alas. He developed another growth on his head about three months after his surgery and died not long after that of a necrotic liver. And if your fish needs an operation, you should know that the price has now gone up to between five and six hundred dollars.

Speaking of animals, some of you may also remember a story from that time about Zippy Chippy the Losingest Race-horse (85 losses and no wins at the time of the interview) and Barney the Dinosaur suing the San Diego Chicken for copyright infringement—not, strictly speaking, an animal story, but so fitting, don't you think, in that most litigious of countries to the south of us. Then there was the Memphis lawyer who was suing his partner for oinking in the office, or was it the other way around? It may have been the oinking lawyer who was suing his former partner for unfair dismissal. Either way, it was rib-tickling fun.

And that, of course, reminds me of Bonnie and Clyde, the pigs on the lam. (*Real radio, not ham radio.*) It was the middle of January 1998 when two wild boar saved their bacon by escaping from an abattoir in Malmesbury, England (about 80 miles northwest of Reading). Jeremy Newman, the abattoir's owner, told us how the pigs had made a break for it when they were being unloaded from a farmer's truck. They went through a fence, across the road and, with several men in pursuit, piggy-paddled across a river and disappeared into the fields beyond. They were spotted a day or so later, hanging out in someone's back yard, but by then, Mr. Newman had made up his mind that these pigs had earned their freedom. He wasn't going after them and neither was the farmer, and that was the right sentiment for residents of the town where Thomas Hobbes was born.

Before Malmesbury a Canadian pig had gone AWOL out west, and the media had dubbed him Francis Bacon. (Bacon was a near contemporary of Thomas Hobbes, by the way. Coincidence?) At any rate, we had only to drop the merest hint—"What should we call the runaway pigs?"—and our phone lines lit up: *Butch Cassidy and the Sundance Pigs, Bonnie and Clyde, Thelma and Louise, Ed and Flo, Runaway Pork and Big Bertha, Piggly Wiggly and Greased Lightning, Rasher and Dancer, Sook Sook and Yuk Yuk, Bubble and Squeak, Bangers and Mash* and *Bangers and Dash* were some of the offerings from our listeners.

A man from Edmonton said he could think of no better names for a couple of fast-moving hogs than *Harley and Davidson,* and a San Francisco caller named our pigs *Footloose and Fancy Free* and wished them, "Good luck if you're listening." I don't think the CBC phone lines had received so many calls on one topic since the day they pre-empted *Coronation Street*.

In the end, I didn't die from exhaustion in the first year and a half, and I didn't kill the show either; I just got hooked.

THREE

Cabbages and Kings

Radio that's a gas

⌐

The genius of *As It Happens* as a concept is that it can be anything you want to make it, and it has always romped from the Grave-and-Important to the Silly-and-Preposterous and back again with great ease. Like a well-balanced diet, it offers up a nutritious daily helping of hard news—the meat and veg—and garnishes it with a variety of other stories—the *amuse-bouches,* palate-cleansing sorbets and desserts. Kings and queens there have been, as well as various other noblemen, presidents, prime ministers, advisors and hangers-on. It was easier to get the high-profile guests on the air before all-news TV, the hundred-channel universe and the Internet made competing demands for their time and attention and before the spin doctors took control of the politicians and their agendas, but the AIH chase producers can still land the big fish when they have to.

But first the cabbages.

In November 1998, *As It Happens* celebrated its 30th anniversary. We decided to put the audience front and centre for the occasion, inviting them to write lyrics for the opening theme and to speak up about their favourite stories from the past. Barbara Frum's interview with former Maple Leaf Gardens owner Harold Ballard was a popular favourite, as were Michael Enright's lesson in worm charming and Al Maitland's moist experience with a beaver, but the most requested blast from the past was Frum's encounter with the Big Cabbage. As regular listeners know, we rarely pass up an opportunity to celebrate the growers of giant vegetables. The standard line of questioning isn't hard to imagine: *How big? How heavy? . . . What did you feed it?* But on one occasion in 1976, Frum's questions to Farmer McLaughlin in Bristol, England, were falling on deaf ears—literally.

BF: How big is big in a cabbage?

FM: It's five foot across the top.

BF: So if you measured around the circumference . . .

FM: No, across the top.

BF: You mean if you cut it in half, it'd be five feet across?

FM: Pardon?

BF: If you cut it in half, would it be five foot across?

FM: Pardon?

BF: Hello.

FM: Hello?

BF: If you stand up next to your cabbage, where does she come to on you?

FM: Up to me breast.

BF: No kidding. You could roll that down a hill and kill somebody.

FM: Huh?

BF: YOU COULD ROLL THAT CABBAGE DOWN A HILL AND IT WOULD KILL SOMEBODY!

FM: Pardon?

[pause]

BF: Have you cut it yet?

FM: I dismantled it anyhow.

BF: How did you dismantle it?

FM: Pardon?

BF: Mr. McLaughlin, how did you dismantle it?

FM: [unclear]

BF: How'd you get it so big?

FM: I'm not telling you. [pause] I talk to it.

BF: Mr. McLaughlin, what do you feed your cabbage?

FM: Pardon?

BF: WHAT DID YOU FEED YOUR CABBAGE?

FM: I don't hear you. What did you say there?

BF: Mr. McLaughlin, I haven't got the strength for you today, I'm sorry. Why don't we call you on Monday?

FM: I'll be working Monday.

BF: You're working Monday.

FM: You oughta come over to see it.

BF: WHAT. DID. YOU. FEED. THE GODDAMN CABBAGE?

FM: I'll send you a picture of it.

BF: I don't want a picture of it! I just want to know what you fed it!

FM: Huh?

The Goddamn Cabbage didn't make it to air that night. The producer wrote it off as a "failed interview" and stuck it in her drawer. But she dug it out again for an end-of-year round-up, and it soared to the top of the charts, profanity and all.

Except in the United States. We love our American listeners, and we love the fact that public radio stations across the U.S. broadcast *As It Happens* in their own markets, but once in a while, we run afoul of the FCC (Federal Communications Commission) in Washington. The FCC have very strict rules about the sort of language you're allowed to use over the public airwaves. They don't seem to object to serial-killer dramas or hate messages or selling crap to kids, but they take a dim view of using words like *crap* or *goddamn* on the radio. It's incumbent on AIH producers to phone Minnesota Public Radio when they think there's something on the show that might bring censure down on our American fellows, so Minnesota can bleep it out before it hits the innocent air south of the 49th parallel.

The Internet, satellite radio and even short-wave radio make all these efforts rather pointless, but you can't blame folks for trying. I even have a certain sympathy for the FCC's attempt to uphold some standards; people have a right to expect that they can listen to the CBC without having a lot of foul language thrust at them. It's just that we think it's possible to draw the line a bit short of a total taboo. We do draw the line, as a country, at Howard Stern and Don Imus and their vulgar mockery of, well, of everyone who isn't Howard Stern or Don Imus really. But goddamn cabbages we can handle.

Cabbages and the like were also remembered by the show's other hosts—Harry Brown, Elizabeth Gray, Dennis Trudeau, Michael Enright and Al Maitland—when we assembled them in our Toronto studio for that 30th anniversary show. Harry Brown recalled that the show was a product of the so-called radio revolution at the CBC, when people like Margaret Lyons and Val Cleary took an old medium that had been overshadowed by its flashy younger brother, TV, and gave it a thorough makeover. Harry said that when he joined *As It Happens,* he was the only one there with short hair and no love beads. Also, he smoked regular tobacco.

The CBC had been founded on the idea that it should help bind Canada together as the railway had done in the 19th century; Val Cleary, Elizabeth Gray told us, had the idea that radio could *be* a train. In its first incarnation, *As It Happens* went on the air at 8:00 p.m. in Halifax, which was 7:00 p.m. in Toronto, and rolled through five time zones until they signed off in Vancouver at 10:00 p.m. Pacific Time. In other words, when the hosts were launching into their second hour in the Maritimes, they'd be saying hello to the listeners joining them from Quebec and Ontario; when they were saying goodbye to the Maritimes, they'd be doing a second hour in Ontario and saying hello to Manitoba and so on.

The fact that Canada has six time zones always made things interesting for us when we had to update a story across the country. Those nights were ones when I paid close attention to the script to try to keep a grip on exactly which part of the show we were doing over, where and for whom. It takes an *idiot savant* to keep track; I played the *idiot* part, and the Desk furnished the *savant.*

When Harry Brown and company signed off in Vancouver at ten, it was, of course, one in the morning in Toronto. So if the show had aired every night, the pace would have taken its toll on even the youngest producers. But in the beginning, it aired only on Monday nights. Harry shared the hosting duties with writer Phillip Forsyth at first and later with artist William Ronald.

In 1971 the Monday night team joined up with the people who were producing another young programme called *Radio*

Free Friday. Barbara Frum and Cy Strange came on board, and the show went to five nights a week, with rotating hosts. Cy, like Harry, would have a long career as CBC announcer and programme host. His biographical notes in the CBC files read like something that Ted Baxter, the news anchor on *The Mary Tyler Moore Show,* might have written:

> *Cy Strange grew up in a farming community in southern Ontario where he pumped vinegar in his father's general store, shot rabbits for dinner and used to hitchhike 35 miles to sing and play the guitar on a 100-watt radio station in London, Ontario.*

In 1973 the format changed again, and *As It Happens* took on the shape it's maintained pretty much to this day: a lively mix of music and talk and interviews with leading newsmakers. Then as now, there were other programmes playing music and talking to people on the phone; what distinguished *As It Happens* from those other shows was that instead of waiting for people to call *in,* the producers and hosts called *out.* "The telephone is a delightful instrument," said Phil Forsyth at the time. "It can go anywhere, doesn't cost that much, and on the air it sounds like a real conversation, rather than an interview."

Which is why, four decades later, *As It Happens* can still sound as fresh as the day it was born.

Al Maitland, the man with the golden voice, claims he was mucking out stables when they called him in to co-host *As It Happens.* He was crazy about horses and always kept one or two about somewhere—not usually in the studio. But one year on his birthday, the crew did bring one in, wearing a blanket that said "Happy Birthday, Al." He was a bit disappointed, he said, that he only got to keep the blanket.

At least the horse didn't mistake the studio for a toilet, unlike the beaver that came calling when the show was campaigning to have *Castor canadensis* anointed as the country's national animal.

"It was," Harry told us on the 30th anniversary, "more fun than I realized at the time." Also on that anniversary show, Barbara Budd recalled Grumpy the Goldfish, who was given the kiss of life by his doting owner (yes, in England); Dennis Trudeau impressed us with his memories of commuting to work every Monday morning from Montreal and returning Friday night; and Elizabeth Gray dazzled us with her ability to pronounce Llanfairpwllgwyngyllgogerychwyrndrobwllllantysiliogogogoch, the name of the Welsh town where her mother was born, which means "the church of St. Mary in the hollow of white hazel trees near the rapid whirlpool by St. Tysilio's of the red cave." Some of you probably knew that already.

Apparently, that's not even the longest place name in the world; the Maoris have a longer name for a hill in New Zealand. It's *Taumatawhakatangi* . . . plus 40 more letters, and it translates as "the place where Tamatea, the man with the big knees who slid down, climbed and swallowed mountains, known as 'landeater,' played his flute to his loved one." More like a short story than a name really.

But to get back to the anniversary. Michael Enright recalled the lady in Alberta who killed and stuffed little prairie dogs and then dressed them up and put them in tableaux: the Battle of the Plains of Abraham, the Nativity scene at Christmas. We talked about the Reading Man and the time they tried to change the theme music and Al Maitland's debut as "Fireside Al" and the struggle that producer Pam Wallin had had to get Zimbabwean guerrilla fighter Joshua Nkomo on the programme.

Pam flirted shamelessly with him, we heard, finally inveigling him into agreeing to an interview with Barbara Frum. Unfortunately, the day he finally acceded to Pam's entreaties, Barbara was away. Enright was filling in for her, and Nkomo insisted on addressing him as "Barbara" throughout their talk.

And we remembered Barbara. More than anyone else, it was Barbara Frum who must get the credit for making *As It Happens* a daily event in the lives of many Canadians.

"She was the consummate journalist," said Harry Brown. "She was meticulous and hard working, and she had a most beguiling tone."

Harry recalled how she had taken him aside one day and told him that she'd been diagnosed with leukemia; she probably wouldn't live to see her grandchildren. But then, he said, she seemed to put it out of her mind and carry on, and she never mentioned the subject again. Frum went on to host *The Journal* on CBC Television (with me) and died in 1992 at the age of 54. She lived long enough to welcome her first grandchild, Miranda.

November 18, 1998, was also the last time we had Al Maitland and Harry Brown on the air together. Al died a couple of months later of congestive heart failure; Harry's heart gave out three years after that. Happily for us, their voices are preserved on tape. CDs of the collected readings of "Fireside Al" and "Front Porch Al" are steady favourites in the CBC gift shop, and Maitland's reading of Frederick Forsyth's *Shepherd* is an absolute must every Christmas Eve.

As It Happens probably gets more questions about *The Shepherd* than any other single thing on the show. *Who wrote it? Will it be on this Christmas? Where can I buy a CD?* (Answers: British author and journalist Frederick Forsyth; it's on *As It Happens* every Christmas Eve; and the CD is now available from CBC gift stores.) A close runner-up would be

Reading, as in *Where did that Reading thing originate? Why do you keep making those references to Reading?*

The "Reading thing" goes something like this: whenever we have a particularly silly story from England—an interview, say, with a woman whose fondness for garden gnomes has led her to establish a gnome sanctuary—Barbara Budd will *extro* it by saying something like:

> *Ann Atkins is the founder and keeper of the Garden Gnome Reserve, and we reached her in Abbots Bickington. That is 240 kilometres west of Reading, and from the Garden Sanctuary it would take 720,000 garden gnomes, lined up hat to hat, to reach dear Reading.*

In other words, Reading is the centre of the universe, and the story's distance from the centre is calculated using a distinctive system of measurement.

There are a couple of explanations as to how this silliness got started. One version is that one day, after interviewing someone in Reading, Al Maitland said, helpfully, "Reading is 30 miles west of London." A few minutes later, there was a story from London, and Alan said, "[Jane Doe] spoke to us from London . . . which is 30 miles east of Reading." It's the sort of thing Al would have done.

Former AIH producer George Somerwill, however, says his is the true version. He'd been working on the show for only about a week, he says, when he booked one of those wacky English people—a "tongue-in-cheek story" is how he puts it—who happened to be somewhere in Berkshire, not all that far from where George himself used to live and not far from Reading.

> *We recorded the item about ten minutes past five, and it was slotted early in the programme, so I had only a few*

minutes to cut it, top-and-tail it and write the green—in those days, we wrote our scripts on five-part green paper. When I came to the extro, *I wrote: "John So-and-So spoke to us from . . . [whatever-the-village-was]."*

Then I thought, No one will know where that is. So I added, "which is nine miles from Reading." And that's what Al read on the air.

Somerwill, in his innocence, assumed that this would make everything clear. He was set straight a moment later, when the show's producer, Bob Campbell, exploded out of the studio, roaring, "WHERE THE HELL IS READING?"

Everyone found this quite funny, so from then on, whenever anyone had a nutty story from England, he would cite its distance from Reading and, well, we've just never stopped. Somerwill, who now works for the United Nations in Liberia, says people still come up to him and say, "Hey, aren't you the guy who used to work on *As It Happens?* Started that Reading thing?"

I rather imagine it was producer George Jamieson who started measuring the distance in supine gnomes and the like; it's the sort of thing *he* would do.

In any event, the Reading references drive one poor soul right around the bend and straight to his phone. We call him the Reading Man.

"You stupid, *stupid* people" is the way his message usually starts. "When are you going to stop these *stupid* references to Reading. It's so STUPID!"

And of course, the answer to the Reading Man's question is: never. Our producers are a sick and twisted lot, I'm afraid; the more abuse they get from the Reading Man, the more determined they are never to stop this admittedly childish habit.

They get such a kick out of it that they decided, one day, to see if they couldn't find a similar reference point in the U.S. I think the idea arose just after we'd talked to the nice man from Menomonie, Wisconsin, about the sudden disappearance of his moose. Moose stories always remind me of that scene in the TV show *Murphy Brown* where Murphy, played by Candice Bergen, is dismissing a rumour that she might be replaced by a reporter from Canada. "Canada!" she snorts. "What do Canadians know about news? MOOSE LOST, MOOSE FOUND. MORE SNOW."

Anyway . . . the lost moose. It was made of fibreglass, about seven feet tall and six feet long, Terry Tilleson told us, and had been fastened to the front door of the local Moose Lodge right under the security light—only it wasn't there any longer. Not only that, it was the second time the moose had gone AWOL, so someone in Menomonie had a thing for that particular ungulate. We were sorry about his missing moose, of course, but at the same time, we were quite taken with the name Menomonie, and since it *was* a moose and all that had taken us there, we wondered if Menomonie might not be the right place to anoint as our American Reading.

Senior producer Marie Clark decided to put the question to our audience. They could nominate alternatives to Menomonie if they wished, and then we'd have one of those totally spurious web elections to determine the winner. In the end, it came down to four places: Peoria, Illinois; Normal, Illinois; Peculiar, Missouri; and Menomonie. Producer Max Paris did the counting, and on June 25, 2002, Barbara Budd proclaimed Menomonie the new official centre of the wacky universe in the U.S., with 41 percent of the vote. Luckily for her, it's easier to pronounce than it is to spell.

But you know, Menomonie never caught on quite the way Reading did, much to the Reading Man's sorrow, no doubt.

We might have fought harder for Menomonie if we'd known then what I've since learned. While trying to nail down the correct spelling of the place, I found that the beautiful *city* of Menomonie (population fifteen thousand) is located partially within the *town* of Menomonie in Dunn County, northwest Wisconsin—NOT to be confused (though it's bound to be, isn't it?) with Menomonee Falls, which is incorporated as a *village* and contains thirty-two thousand people, in north*east* Wisconsin, although it's north*west* of Milwaukee. Wherever and whatever it is, Menomonie sounds like our kind of place.

Don't ask me if they ever found their moose; I don't know. One thing I should add, though, is that in September 2000, I had my own Big Cabbage moment: Barbara Everingham in Wasilla, Alaska, told me about winning a local Big Cabbage contest with a specimen that weighed 105.6 pounds (47.9 kilos for the metric crowd). I was surprised that they could grow such big vegetables in the short growing season they had, but she reminded me that they also had sun 24 hours a day during the summer.

FYI, the Big Cabbage world record holder is Bernard Lavery, formerly of Llanharry, Rhondda Cynon Taff, Wales, who grew a plant that weighed 124 pounds in 1989. In the account he posted on the Internet, Dr. Lavery says it would have weighed more but the movers kept losing pieces of it as they were hauling it to Alton Towers, 210 miles away, where the Worldwide Giant Vegetable Championships were being held that year.

> *So all in all, it was a disastrous harvest. Although I broke the world record, I should have chalked up one of at least 150 lb. The huge cabbage ended up in a sorry state, with thousands of visitors poking at it over the four days that it was on exhibition. At the end of the show, I gave bits and pieces of it away as souvenirs to whoever wanted it.*

This cabbage abuse seems to have soured Dr. Lavery on growing big vegetables. According to his posting, he subsequently went to work for Sheik Zayed in Abu Dhabi and then settled in Sutton St. Edmund in Lincolnshire, England, where he grows "a few pumpkins and sunflowers for the children."

As of this writing, Barb Everingham's cabbage still holds the state record in Alaska—and she didn't feed it anything special.

FOUR

Tim and Colin and Julie and Yulya

Radio that takes hot air to new heights

⌒

It's May 2004, and Canadian adventurer Colin Angus is telling us about a little trip he's planning to make from Vancouver to Moscow with his friend Tim Harvey.

CA: We're going to be leaving from Vancouver up to Fairbanks; that's 3,600 kilometres on the bikes. It's going to be an interesting trip but fairly straightforward; it's your typical sort of highway biking. And then from Fairbanks, we'll continue down the Yukon River in a rowboat for about 1,800 kilometres to the Bering Sea and then we'll cross the Bering Sea in a rowboat, which is about a 400-kilometre crossing, and then follow the Siberian coastline in our boat until a town called Anadyr. Then we hop onto our skis and we ski for about 800K and then back onto our bikes again.

ML: It all sounds challenging to me—what is going to be the most challenging part, do you think?

CA: I think the toughest part is going to be our travel in Siberia. Often people think the Bering Sea crossing is going to be the toughest, and it sounds intimidating, but we've really prepared for that. It's actually fairly calm in August when we do the crossing. But Siberia itself—it's very remote and it's cold. We're going through there in the middle of winter, and the average temperature is minus 50 in January. That's the average; Winnipeg, by comparison, is minus 20, so . . .

ML: That's not good.

CA: No, no. We've spent a lot of time preparing for this section, too. It's all about having the routines in place and making sure that your equipment isn't going to break down on you, because you can't really take your gloves off and repair it.

ML: How much food are you taking? How long is it going to take you, first of all—the whole trip?

CA: The duration of the trip is going to be approximately 11 months. We've dropped off caches of food all the way up to Fairbanks for the cycling leg, and then we're going to be carrying almost 4 months of provisions in our rowboat. The boat is packed: it's got all our gear for Siberia and enough food to take us right into the heart of Siberia, and that's pretty much when our own rations end. We're using freeze-dried food; it's approximately 1.2 kilograms per day per person, which is about five thousand calories, which is a lot of energy, but it's necessary when you're trudging through the cold conditions.

Once we get to Irkutsk, which is where our food's going to run out, we'll have to start using local supplies, but it's a lot more difficult using local provisions, because it's things like potatoes and meat, which, when it's minus 50 out, it's pretty hard to chop the potatoes up, so we'll have to do as much prep as we can before we embark from the cities or towns we purchase the food from.

ML: You've made some extraordinary journeys in the past. Did you canoe down rivers in Russia before?

CA: Yeah. Our most recent river journey was a descent of the Yenisey River, which flows through Mongolia and Siberia. The thing I like about rivers is that they offer you a unique view of the land. It's almost like an inanimate guide taking you along, showing you all sorts of aspects of the land you're going through, and this, in some ways, has some similarities—we are descending a river, but it's almost like a whole bunch of expeditions thrown together.

ML: And Tim? Has he had some experience with this kind of adventure?

CA: Tim's spent a lot of time in boats and kayaking. I mean, he hasn't done any extended adventures exactly like this; the most recent trip he was on was working as a photojournalist in Central America. The most important thing, though, is to have the right kind of attitude and spirit, which Tim definitely has: it's a combination of being tough, being able to endure the hardships that are definitely going to be encountered, but also having a passion for the outdoors, a love for the environment around you. . . .

Why did they want to do this? Colin said it was to save the planet—to encourage people to mount their bikes and leave their cars at home in order to reduce greenhouse gases and slow down global warming. But I think they may be addicted to adventure. I mean, other people sell raffle tickets or write pamphlets to save the planet; they're not skiing across Siberia. Since Colin and Tim's trip was sponsored in part by a satellite phone company, it was not going to be hard to contact them along the way, and we thought it would be interesting to stay in touch, but we had no idea how interesting the trip would get.

Before they even got out of British Columbia, forest fires forced them off the road, so they bought a canoe to carry them northward. Getting across the Bering Sea in an 18-foot rowboat also proved to be more challenging than Colin had anticipated, as wind and stormy weather kept blowing them in the wrong direction and threatening to cast them into water that was cold enough, Tim said, to bring on "an ice-cream headache in your hand" if you trolled it overboard for a moment.

This is definitely my kind of story. I'm the original arm-chair traveller; I love adventures, provided they're someone else's. I love talking to people like Tim and Colin and reading books like Joe Simpson's *Touching the Void,* which is an account of a harrowing adventure Simpson and his friend Simon Yates underwent in 1985.

Simon and Joe have just completed a first ascent of the west side of Suila Grande in the Peruvian Andes, they're heading back down and Joe falls and breaks his leg in several places. At first, they proceed downward, with Simon and Joe roped together, Simon lowering Joe ahead of him a few hundred feet at a time. This is agonizing enough, but then Joe goes over a cliff and is caught hanging in mid-air. Simon realizes that either they will plunge to their deaths together or he can cut the rope, let Joe go and hope to save himself. He cuts the rope. He hears a yell, then nothing. Simon continues his descent and returns to base camp, feeling devastated because he has had to leave his friend for dead.

Joe, meanwhile, lies at the bottom of a crevasse, not dead but without much hope of getting out. Miraculously, he does get out and then gets himself, broken leg and all, back down the mountain alone. It takes him three days. At the end of it, he is dehydrated and starving and half-frozen, but he is alive.

Touching the Void is a thrilling tale of adventure and extreme peril, of human ingenuity, grit and determination. The title describes the feeling you get whenever you take a leap into the unknown, which is what we all do every time we embark on something we haven't done before and aren't sure we can do—starting a new job, getting married. But some people aren't satisfied with the ordinary challenges life offers; they crave extreme challenges, and I crave the vicarious pleasure of hearing about them.

They must be a bit crazy, though, don't you think? These climbers and sailors and the people who get themselves perched atop a million tons of rocket fuel and blasted into space? How else to explain why a young woman would wager her future against a race into the Southern Ocean, alone aboard a 60-foot yacht in high seas and biting, gale-force winds, knowing that if you have the good fortune to come out the other end alive and in one piece, you're still not likely to have won the race?

That's the race called the Vendée Globe, about which Canadian sailor Derek Lundy wrote a mesmerizing account in his book *Godforsaken Sea*. He was motivated to write it, he said, by the death in 1997 of fellow yachtsman Gerry Roufs, a former Olympic sailor from Hudson, Quebec, who was ploughing through a fierce South Atlantic storm in the Vendée Globe race when he lost radio contact. Roufs was never heard from again. Pieces of his boat were being collected by the Chilean navy at the very time that Derek Lundy came into the *As It Happens* studio to tell us about the book and the race.

The Vendée Globe is always exciting, but the '96/'97 race was particularly intense. There were three sailors apart from Gerry Roufs who might have been lost had it not been for some remarkable rescue operations. The most daring involved

British racer Peter Goss's rescue of Raphaël Dinelli, a French sailor whose boat capsized 1,200 nautical miles south of Australia in the same storm that killed Gerry Roufs—a "survival storm" Derek Lundy called it.

> DL: A survival storm is essentially a storm in which wind and wave have reached the point where the sailor can't make any choices. He or she is really just hanging on, adopting storm tactics—that is, probably running off before the wind and waves. You're really at the mercy of whatever happens. I mean, if you get through a survival storm, there's a little bit of skill involved—well, a lot of skill involved—but there's a heck of a lot more luck involved.

> ML: So you're bobbing along on the ocean, just praying to God that you'll survive it.

> DL: You're surfing and screaming along on the ocean, praying that you'll survive, yeah.

> ML: So they're in this condition and Pete Goss has to turn his boat around and beat *up* into these gale-force winds?

> DL: He had to beat into winds that were blowing in excess of hurricane force, probably around 70 knots or so. The seas were described as anywhere from 50 to 65 feet. The Vendée Globe boats are strong, but they're not designed to do that; they're designed to run ahead of weather like that, not go back into it. So he really put himself into a position where he wasn't sure whether his boat would hold together.

Peter Goss was about 160 miles past Dinelli when he heard his distress call, and he did turn around into the howling wind. It took him two days, but he got there in time. Goss finished the race in fifth place, but he was rewarded with a hero's welcome in France and the knowledge that he had acted nobly. Raphaël Dinelli, for his part, showing the steely determination that characterizes so many of these adventurers, entered the next two Vendée Globe competitions and, on his third try, finally made it all the way to the end. He finished the race in 12th place, 37 days after the 11th-place finisher, Anne Liardet.

In 1997 someone also tried to save Gerry Roufs. Like Peter Goss, Isabelle Autissier reversed course and beat back toward Roufs' last known position, but without any radio signal from Roufs' boat, she couldn't find him in the raging storm, nor could any of their fellow sailors in the area.

I asked Derek Lundy why people signed on for the Vendée Globe.

ML: Given how awful it is out there, you ask yourself, *Why do they do it?* Why would anybody put himself through such pain and terror and take such a beating?

DL: That really is a good question. I think they do it for a number of reasons. First of all, they are professional sailors, and this is sort of the apogee of the profession. You know, you sail the Vendée Globe, you've reached the top. But there are also people who just like adrenalin; they like the thrill of coming close to death or appearing to. It must seem to them quite often that they are.

ML: But are they crazy?

DL: No, they're not. I thought they might be, or I thought they were before I started talking to them and reading more about this sort of racing, but in fact, I found myself talking to people who were extraordinarily sane, calm, centred, modest people. There was nothing pretentious about them. One of them said to me once, "When you've been out there on the edge of the world, you know you're insignificant; you know you're just the ordinary human being you are; it's impossible to think otherwise of yourself or of humans in general."

And I think there's another element, too. You know, the Southern Ocean itself can be a terrible place, but it is a beautiful place in a way as well, in the sense that it probably is the last true, great more-or-less untouched wilderness on earth. So people who are out there are in a place on earth where hardly any human being living today has been. It must be a unique sensation.

All right, but still. Forget the Vendée Globe. I have always wondered, who but a madman would willingly—*willingly*—expose himself to the brutal cold of Mount Everest, where if you don't die of exposure or a fall, the altitude alone could kill you? In May 1996, several people paid a small fortune for the privilege of dying an agonizing death on the roof of the world. That season on Everest was notorious for the loss of life—8 in one day, 15 by the end of the climbing season—and people were wondering how much commercial exploitation should be permitted on the world's highest peak.

The traffic doesn't seem to have diminished. In 2005 Canadian climber Pierre Bourdeau was one of three hundred would-be Everest summiters. We spoke to him just after he'd narrowly escaped being wiped out by an avalanche that had come down on his camp on the Kumbu Glacier.

It was 5:30 in the morning when Bourdeau was awakened by something that sounded like thunder. Two or three seconds later, his tent was being pelted by rocks and debris. He knew what was happening, and he was sure he was going to die; if the rocks didn't kill him, he'd be buried alive in the snow. The next thing he remembers is being about a hundred metres away from where the tents had been, and alive. The tents were all destroyed, but by some miracle, he and his fellow climbers had escaped with only a few bruises.

"We don't know why we're alive," Pierre Bourdeau told us.

"So are you done with climbing for a while?"

"For a short time, yes."

Another very cold place to visit is the North Pole, which is where British adventurer David Hempleman-Adams got himself in April 1998, making him the first person to climb the highest peaks on seven continents *and* reach the magnetic and geographic North and South poles. He spoke to us from Resolute Bay after being air-lifted off the ice, together with his Norwegian travelling companion, Rune Gjeldnes.

ML: How did you know you were there [at the North Pole]?

DH: We had two systems: we had a global positioning system and an argos positioning system. So we were within three metres, actually, of the Pole. And what happens, it's drifting all the time, and by the time the airplane the next day came in, we'd drifted off seven miles, so we had to walk through the night to get back to the North Pole again, so we went there a couple of times.

ML: Let's make it clear to everybody exactly what kind of an ordeal this is. Some four hundred miles on skis? . . . How heavy was the sled?

DH: Mine was about 150 pounds; Rune's was probably nearer 200.

ML: And the weather's not nice.

DH: Well, when we started, it was dark and it went down to—we recorded minus 55. Well, we think it was minus 55, because we could only record minus 55; it was right on the backstop, so it might have been lower. You got open water and wind, so the actual winds will take the windchill factor much lower. But it warmed up. We were picked up on a beautiful day; it was minus 20, no wind. . . .

ML: You probably had your shirt off at minus 20.

DH: You could certainly feel the difference, because by that time, we'd got acclimatized, of course, and we used to have two sleeping bags [each] and we threw away the inner sleeping bags, so, yeah, it was much warmer.

ML: What did you eat?

DH: Well, we had to get in six thousand calories, because we were burning twelve thousand up.

ML: Every day?

DH: Yeah. Good place to go for a diet. I lost about 24 pounds. But in any event, we had dehydrated food and what you do is you mix a lot of oil with it to try and get the caloristic value up, and it was the same food every day, so it got pretty hard to eat in the end.

ML: You fell in the water at one point.

DH: Yeah, that was probably the lowest point of the whole trip.

ML: No kidding!

DH: I thought, *Boy,* you know, *this is it.* It wasn't a problem falling in the water, but I had my skis on as well, and I didn't want to lose my skis, so I was lucky Rune was there to fish me out. And we had to start walking pretty quickly, and what happened was, the water freezes and then you just crack the water off, but you just have to get going quickly to get the heat back into your body.

ML: You must like the cold.

DH: Uh, I don't—I'm just not smart enough to realize that I don't like it. I seem to keep coming back here, but it's a beautiful area, I have to say, and this thing that you just can't describe to people—it really is a wonderful place.

ML: Try.

DH: Well, you've got this raw beauty. You're on the limit, basically. You've got the mountains—so beautiful—and very few people visit them. The nicest thing about Canada, it's so big; up in these national parks, you see these mountains that have never been climbed before, that are just stunningly beautiful. And then you've got the different colours of when the sun starts to come back in the North here—these oranges, and mauve and purple skies . . . it's beautiful. And then you've got the sheer beauty of the sea ice itself that's always moving and changing shape and consistency, and every day is different, completely different.

And then you can get the raw savagery of it with the wind blowing 30 miles an hour. So it goes from one extreme to the other, and we've always said it can be hell and heaven in one hour, the weather changes so quickly. And the conditions as well. If you've got a lot of rubble and you try to pull your sleds through, it can be hell, and then you got a pad of ice which you could land the Concorde on, which is heaven, of course.

ML: I don't need to ask you why you do it—you've already said you're crazy—but have you done it all now? What challenges are left for you?

DH: Well, there's always a challenge for man. I think Browning said, "A man's reach should be beyond his grasp," and I think he meant it doesn't matter what you do, be it trying to get to the top of the stairs for the first time or walking down to the end of the street for the first time. Man has to have a challenge. I think maybe now I'm 41 and I've got young children, I have to start slowing down. Hopefully, there'll always be some challenge, even if it's going down to the local pub. I owe Rune a few pints, so I suppose that'll be the next expedition.

The next time we talked, in March 2004, David had just set a new world record, flying a balloon 13 kilometres into the atmosphere above Colorado, so I guess he did find another challenge after leaving the pub. It was cold up there, too, he said—minus 70 degrees.

David's countryman, or rather -woman, Fiona Thornewild, also walked into the history books in 2004 when she became the first British woman to walk solo to the South Pole. She walked a thousand kilometres in 42 days, dragging a 130-pound sled behind her. She had a radio phone for company for the first 10 days; then it conked out and she had only herself to talk to for the rest of the journey. The lowest point for her, she told us, was when her GPS directional device broke down and she couldn't immediately lay her hands on the spare.

Why go through it? She said it was because it was the biggest challenge she could set herself; because of the sense of personal satisfaction it gave her; and because after her first husband had been killed in a car accident at the age of 26, she'd promised herself to live life to the limit.

We talked to people who'd made their way across the great Arabian desert known as the Empty Quarter—the name tells you all you need to know about *that* particular piece of real estate—and people who have kayaked and rowed and paddled their way across oceans, or tried to, and people who prefer to travel by balloon, and whenever I talked to these men and women, I reflected on how nice it was to be warm and dry and cozy in the studio. But if I had to choose from among these torturous adventures, I'd probably opt for being baked in the sand or frozen on a mountaintop over being smashed around in a cold, dark sea at the bottom of the world or sinking to a watery grave. Maybe that's why the sailing stories thrill me most. When Adam Killick joined the programme, I had a new ally in my quest to get more sailors on the air. An enthusiastic sailor himself, Adam was keen to have us follow the progress of Derek Hatfield aboard *Spirit of Canada* in the 2003 Around Alone race, which is like the Vendée Globe, only you're allowed the occasional landfall. The low point of Hatfield's passage came when he lost his mast while rounding Cape Horn. We heard all about it when we reached him a few days later in Ushuaia, Argentina.

> DH: It started with a hailstorm and a big black cloud—blew 60, 65 knots out of the west—and that was approaching the Horn. . . . I arrived on the shoals of the Horn with waves up to 45 feet breaking. I battled the storm all Thursday night and into Friday and actually battled my way all the way around the Horn, and midafternoon on Friday, was struck by this really difficult

wave that, in hindsight, was kind of an odd thing—one of those things that obviously had the *Spirit of Canada*'s name on it. It picked up the back of the boat—what we sailors refer to as a semi-pitch-pole—and the boat went vertical. The bow went down, and the boat basically stood on its head, then fell off to the side and was rolled upside down by this wave, which wasn't particularly big—20 feet or so, I guess. I'd been dealing with those waves all day long.

ML: But you didn't have your harness on? How did you manage not to get thrown overboard?

DH: It was one of those—I want to make it clear that I always wear the harness, especially when I'm sailing in conditions like this—but I had just come up from down below. Because I'd been hand-steering the boat through these big waves all day long, I was dashing down below in the lulls. In this case, the wind was going from 65 to 70 down to 40—to me that was a lull—and I was grabbing some quick energy foods and trying to get a little bit warm and rushing back on deck for the next blast of wind. But I rushed back on deck just as the wave hit and before I had a chance to clip on and—bang! The boat went over. I went across the cockpit to the far side up against the lifelines. It was the lifelines that saved my life. I guess that's why they're called that—

ML: You managed to grasp the lines.

DH: Well, no, I didn't have a chance to grab anything. It's one of those situations similar to a car crash; you really don't have a chance to do much.

ML: They just caught you.

DH: They just caught me and kept me on board. I was under the water momentarily, and I could hear the gurgling of the water, as I was not really swimming, just kind of floundering around under the water there and— the real memory that I have is the splintering carbon of the mast exploding. I think it broke in three or four places. By the time I came to my senses and back inside the boat, the mast was gone over the side but still being held on to the boat with the rigging. The mainsail and all the lines and the halyards and everything were still attached, so the boat is going sideways in 55 to 60 knots of wind with these huge monster waves trying to roll the boat again. But it didn't roll, and it took me about 45 minutes to go around and systematically cut all the lines and pull all the pins on the rigging and let the rig go. Then I started to motor—and luckily, I was not far from the coast—and motored straight up the Beagle Channel here to Ushuaia.

ML: Your engine was still working!

DH: Yeah. Miraculously. But the inside of the boat was total carnage. Everything that was in the boat, in the back or in the main salon, the cabin, landed in the nav station because the boat stood on its bow, smashing a lot of the instruments and, at that time, took out the sat [satellite] phones, basically. The one sat phone continued to work for a little while, but the charging system was not working, so the battery went dead very quickly.

ML: We think that's what happened to Gerry Roufs back in 1997, huh?

DH: Yes.

ML: That he was thrown out of the boat in a storm. Did you think about him at all?

DH: I remember Gerry a lot. I'm not sure how close I was to where he was lost, but I sailed through that part of the world as well. Because of that incident with Gerry, the boats are much safer now. I suspect that if my boat had stayed upside down, I wouldn't be talking to you today.

Derek Hatfield did manage to get a new mast and gear—thanks, he said, to the amazing outpouring of support he got from folks back in Canada—and made it home in one piece.

As for Tim Harvey and Colin Angus, the Vancouver-to-Moscow trekkers, in September 2004, after taking a month to cross the Bering Sea, our lads made landfall on the coast of Siberia, at Provydenya. The townspeople made them welcome and gave them a small apartment, where they spent a couple of weeks building up their strength and provisions for the next leg of the journey. Until this point, although there had been difficulties, the voices on the radio still conveyed some of the exhilaration and optimism we'd heard at the outset. But somewhere between Provydenya and Anadyr, their next stop, things started to go a bit sour. On October 11th, Canadian Thanksgiving, Colin described a frustrating daylong hike down the length of a spit on the Siberian coast and a two-day hike back up after they found they couldn't get to the mainland that way. We also heard the first mention of Yulya, the Russian interpreter who had joined them.

Tim reported that it was overcast and grey, with blowing snow. No trees or bushes, just gravel and tundra. He also talked about the wildlife they'd encountered—walruses, grizzly bears, a wolf—and sent Happy Thanksgiving wishes to his grandmother and granddad in Shawville, Quebec. I felt thankful not to be in Siberia.

After that things got worse. A warm spell turned the tundra into mud. Colin developed a severe urinary-tract infection and had to fly home to Vancouver for treatment. At Christmas Colin was still in Canada, and Tim was still waiting for him in Siberia. Colin rejoined Tim in January, but something (or someone?) seemed to have come between them. When we reconnected on February 17th, they told a harrowing tale of nearly having lost Colin in the Siberian wasteland.

Colin had left Tim and Yulya to make his own way to a shelter they were aiming for at Kilometre 86—about two hundred kilometres east of Egvekinot. Along the way, he got lost in a blizzard. Just as darkness fell, he came across the "86" marker he was looking for, but there was no hut. Suddenly, he felt very, very scared.

Alone now in the freezing darkness, the Siberian wind shrieking, Colin began to contemplate his death and how sad it would make his fiancée and his mother. Then, like Ignacio Siberio, the man who wouldn't drown, he focused his will on how to make it through the night. First thing, dig a hole in the snow and get out of the wind. This he did with the aid of a penknife. For the next eight hours, he alternated between huddling in his cave and jumping up and down in the wind to restore his circulation. At around 1:30 a.m., when he emerged from the cave to revive his limbs, he thought he saw a faint glow in the distance.

What to do now? It was an agonizing decision: whether to strike out toward that faint glow in the hope that it was coming from the hut he was looking for, or stay where he was until daylight. If there was no hut, he would certainly die. He struck out.

Luckily for Colin, it was the right move. Tim and Yulya had organized a search party, but they had almost given up on

Colin when he staggered into the building, half-frozen and looking like the Abominable Snowman.

Getting separated was a mistake, they agreed. "You gotta stay together as a team," they told us over the phone. But that was the last time we spoke to Tim and Colin together; shortly afterwards they parted company for good. Tim and Yulya went one way, Colin another. Colin kept the sat phone, and we were able to stay in touch with him. Tim kept the camera, and Yulya. In the office, we speculated about the possibility that three had become a crowd, but perhaps the guys would have split up anyway. Our producer Kevin Robertson reported that on their website and in the Vancouver papers, the two adventurers and their respective allies and supporters had taken to bickering and hurling insults at each other.

Having abandoned their original mission—to trek together from Vancouver to Moscow—the travellers did all reach Moscow eventually. There they regrouped and made separate plans to continue the man-powered journey all the way back to Canada. Man-and-woman-powered. Colin acquired another camera and a female partner, his fiancée, Julie Wafaei. When I last spoke with Colin and Julie, they were a thousand kilometres off the west coast of Africa, breathing a collective sigh of relief after weathering two tropical storms. They'd been rowing for 65 days and had found about 50 ways to cook dorado. Julie said they were getting on very well, which we were glad to hear, as they had another two and a half months of rowing ahead of them before making landfall in Miami.

Tim Harvey, meanwhile, had got himself a new phone but had lost Yulya—some problem with her travel papers, I think—so he had a new travelling partner as well, a chap by the name of Erden Eruc. When we last spoke, they were about 80 kilometres off the Moroccan coast and making a beeline for shore in the face of an approaching storm. They'd already been held up for weeks by high winds and waves, but Tim said, "Today was great. We've seen whales and sea turtles and dolphins, beautiful sunset. . . . There's nothing I'd rather be doing."

Everyone made it back to Canada eventually, and you can learn more about the adventures of Tim and Colin and Julie and Yulya and Erden by checking out their own accounts on the web or on film or in their own books. Last I heard, Colin and Julie were planning a trip through the canals of France, and I thought, *The food will be much better there!*

A few weeks after we talked to Derek Lundy about the Vendée Globe, we heard of another adventure on the high seas. This one involved a Russian sailor who was taking part in the 1998 Around Alone race. Russian sailor Victor Yasekov was about 950 miles west of Capetown when he radioed for help. His right arm had got infected; it had turned red and yellow and was badly swollen. Boston physician Daniel Carlin was one of the doctors on call for the Around Alone sailors, and as he tells the story, he answered Yasekov's call for help and proceeded to tell him, via email, how to operate on his arm. Yasekov had to lance the abscess with a sterile scalpel, pour iodine into the wound, insert a drain and then dress it.

The operation seemed to go well, but when Yasekov sent another message a few hours later, the news was not good. Now his arm was white and limp and utterly useless. Carlin figured it this way: Yasekov had probably taken a lot of Aspirin to ease the pain in his arm, which had led to profuse bleeding after the operation; then, in trying to staunch the bleeding, he had bound his arm too tightly and cut off the circulation. Carlin was worried that the sailor might now lose his arm. He told Yasekov to remove the tourniquet, and Yasekov reported that he had started to get some feeling back in his arm, but it still wasn't much use. He ended up sailing pretty much one-handed all the way to Capetown.

Daniel Carlin had a different answer when I put the question to him on the radio:

"These people are nuts, right?"

"Yeah."

He, it turns out, is a fine one to talk. I was curious about whether Yasekov's arm ever did heal completely and also about whether Dr. Carlin was still practising long-distance medicine, so one day I tracked him down to a clinic in New London, New Hampshire. We didn't know it at the time, but our interview had caught Carlin in the middle of his own adventure, and his journey was just as exciting in its way as the Around Alone race. He began by telling me how important the Yasekov case had been for him.

That was the sentinel case for a sweeping change in medicine. That was the first time, basically, that the Internet came to someone's rescue very quickly and that there was actually an infrastructure—my practice—built around that capability. Back then I had really high hopes for this. I had been a refugee camp doctor and had lived overseas and I thought, Holy cow. If I make this work on a simple practice basis, then it's just purely a question of scaling this up in the years ahead and recruiting medical centres to participate so you could have a portal like my practice and use that portal to focus real expertise on some distant patient or clinic to the benefit of that patient.

At the time he treated Victor Yasekov, Dr. Carlin told me, he was just finishing a long-distance medical project in

Ghana—part of what he was now calling his World Clinic—
and he was working out of the New England Medical Center
in Boston. Three weeks later, they let him go. Carlin believes
that some of the older doctors there didn't understand what
he was trying to do, marrying medicine and the Internet.
Maybe, too, they resented all the publicity he was attracting.
Ironically, his face was on the cover of *Tufts Medicine* the very
day he was clearing out his office.

Whatever the reason, Carlin was reduced to running the
World Clinic out of his living room, which he did for about
five weeks. Then he forged a new association with the Leahy
Clinic on the outskirts of Boston. He also landed some private funding for his World Clinic experiment, and for about
20 months, the business grew nicely. Then, in April 2000, the
tech market crashed, and his investors pulled up stakes and
fled. In June he started laying people off, and by the following April, he was almost back where he'd started: a one-man
company running everything from his own computer.

Except that his experience had taught him that the service
he was trying to offer was really needed. So Dr. Carlin
reclaimed the company's title for himself, determined to keep
it going. From 7:00 in the morning until 3:15 in the afternoon,
he told me, he would work on his World Clinic practice; from
3:30 to 3:50, he would nap; and from 4:00 p.m. until 1:00 a.m.,
he would work as an emergency room doctor. This is what he
did for two years to support his wife and kids while he was
putting his World Clinic on a solid footing again.

> *I acquired the ability to really, solidly focus on what
> exactly needed to be done to survive. You're walking in a
> holy light, so to speak. You know how they used to say the
> saints walk in a holy light? It's somehow analogous to that,
> because you have absolute clarity.*

This ability to focus and to make it past the most horrendous obstacles was something Daniel Carlin had in common with the sailors he liked to help, I observed, and he agreed.

It seems to have paid off. His World Clinic in New London, New Hampshire, now boasts 3 full-time doctors and 5 support staff and can call on the help of 20 other physicians for consultation, including 8 specialists. Their clients include crews, island populations, top executives and families with "high net worth" who travel a lot and maybe keep several residences in different parts of the world. The money the clinic brings in from well-heeled clients goes to support projects in Madagascar and Cambodia and a street clinic in Boston. Carlin even has a few sailors still on his list, including a bunch of "old guys in their 70s," who had just called him from Gibraltar the day we were chatting. They were in the process of planning "their last hurrah"—a voyage from Portugal to Hawaii.

As for Victor Yasekov, his arm's fine, apparently. Carlin met up with him in Charleston, Virginia, when the race was over. Isabelle Autissier, the French Vendée Globe racer, was also there, and Carlin said he was thrilled to find himself in such terrific company.

They're such great people. They're humble, soft-spoken, easy to work with—you can tell them to do anything and they do it. They're a unique group of people.

Not so crazy after all? I'll let you decide.

FIVE

Touching the Earth

Radio that has all the right stuff

❦

Space pilots, or space sailors as they're sometimes called, aren't adventurers in the way the Vendée Globe sailors are. In some ways, astronauts are the antithesis of what we think of as venturesome: they don't work alone, they need the backing of hundreds of people and billions of dollars and so on. Not to belittle them at all, but the first astronaut was actually a monkey called Able—the first one to survive anyway—and he was followed by an assortment of guinea pigs, other monkeys, frogs, rats, and cats and dogs—as well as *Homo sapiens.*

That said, you have to have a certain amount of the right stuff to ride an aircraft straight up until you run out of air and the sky turns black around you—as Joe Walker did when he piloted the X-15 into space—or to plop yourself down atop a rocket and head for the moon.

Roberta Bondar, a neurologist by training, was the first Canadian woman in space, a mission specialist aboard the space shuttle *Discovery* in 1992. Her book about that experience was called *Touching the Earth,* but when you think about astronauts hurtling through space, you think, *Here's another group of people who are also touching the void.* We were especially conscious of their bravery the day in February 2003 when we talked to Bondar about the fiery descent of the shuttle *Columbia* and the loss of its seven crew members.

I asked Dr. Bondar if there had ever been a moment during her trip when she believed she wouldn't make it home. She said that one day they'd heard a loud bang, like an explosion, and immediately everyone started rushing around to get the shuttle ready for what she called "an emergency de-orbit." It turned out that what they'd heard was only the noise of metal tanks expanding—but it sure scared them.

Astronauts don't often talk about the fear they must feel, especially at the time of launch. Bondar was more candid than most. "If you don't have respect for the seething monster that's about to engulf you," she said, "there's something wrong with you." What gets you through is that you're very focused on the job you have to do. In eight and a half minutes, the blast-off is over, the fiery engines have been dispatched and you're sailing through space. Even so, everyone who flies the shuttle is very much aware that it's still an experimental system.

"We're all test pilots. We're sitting on a rocket. It's not licensed by the FAA (Federal Aviation Administration). We get our affairs in order before we fly."

But fly they do, and I, for one, am quite envious. It's the one kind of exploration that I can imagine myself doing if I were qualified, notwithstanding the fact that I'm a total coward. Quite a few people with the means have already flown as "space tourists," and many more are reserving places on the first private commercial tours, so I guess the idea of exploring outer space appeals to a lot of people. My own interest probably stems from nights spent with my father on the roof deck of our house in Ottawa when I was growing up, the two of us mesmerized by the night sky and speculating about what other kinds of life might be out there. (You could see the night sky in the city in those days! And we often saw the Northern Lights.) No doubt these moments also explain why, when I was old enough, I had to get a pilot's licence and why I never pass up a chance to watch Canada's incomparable aerobatic team, the Snowbirds, in action. To this day, a chill runs up my spine when I picture Neil Armstrong and Buzz Aldrin walking on the *moon.*

My son, David, had an even greater passion for space when he was small; he was especially taken with the space shuttle. Before he could read, he knew his little shuttle book by heart and could have worked as a tour guide at the Kennedy Space Center. The day he and I and my mother drove up to the gates of Cape Canaveral in Florida for the first time and he caught a glimpse of the towering Redstone rocket guarding the entry, he was beside himself with excitement. (I'd agreed to deliver him to Canaveral if he would accompany me to Disneyworld, not too far down the road.) We were both thrilled to attend an actual launch a year or so later and grief-stricken when the *Challenger* blew up in January 1986. We were then living in Cambridge, Massachusetts, and since there was a New Hampshire teacher aboard the shuttle, every classroom in New England had tuned in to watch the launch. Many hearts were broken that day, ours among them. David never talked very much about it; in fact, we didn't talk much about space ever again.

The old Redstone rocket later fell down in a storm.

The shuttle's image had been tarnished anyway, for me, by Ronald Reagan's attempt to link the shuttle flights with Star Wars, the popular name for his missile defence programme. I don't know if there's any compelling reason to oppose missile defence research today, but during the Cold War, critics feared the U.S. project would spark a new round of weapons building on the part of the Soviet Union, and since the U.S. and the

U.S.S.R. already had about eighty thousand nuclear warheads between them, there seemed to be more than enough on tap to blast the earth out of its orbit. There were others who thought Star Wars was just impractical and a waste of money.

The astronauts, though, were like members of some master race. They were not tarnished in any way by the schemes of their political masters, and I was always pleased to talk to them, especially to the Canadians among them, like Bondar and Marc Garneau and Chris Hadfield. Hadfield was the voice of Mission Control on the ground for the flight that would take a 77-year-old John Glenn back into space, making him the oldest person to venture beyond our atmosphere. I asked Colonel Hadfield what were the major differences Senator Glenn would experience between his first flight and the one he was about to make, and he said, "Room, for one thing." On his first flight, 36 years earlier, Glenn had been wedged into a compartment the size of a go-cart; now he'd be able to unstrap himself and float around, weightless, with the rest of the crew.

And this time he was going as a scientist, not a pilot. Everyone experiences osteoporosis and loss of balance in space, Hadfield told us, but in younger astronauts these conditions reverse themselves after they've returned to earth; no one knew what would happen to Glenn's body after he returned. *Like giving your body to science while you're still alive,* I thought. Hadfield added that Glenn was tickled pink to have a second chance to fly. Hadfield himself was 36 years old when he got his *first* flight, and now he was hankering for another.

Julie Payette, a mission control specialist aboard *Discovery* in 1999 and the second Canadian woman in space, tried to convey to us once how really weird it was to be weightless. Even though we're all familiar with the concept, even though you train for years before you fly, your reflexes just aren't prepared for the experience, she told us. So if you drop some-thing, you look *down* to see where it fell, when in reality, of course, it doesn't *fall* anywhere. Payette said that when she went to sleep the first couple of times in space, she got into a "horizontal" position, or what seemed like horizontal in the context of the ship, just as though she were lying down on a mattress. But there was no mattress and there was no hori-zontal and you could go to sleep in any position. In fact, said Dr. Payette, she came to appreciate that sleeping in space was one of the great aspects of weightlessness.

Payette also said she would never get over the sight of the planet Earth from space. She would look up from her work and think, *Oops, there goes Australia. . . . Oops, there goes a small island in the Pacific.* The immensity of the desert in northern Africa, the greenness of Canada, the way the sun rises instantaneously—they had 16 sunrises and sunsets a day—were things she thought were etched on her soul for all time.

Nowhere were the stamina, ingenuity and courage of space sailors more tested than aboard the Russian space station *Mir* in the months between February and June 1997, when a fire and then a collision with a docking cargo ship put the Russ-ian and American crew members in great peril. *As It Happens* covered the accidents when they occurred, but it wasn't until journalist Bryan Burrough took us behind the scenes in his book *Dragonfly* that we really understood what had been going on at the time—and we, of course, invited Burrough to paint a picture for our listeners.

Burrough told us about the strains that existed between the Russians and Americans, in space and on the ground. The strains were caused, in part, by personality clashes among them and, in part, by cultural differences. As Burrough described it, NASA chiefs were intent at that time on getting more bang for their bucks—a kind of *higher, faster, cheaper* policy—but even so, the Americans went to great lengths to make space travel as safe as possible. The Russians, on the other hand, were used to stuff breaking and making do, and they seemed to think that some of their fellow travellers were sissies. Burrough had got access to transcripts of all the Russian radio traffic during this time, and he did a brilliant job of recreating the tension and danger aboard *Mir* during the crisis.

A poignant aspect of the *Mir* story was the fact that, although the space station was launched and assembled by the Soviet Union when it looked like a superpower, it was a bankrupt and demoralized Russia that was trying to keep the space programme going. The cosmonauts, as the Russians call their space pilots, held all the records for endurance in space, but by the time the Soviet Union collapsed, they were already being pushed to their limit, operating on a shoestring. Indeed, there was a lone cosmonaut aboard *Mir* when the U.S.S.R. came to an end, and for a time it looked as though he might be forgotten up there.

In 1999 I went to Russia with *As It Happens* producer Thom Rose to report on how people were coping with a faltering economy and all the other challenges of adjusting to life after *glasnost*. The trip was memorable in several respects, but going out to the Yuri Gagarin Cosmonaut Training Centre in Star City to meet cosmonaut Sergei Krikalev was both memorable and thrilling for me. Apart from his charm and good looks, Colonel Krikalev, it turned out, was the very man who had been stranded aboard *Mir* in 1991. The mission lasted more than 311 days as a result. When Krikalev finally stepped out of his Soyuz capsule back on *terra firma,* he was wearing the badges of a country that had ceased to exist.

When I met him, I asked Krikalev how he had kept from going crazy, alone in space for months at a time. He said it wasn't as hard as you might think. There was the view, for one thing—always spectacular. And he'd had lots of communication with the ground—with Russian space officials, of course, but also with ham radio operators who would call him up to chat.

Krikalev had a practical view of the problems the space programme was facing at a time of widespread economic hardship. As I reported back to Barbara Budd and Jennifer Westaway in the *As It Happens* studio in Toronto, the budget for the space programme that year was $290 million, a tenth of what it had been in 1989. The Kremlin had decreed that *Mir* could be kept aloft only if they could find a private backer to pay for it. (Would they consider re-naming it the Ted Rogers Space Centre?) The buildings at Star City looked shabby and neglected; people were scarce. I thought all this must be very hard on Russian pride, but Krikalev said he understood that times were hard and that the country had other priorities. He added, though, that he was concerned about the lost opportunity.

"Space is our future," he told me, "our science, the education of the next generation."

The Russian space programme was an important symbol, but it was also more than a symbol. Obviously, he hoped the programme could be saved. For Sergei Krikalev, at least, the ride was not over. He continued to go into space and was involved in a number of missions with the Americans, including, in 1994, the first joint U.S.-Russian Space Shuttle Mission. The much-decorated (did I mention also charming and handsome?) cosmonaut has spent more time in space than any other person—803 days to date—and is slated to fly again in 2009, although his appointment as Vice-President of the

Energiya Corporation, which now runs the Russian space fleet, may preclude that.

Listening to Chris Hadfield and Julie Payette and Sergei Krikalev talk about their experiences made me realize I was still very much caught up in the romance of space travel after all, but my love affair with the shuttle took another bashing when *Columbia* burned up somewhere over Texas. Texas, George W. Bush's home state, and just before the invasion of Iraq . . . the symbolism was haunting. Once again it looked as though the gods were angry and the brave space pilots were somehow being punished for the sins of their commanders on the ground. That's not just superstition, by the way: dollars spent fighting wars are often dollars that don't get spent somewhere else, like maybe making space travel safer.

The immediate cause of the disaster had to do with *Columbia*'s heat shield, which had sustained some damage on take-off. One might have imagined that this would set off alarm bells at NASA, but as Roberta Bondar reminded us, such things had happened before without consequences. This might explain why no one thought it necessary to try to find out exactly how much damage the shuttle had sustained. Tragically, it was too much.

Bondar also told us it wasn't the first re-entry that had gone badly wrong. It had happened to the Russians, she told us—only they had managed to hush it up at the time. In that episode, the cosmonauts knew well in advance that they weren't going to make it back alive. They radioed their families and said their goodbyes and awaited their awful fate.

Would anyone at NASA have known that Columbia *wasn't going to come back in one piece?* I wondered. Roberta Bondar didn't think so.

SIX

Rugged Roses

Bittersweet radio

⁓

ML: Hello, I'm Mary Lou Finlay.

BB: Good evening, I'm Barbara Budd.

This is *As It Happens*.

THEME THEME THEME

BB: Tonight:

ML: Defending the commissioner's work ethic. A Liberal MP says Bernard Shapiro is the right man for the job.

BB: A web of influence. An Iranian exile in Toronto uses his blog to say what he couldn't say back home.

ML: Ferreting out those weapons of mass destruction. A British government memo reveals that pilots were told to goad Saddam Hussein into war by firing on Iraqi installations.

BB: The eagle has landed. With a thud. An Alaska man looks on as a bald eagle crashes through his neighbour's window and drops its fish.

ML: Mortar-fied. An Ontario man is surprised to learn that an old shell he kept in his garden shed was armed and ready to detonate.

BB: And a Canadian journal settles an ontological

question that has puzzled great thinkers for centuries: what is the funniest philosophy joke?

As It Happens, the Wednesday edition. Radio that is.

This is what the first page of script looks like for a typical *As It Happens* show. We say hello; we play our opening theme (Moe Koffman's "Curried Soul"); and we read "the bills." Barbara always gets the last word, and it includes "the tie-off line," which always includes the word *radio* and refers to one of the lighter stories in our lineup. I've no idea how long we've been using "radio that . . ." tie-off lines, but it's now as much a part of the show's signature as the theme music, as venerable a tradition as Reading.

But the point I'm making here is that we hosts don't just make it up as we go along, not when we're introducing things anyway. We have scripts, scripts need writers—and *As It Happens* has had some of the best writers in the business. Occasionally, they have a bad day. Many of us remember Al Maitland announcing one night in apparent exasperation, "I would like to inform listeners that, although I read this stuff, I do not write it."

But even that line, I have learned, was written for Al by the show's writer at the time, George Jamieson. When I joined *As It Happens,* George was the senior producer. He was responsible for writing the bills and tie-off lines, which he did between bouts of consulting with the chase producers, briefing me on dead blues musicians, listening to interviews being taped, keeping tabs on developing stories, making popcorn and watching the webcam located at the corner of Bourbon Street and St. Peter in New Orleans. Except for the webcam part, George had been doing this for as long as anyone could remember; he made it seem easy. In fact, the only time I remember seeing George break into a sweat was the night we lost Dalet about five minutes before air time.

Dalet was the name of the digital recording and editing system that replaced the old quarter-inch audiotape we'd used since around the time of Alexander Graham Bell, or slightly after. What I found disconcerting about digital recording was that, in my view, it didn't actually *exist*. There was no nice solid little reel of acetate that you could hold in your hand, cut up, splice back together, carry to a machine and *play*. A digital recording was just a computer file—and we all *know* what happens to computer files.

True to their form, all the radio news computers would occasionally get clogged up or crash or threaten to crash, and everyone would scramble to save what they were working on, but nothing really disastrous happened to us . . . until the night we lost the whole show just as we were about to go live to the east coast. Happily, I wasn't the only techno-skeptic on the floor. When we'd switched to digital, Linda Groen, the show's executive producer at the time, had decreed that until further notice every interview would continue to be recorded on our old tape machines, as well as on the computer. So when Dalet crashed, we had hard versions of all the material we'd collected for the show that day, but none of it was cleaned up or edited or timed or in any way ready for broadcast. And by the way, was there anyone in the room who still knew how to cut tape with a razor?

At times like this, I would just go and sit down in the studio with Barbara; we'd cast a hopeful glance at each other, cross our fingers . . . and trust in our colleagues "out there" to get us through. The night we lost Dalet, there *were* a couple of people left who knew how to edit tape. Someone threw the first reel on—the interview was perhaps a tad too long—and while it was running, someone else was cleaning up the next bit, and so we got through it. If memory serves, our digital files were recovered before we hit central Canada, so the show was clean for the rest of the country.

Later, George and Kent Hoffman, our technician at the time, rigged up some sort of back-up system with guitar cables and duct tape to ensure that if the computer in the studio crashed again, they could still play back the show from another computer at the Main Desk. It worked like a charm.

When George decided it was time to move on, the rest of us were dismayed. Not only did he have the writing and journalistic and people skills that made him an ideal senior producer, he was also the show's memory. When there's a turnover of producers and hosts, as there often is, it's important that someone remain who can say, "We did that story last May." Or when a Big Name dies, "Liz Gray did an interview with her in 1987. Ask Archives to find the tape." Or in some cases, "Whatever you do, don't book *him* for an interview. No one can understand a thing he says."

George had the memory, because his days with *As It Happens* dated back to when the show came out of an old mouse-infested former girls' school on Jarvis Street in Toronto, where they'd had to gallop up and down stairs to hustle scripts and tapes from the production office to the studio.

Those were the days when you had to enlist the help of a Bell operator to find the number for the newspaper editor you were trying to reach in Katmandu or the FARC spokesman in Colombia. Some operators were very good at it. They probably thought of themselves as part of the production team—and so did the radio people. George recalls that one day when he called Bell to ask for a line to Africa, the operator came back with, "Isn't it Mr. Somerwill who usually calls Africa? I hope he's not ill."

In the event, the show didn't crash when George Jamieson left, but it did require two people to take his place. Leith Bishop took on all the responsibilities of senior producer except the writing; that task we entrusted to a skinny, pony-tailed guy called Bob Coates. Bob was in his 30s and had been loping about the place for several years at that point, though so quietly you hardly knew he was there some days, until he started serving up his little gems. Like all good producers, Bob could turn his hand to almost any kind of assignment, but his preference was for music and art and quirky marijuana stories, and he had a talent for finding something amusing in almost any situation. It was when he moved into the writer's chair at *As It Happens,* however, that Bob really found his stride.

I don't know where or how Bob learned to write the way he did, but maybe his early exposure to Harlequin romances had something to do with his literary development. Harlequin was where he met fellow producer Greg Kelly in 1989; Bob worked nights and Greg worked the day shift. As Greg recalls . . .

> . . . *from time to time, our paths would cross. And the only way that I could keep my sanity throughout the day, doing this drudgery of proofreading Harlequin novels, which is what Bob was also doing, was to keep a rogues' gallery of the worst sayings and abuses of the English language that you'd come across reading these things, and I would record them or get people to hand them in to me. You'd get things like, "She walked past him at a run." Or "Bitch," he said, "but the word was a caress."*

When I met Bob, I found that he was keeping his own rogues' gallery. Bob maintained that one of the hallmarks of really bad writing was the prevalence of "ly" adverbs. So, instead of conveying speed, you would simply say "quickly." And if you got a lot of these "ly" adverbs going on, you knew you were going to get bad writing. The most egregious example of that that Bob ever came across is one that I will always remember Bob for: "Aaron raised his eyebrows evaluatively."

And that, to me, sums up Bob's sense of humour.

His sense of humour and his sense of style. Not that Bob found it easy to write the show. No one does; it can be a terrible grind. The writer's responsible not only for the bills and tie-off lines, but also for all the other scripts in the show, including the introductions. The individual story producers submit drafts, but they often need a lot of rewriting. Former *As It Happens* producer Neil Morrison remembers what it was like to have Bob Coates as a mentor:

After I'd written an introduction, Bob would clean it up and do a lot of work on it. And in the beginning there was a lot of work to do; Bob always made it a completely different piece of work. And I used to study, study, study how Bob did this. I would look at my version and then look at Bob's version and be depressed and discouraged by how much better it was. Then at one point—I think I'd been sending in scripts to him for about three months—he came to me and let me know that, for the first time, he didn't have to change anything in my intro. It was a crowning moment for me. I thought, Finally I've got something that passes the Bob test.

Neil was one of the people who filed his scripts early enough for Bob to polish them. There were others who didn't quite manage to file sometimes until just minutes before the *intros* were due to be read on air by Barbara. So . . . it's ten minutes to showtime, the writer's scrambling to finish the bills and the tie-off line and to make sure the first scripts, at least, have been delivered to the hosts—and maybe the topics aren't so inspiring that night.

"I need your *intro*, Laurie. Now!"

"*You* try writing a fresh lead to your 32nd story on mad cow!" Laurie wails.

"DOES ANYONE HAVE A TIE-OFF LINE FOR THE GUY WHO DID THE NOSE JOB ON THE DUCK?"

"Who burnt the popcorn?"

"Has anyone seen Barbara and Mary Lou?"

"Have you checked the smoking room?"

There is no longer a smoking room at the CBC, of course, and Barbara and I have both quit, in spite of our convictions that inspiration—to paraphrase American writer Fran Lebowitz—is coded into the inside of the cigarette paper. Bob found his elsewhere—from staring at a blank computer screen. When he started chuckling quietly to himself, you knew he'd nailed it.

When he wasn't wrestling with scripts, Bob was still chasing the stories he loved: feature interviews with the glass artist Dale Chihuly when he came to town to open a new exhibit, or with architect Frank Gehry when he agreed to design a winery in the Niagara region. For some reason, these interviews always seemed to be scheduled for a day off, but it was never an issue with me. Bob's enthusiasm was too persuasive.

Bob never said so to me, but it must have been painful for him at times to watch me struggle through an interview with an artist whose work he loved—and which I admired but didn't really understand. I was more comfortable with politics and science than with the arts stories. Like the other producers, he did his best to brief me, but there's only so much you can do with me as raw material. I've seen Barbara wince at some gaucherie I committed when chatting with an actor or musician. I'm so un-hip that my "secret Santa" one year—Laurie Allan—presented me with her own Idiot's Guide to Pop Culture. It listed critical facts about such pop icons as Lindsay Lohan, Fantasia, Dr. Phil and Prince—along with their photos.

One day Laurie also provided us with a perfect example of why it's always good to have people of different vintages on the production team: when the name *Tito* came up in a story, she didn't connect it with the former President of Yugoslavia, while I had no idea it could also be referring to one of the Jackson Five singers.

Bob, on the other hand, was very hip. His finger was on the pulse of everything that was happening in music and art and design—especially music. He loved blues and bluegrass and jazz and rock, and according to those who might know, he had a finely tuned ear for the best. When he had time to pick music tracks for the show, as well as to produce stories and write, the product sounded very good indeed. With all that talent, he might have been an arrogant shmuck—but he wasn't. The truly amazing thing about Bob—the reason we all loved him—was that he was invariably patient with us lesser mortals. The only time I saw him angry was when a senior producer was being too hard on a young recruit, but even then he didn't have it in him to be rude.

We were lucky to have Bob with us, and we knew it. And then our luck ran out.

"I had to go for a biopsy," he told me one day when we were standing together at the photocopier. "There was a spot on my ear . . . and I have a swollen gland." My blood ran cold. Bob looked really worried, and I could understand why. I think I knew at that instant that this story wasn't going to have a happy ending. Still, it was a shock when he called us a week later to tell us that his doctor had just confirmed the bad news: it was a malignant melanoma. A few days after that, Bob's partner, Karen, was told she had breast cancer. *This can't be happening,* we thought. *How could this be happening?*

And how could we carry on at work as if nothing were happening?

We did carry on, but the programme wasn't at its peak in those days and no wonder. Everyone's mind was elsewhere a lot of the time. Everyone wanted to be with Bob and Karen as much as possible, for as much time as Bob and Karen could put up with us. They were very generous with their time, the two of them. They shared almost all the time they had left together with many other people—with Bob's family and Karen's family; with Bob's friends from the CBC and Karen's friends from Nelvana, where she worked as an animation editor; with other friends from other parts of their lives. They did it as much to make us feel better as for their own distraction, I know. And all the while, Karen was getting radiation and chemo, and Bob was getting radiation and chemo, and both of them were generally feeling pretty damn awful.

Karen, I'm happy to report, recovered from her cancer. Bob died at home on Saturday, November 30, 2002.

Monday morning at *As It Happens,* we turned our attention to the tribute we would air that night. Producer Brooke Forbes offered to go around the building and record goodbyes from all the people who had worked with Bob. (The memory of this became especially poignant to us not long afterwards when Brooke also died of cancer.) Mark Ulster wrote a script; Barbara and I set down a few thoughts of our own; others resurrected some of Bob's productions from the archives and selected the music. Actually, Karen picked the music, a song she and Bob both loved: "Rugged Roses," by a Texas band called the Gourds. It starts like this:

> Tell me with yer eyes
> In silence let them ring
> The precious humming of our hearts
> In silence let them sing
> May our phantoms find their places
> Where ever that may be
> Let only the sound of love dear echo endlessly.

The *As It Happens* tribute to a favourite son lasted half an hour. We could have done more but—grieving though we were—we didn't want to embarrass Bob's memory by appearing too self-indulgent on the air. The audience reaction told us we'd got it about right. There were no complaints, and many people called and wrote to tell us how moved they had been by the tribute and how grateful they were to have been given an insight into the people behind the scenes—and how much they wished they could have known Bob Coates, since he was obviously a very special person.

Bob Coates set high standards, but I think he'd be pleased to know how hard people have worked to maintain them. Chris Howden and Adam Killick and Robin Smythe all occupied his writer boots when I was there and proved they were as devoted to words and language and laughter as Bob. Mark Ulster wrote the show for a while, then became its senior producer—an excellent one, by the way. I don't know which one of them wrote the opening bills I reproduced at the beginning of this chapter, but I love the tie-off line—and I thought you might like to know how that whole philosophy joke thing turned out.

The interview, in June 2005, was with a woman named Christine Tappolet, professor of meta-ethics at the University of Montreal, who had organized a contest for the magazine of the Canadian Philosophical Association. The aim was to find the funniest philosophy joke. She had selected four winners and—just to give you an idea—this was her favourite: QUESTION—*What's brown and sticky?* ANSWER—*A stick.*

"What was the joke?" I asked her.

"That's it," she said.

To be fair, the pickings were slim. Dr. Tappolet said that only 18 of the 700 members of the association had responded to her request. The problem was, she told us, "No one reads the bulletin; one of the goals [of the contest] was to beef up the readership."

But Talkback didn't let us down. Here are my Top Ten listeners' submissions for consideration as Best Philosophy Joke:

Q: What did the Zen Buddhist say to the hot dog vendor?
A: Make me one with everything.
                                    —Bob McLeod, Stittsville, Ontario

"Nietzche is dead."—God.
                                    —on a T-shirt spotted by Linda
                                    from Georgetown, Ontario

Q: What's the difference between a Stoic and a Cynic?

A: A Stoic is what brings the baby, and a Cynic is what you wash him in.
                                    —a Ms. McQuarry from Calgary, Alberta

The funniest philosophy joke in the world? I think it is simply this: "Define your terms" as the response to any philosophical question.
                                    —Tom Norris, Vancouver, British Columbia

Q: How do you get a philosopher off your porch?
A: Pay for the pizza.
                                    —Dave from Ottawa, Ontario

René Descartes is sitting in a bar, and the bartender says, "Last call, René. You want another one?" Descartes says, "I think not"—and disappears.
                                    —David Gearlock, Frankfurt, Kentucky

Q: What do you get when you cross a dyslexic agnostic with an insomniac?
A: Somebody who stays up all night wondering if there is a dog.
                                    —Stewart Dudley, North Gower, Ontario

Did you hear the one about the philosophy student who declined an invitation to a brothel in order to study for his finals? He wanted to put Descartes before the whores.
                                    —Ian Bowater, Los Angeles, California

Did you hear about the student who left a note on the kitchen table? "Gone to philosophy class; your dinner doesn't exist."
                                    —Jill McCabe

"If a tree falls in the forest"—*shit, I screwed it up. The joke goes, "If a man speaks in the forest and there's no woman there to hear him, is he still wrong?"*

—this version called in by Duncan
Thompson from McLean, Virginia

I think I hear Bob laughing.

SEVEN

The Man in the Bear Suit

Radio with all the grizzly details

〜

I'm not sure just when or why Troy Hurtubise decided to dedicate his life to making a bear-proof suit, but he's been at it for quite a while and has acquired an international reputation for eccentricity. He's also acquired an Ig Nobel prize at Harvard and attracted a fair amount of investment capital over the years. When I first spoke to him in November 2001, he was about to test the Ursus Mark VI bear-proof suit, i.e., a suit that he could wear for a date with a very large bear—a grizzly, say, or even a Kodiak, which is a brown bear the size of a polar bear.

ML: Mr. Hurtubise, you have your suit all pressed and polished and ready to go, have you?

TH: Suit's all prepped and everything, yes.

ML: Now, how are you going to meet your challenger? Are you just going to pour honey over it and stand in the woods or what?

TH: No, I'll basically just stand there and the handler will say, "Go at the suit," and the bear will go at the suit.

ML: What handler? Where are you going?

TH: I'll be going to British Columbia, and the attack itself will be a controlled attack.

ML: Oh, it will.

TH: Oh, absolutely. Getting in close to grizzly bears in the wild, doing research alone, is hard enough, never mind counting on the bear attacking to see if, in fact, the suit would work if things went awry.

ML: So you're going to be attacked by a *tame* bear?

TH: Yes. A 1,300-pound Kodiak.

ML: And what kind of a test is that?

TH: It's a test that could kill you if it doesn't work.

ML: Okay.

TH: You've got 1,300 pounds, 10 feet, real claws, real teeth—real power. So basically, the suit's a toy to the bear.

ML: Okay.

TH: And when he's told to go at the suit, it will rip apart the suit. I've no illusions that the outside skeleton will [not] be ripped apart, which is the rubber base that holds the electronics in place. That'll be completely ripped apart.

ML: What are you saying? You think it will be ripped apart?

TH: Oh, the outside of the suit—absolutely. He'll make his way to the titanium and then that's, of course, what'll stop him. I'm not so much worried about the claws and the teeth as I am about the power. Basically, what I wanted for 15 years is [to see]: could the suit withstand that kind of force? I mean, I've tried against trucks and everything imaginable to man, but never against the power.

ML: The weight and power.

TH: No, not so much the weight. I mean, we've done 3-ton pick-up trucks at 35 kilometres an hour, and that's not a problem.

. . .

ML: What did it feel like—getting hit by the truck?

TH: Oh, I guess the equivalent of being in an inner tube. You know, rolling-down-the-hill type of thing, maybe hit a tree. . . . You know you were hit only because you hit the ground, because you left the ground and flew back 50, 60 feet. . . .

ML: So how will you signal if you're in some distress?

TH: Well, that's basically a voice command. And if he's knocked the wind out of me, there's not much you're going to be able to do about that. I mean if I can't talk, there's no way the handler's going to be able to know. He can't get face signals, because I'm enclosed in a titanium shield.

ML: Yes. . . . Do you not think the bear might just be scared out of his wits and run in the other direction . . . when he has a look at you?

TH: You've hit it on the head. In all the research that I've done with grizzly bears—you know, winter den studies and testing the deterrent sprays and that—you're right: a wild bear might, possibly, nine out of ten times, look and say, *That's a formidable thing in front of me, and I don't like what I'm looking at*—and actually take off.

ML: Of course, it *works* that way. I mean, if that's what happens, if that's how you protect yourself, it works—right?

TH: Yeah. So when you're talking about a controlled attack, where you have a handler, the bear will do what the handler says, so I don't have to worry about the Kodiak looking at me and saying, *I don't want to play with you.*

ML: Now, Mr. Hurtubise, I sort of forget why you started this. I mean, why would a can of Mace not do the trick if you're trying to protect yourself against a bear?

TH: Well, that's why I originally built the suit. I tested deterrent sprays under actual field conditions. I'm the only one able to do it in the world for companies that market it to the public . . . who are told that, if you're in the backcountry and things go awry, just simply spray the bear and it goes away. Well, that's a fallacy, of course . . . But to test that, you'd actually have to do it against a grizzly bear. Well, nobody could do it, because if it doesn't work, you're going to get killed.

ML: Yeah.

TH: So they come to me and I have this suit. And I start out with black bears—I don't wear a suit with black bears. You don't need it. It's a totally different species. And then you move your way up to grizzly bears. And I'm able to say whether it works or not, and of course, it wouldn't stop a dog, let alone an enraged grizzly.

ML: So it's not as though your life will be totally without purpose if you meet the bear challenge coming up.

TH: Oh no. We're already into the next suit. My whole point is, after all these years, I would like to know— though I tested it against everything man can throw at me—would it have survived what a grizzly can do? And now I have the chance, a safety-controlled chance, and I'm more than happy to do it.

Troy Hurtubise was as good as his word: he went out west to test his suit against a Kodiak bear, and a couple of weeks later, we called him back to find out how it went. It turned out that I had indeed hit the nail on the head with that question about the bear maybe being more frightened of Troy in his suit than the other way around—sort of.

ML: Mr. Hurtubise, how'd it go?

TH: Well, I didn't get actual contact, but I got everything else I needed. I found out whether the suit would be able to handle the pressure. The other fascinating thing was— I guess the irony of it all—was that the bears are terrified of the suit. They wouldn't come near it.

ML: Well, I told you that!

TH: I sensed that over the years, but I didn't think against a Kodiak . . .

ML: Tell us in detail what you did. You were going to go against this Kodiak . . .

TH: Yes. The handler himself had never seen the Ursus Mark VI other than on TV, so when I got up there with the suit, he looked at me and said, "Well, I want to get my bear accustomed to the suit. So without you in it, I'm going to bring it into his cage."

I said, "Sure, no problem at all."

So he brought it in, and we slowly worked the bear to get used to the suit, and at one point, he said, "Okay, you can have it," and to our surprise, the Kodiak actually claimed the suit. And if you know bears "claiming," it's like a kill. It's *his*. He took it underneath him. So that was pretty scary.

ML: Oh. Aren't you glad you weren't in it?

TH: Well, yeah, at that time, yes, because what I wanted to know was—it wasn't built for a Kodiak—so I wanted to know, would he be able to crush it like a pop can?

ML: And?

TH: No. He tried everything he could. That got him mad, so he started to go at the rubber, and of course, he was taking pieces of the rubber off—we expected that—and then he got to the chain mail, and that's where the problems started. He was peeling back the chain mail like it was a banana.

ML: Uh-oh.

TH: Because it's not shark chain mail.

ML: It's not *shark* chain mail?

TH: No. You see, real chain mail is shark chain mail used for great white sharks.

ML: Right. That has to be strong.

TH: When we shot the movie with the [National] Film Board and I was building the suit, we didn't have time to get that, so I went with butcher's chain mail, which is fine against a grizzly, not a Kodiak. So we had a heck of a time getting the suit back from him. We finally got the suit out, and I mean there was chunks taken out of it. . . . No problem; once he got to the titanium, it wasn't a problem.

ML: The titanium held up. It wasn't squashed.

TH: It wasn't squashed, which was a great success for me. So he took me aside and said, "Listen. Not against this bear; not with this chain mail. I will not allow you to do that."

ML: "Don't want to see you killed."

TH: Sure. So he said, "But I have a 320-pound grizzly . . ." And I said, "Wow. That's great."

He said, "I have more than enough confidence in your suit against the grizzly bear, without even me here—like, inside the cage—that if she actually took you to the ground and had fun with you type of thing, you'd be okay. And I said, "Well, that's great." So I got in the suit, walked in the cage by myself—there's this 320-pound grizzly—and, sure enough, not so much to my surprise but to his, there was no way on this earth that that bear was going to come near that suit. There was no way. See, he assumed that, okay, if she becomes accustomed to it, then she'll investigate. No. I mean, forget it.

So now Troy Hurtubise had the grizzly thoroughly cowed by his bear-proof suit, and the Kodiak, at least, had managed not to completely destroy it, but still he wasn't satisfied. He persuaded the handler to give him another crack at the Kodiak, and this time he *would* be wearing the suit. He thought the bear might have more respect for the suit if it was standing up, and he wasn't wrong.

TH: They let the Kodiak out, and it's just me and the Kodiak and—no way. I mean, for ten minutes that bear was not coming near that suit. I mean, he was scared. I'm six foot two and I'm formidable in this suit; he's on all fours. There's no bear in the world that's bigger than me when they're on all fours, so when he's on all fours, he's looking at me and saying, *I don't like this.*

But now the handler yells back to me. He says, "How long can you stay in the suit?"

I said, "25, 30 minutes."

And he said, "Good. Stand there and chew some gum, because in about five minutes, this bear is going to figure out that he's bigger than you and it's going to turn into curiosity and then it's going to turn into, *I'm not scared of you anymore.*

And, sure enough, five minutes pass and he's catching my scent and he's looking at me and you know what he's saying—

ML: *Crunchy on the outside, soft on the inside?*

TH: No, no, that's not what he's saying. He's saying, *I know you smell like a human. I know what a human smells like and I know what a human looks like—but you don't look like a human. What are you?* So he starts to get more curious and more curious. Finally, he makes it to five feet and then he gets a huge whiff of me and stands up all on his own, ten feet tall—

ML: Uh-oh.

TH: At five feet away. Now I'm terrified. I'm terrified. The grizzly I had no fear of, because I knew the suit could handle a grizzly. The Kodiak blocking out the sun in front of me . . . Okay, this isn't a good thing here; I'm getting scared. So he's up there ten feet, and he comes back down, and in that instant we both knew he knew he was bigger than me. He says to himself—I mean, you just know, the way the look was—*I am bigger than you and I betcha I'm stronger than you.* So he starts to get very curious to the point of brave enough to get within six inches of me, on all fours. His mouth's open and I'm looking down at these canines—I mean, just huge—

ML: You're waiting for the handler to say, "Here, Rover!"

TH: There was a couple of instances the handler knew that he was ready to take a shot at me and would say, "No! No!" and the bear would back off. It's like a mother to him, the handler. So the bear's looking at the handler and me at the same time and thinking, *Geez, I wonder if I can slip one in there.*

So we went at this for a half-hour and it was just, you know, teeth and standing up and this and that. . . . So we ended that, we got out of the cage and—it was a big compliment to me—the handler said, "Listen, it's not over. I have full confidence in your suit. I honestly thought that he'd crush it. He can't do it; I'm shocked. But if you switch the chain mail—get rid of that garbage you've got on there and put the real shark chain mail on—you come back in the spring and I have full confidence that if the bear goes beyond curiosity to taking you to the ground, he won't be able to do nothing to you."

ML: So back to the shop.

TH: So yeah. I'm going to strip it down, put the real chain mail on. I'm going to go back in the spring, be fully confident that I'm going to be able to do what I'm going to do.

ML: And we'll talk to you then.

TH: Absolutely.

ML: You know you're crazy, don't you?

TH: Oh no, just a researcher who does things a little different.

Different . . . yeah.

We did talk to the Bear Suit Man again, when he was about to test the Ursus Mark VII. It had no chain mail whatsoever, but it was much stronger, he told us. Plus, it had air conditioning and on-board computers—oh yes, and *fingers*. The better to climb up and out of the cage, I figured, when the bear came after him.

That was in May 2002. When I checked back the other day to see how his quest was doing, there was good news and there was bad news. The good news was that his bear suit days were over; he felt he'd topped the charts in the bear suit category and no further improvement was required.

As it happens, though, there isn't a huge market for bear-proof suits, and since a guy's got to eat, Mr. Hurtubise has been trying to interest the military in a modified version of his body armour. According to an article I saw in the *Hamilton Spectator*, his new suit is called the Trojan. It's described as a "practical, lightweight and affordable shell to stave off bullets, explosives, knives and clubs." In the picture accompanying the story, the Trojan doesn't *look* very lightweight, but there are other great features that come with it: a knife, a pepper-spray gun, emergency morphine and salt, a laser pointer, a solar-powered fresh-air system and a detachable transponder that can be swallowed " . . . in case of trouble." And all this could be yours—or the Canadian Armed Forces'—for the bargain-basement price of two thousand dollars a pop.

This is where the bad news comes in. The Canadian military aren't in a rush, apparently, to phone in their orders for the Trojan suit—maybe because Mr. Hurtubise doesn't seem to have a regular phone line. He does have other inventions to peddle, though—like the spray-on Fire Paste that would prevent anything coated in it from burning up. He says it costs next to nothing to make and it's biodegradable. That sounds pretty good, no?

EIGHT

There'll Always Be an England

. . . and a radio

⤸

If the Bear Suit Man's clothes weigh a little more than normal, Stephen Gough's weigh less. In fact, he feels that any clothes at all would be an unnecessary encumbrance when he's running cross-country: a birthday suit, rather than a bear suit, is more his style. Mark McKelvey, on the other hand, doesn't feel dressed unless he's wearing a fridge, which is what he sported on a 160-kilometre trek from Liverpool to Mount Snowdon in Wales back in 2003.

Gough and McKelvey belong to the species *Eccentricus britannicus.* Most of the eccentrics who turn up on *As It Happens* are British, and that's because the British Isles possess by far the greatest number of odd people per capita in the world. We don't know why; maybe it's their diet. You know the sort of people I mean: people who roll cheeses and eat nettles, people who shelter hedgehogs and hate hedges, people who play bagpipes and people who hurl haggis . . . people who see haggis as an *aphrodisiac.*

Once, when I was speaking to a group about how our show gets put together, I described the story meeting we had each morning, where everyone was invited to bring ideas about what to put on the air that night. I told them that the senior producer would run through a list of categories: Lead Story, National, International, Science, Entertainment, Dead Blues Musicians and so on—at which point a woman in the audience put up her hand and asked, "When do you do your Crazy People from England?"

The answer, of course, was: whenever we could. Before I started hosting the show, my all-time favourite guest was the English bloke who had a stuffed fish—a marlin—mounted on the roof of his house, and although its presence had spawned a pretty intense campaign on the part of local councillors and some of his neighbours to get the thing removed, he was not at all inclined to give way. In fact, the more they went after him, the more stuff he acquired for display on his property, up to and including, if I'm not mistaken, a Sherman tank.

A man's home is his castle, he told *As It Happens,* and how he chose to decorate it was his own affair entirely.

The King of Redonda didn't have a castle as such, but he did rule over a small island near Antigua in the Caribbean. We talked to King Robert the First—actually, to the Pretender to the Throne, as he then was—just as he was preparing to sail over from Antigua and plant his flag. He told us that the island, populated chiefly by rats and boobies (tropical birds), had been named by Columbus and established as a kingdom in 1865 by an Antiguan citizen as a legacy for his first-born son, Matthew.

The royal line gets a bit confused after that, since several people not descended from Matthew have claimed to be the King of Redonda. I asked King Robert (*aka* Bob Williamson) what he based his claim on, and he explained that he'd been anointed directly by his predecessor.

Robertus Rex (RR): I met the then king, Juan the Second, early last year, and we got along famously. He was here in Antigua on holiday, and over lunch one day, he said he was fed up being king.

"I'm going to retire soon; I'm going to abdicate."

And of course, I asked who the next king might be, and he said, "Well, I've drawn up a short list, and a very rich Spaniard is at the top of the list; he bought all the regalia at Sotheby's last year."

I refrained from asking him why he flogged the royal gear, but I was a bit upset, and he said, "What's the matter?"

I said, "Thousands of lives and millions of pounds sterling were spent kicking the Spanish out of the Caribbean, and now you're giving a piece of it back? You should be ashamed of yourself."

"Oh God! Didn't think of that."

He then went back to England. I wrote to him, applying to get on the short list, for the following reasons: I'm as brown as the first king after living here for three years; I'm also a writer—which all the kings have been, incidentally. And I have a boat, an 18th-century Baltic trader.

ML: So you can get to the island.

RR: Sure. And it's much the same kind of boat as Matthew's father had.

ML: Well, that would seem to qualify you.

RR: Yeah. "Also," I said, "I'm five foot six, so please put me on the short list." So he did.

ML: You claimed the throne.

RR: That's right, with his blessing. He then told me how to go about it. On Sunday, the day after tomorrow, 65 of us are sailing over to Montserrat in a 120-foot square rigger, *Sir Robert Baden Powell,* and we're going to invade the island and plant the flag. It's one of the several things I have to do to secure the kingdom.

ML: Apart from the Spaniard who bought all the things

at Sotheby's, I'd heard that there was another claimant to the throne.

RR: In fact, there are nine claimants to the throne, all of them totally spurious, of course.

ML: Naturally. Who are they?

RR: Mostly English, and they've never been to Redonda. But the second king was a poet called Gosworth, who was a real rascal. He had his throne in a pub in Soho, in London, and whenever he ran short of the price of a glass of Burgundy, he'd flog a title.

ML: Uh-oh.

RR: So there are more dukes from that era than there are in the British College of Heralds. He apparently sold the throne five times.

ML: Oh, how awkward.

RR: Yeah. I mean, don't buy a used car from him.

ML: No. Is there a national broadcasting company on Redonda yet?

RR: Not yet, although that's been proposed.

ML: Well, you certainly should have a broadcasting company.

RR: Right. You would like to run it, I suppose. Are you unhappy in your job?

ML: No, not in the least, but we could have our meetings there—in February.

RR: I must tell you, it's not very hospitable, though.

King Robert didn't sound overly enthusiastic about our coming down to set up a radio station on Redonda, so we didn't pursue it. Speaking of pubs, though, we once talked to a chap who married a pub. Thomas Sisson spent so much time at his local watering hole that his wife told him he might as well marry it—and he did.

Lyndon Yorke of Marlow Bottom is a tad eccentric in his modes of travel. He once drove a Model A Ford from New Zealand to England—130,000 miles without shock absorbers—and in nice weather, he likes to pedal a sort of Bath chair/boat up and down the Thames. In October 2001, when we spoke to him, he had just shown up on a list of the Most Eccentric People in England, so I asked him what he thought about the others on the list.

"There are a lot of nuts out there," he told me.

Among the so-called nuts were a collector of British mailboxes, a chicken whisperer, a snail racer, the gnome sanctuary lady I mentioned in Chapter 3, Captain Cutlass and Captain Beany. The Most Eccentric list was a goldmine for us, and we proceeded to talk to as many of the award winners as we could. This way we learned, for example, that Captain Cutlass, a pirate, lives aboard a galleon—"a fishing boat to some"—from which he sponsors an annual plank-walking contest. Entries are judged, he told us, on their dress, their *piratese,* the size of the splashes they make when they go into the water and their screams. He didn't see this as especially eccentric.

"All I can say is that I got an award for being myself."

Captain Beany *did* admit to being "very, very slightly touched" when we talked to him about his beany-ness. It all started, he explained, when he was lying in a bath of baked beans (as one does) and the thought came to him, *I want to make a mark for myself in the world.* So he took to dressing up like a giant bean and running marathons for charity—a sort of Baked Bean Crusader for the benefit (bean-a-fit?) of mankind.

Ann Atkins didn't seem to mind being counted among the Most Eccentric. As founder and keeper of the gnome sanctuary in Abbots Bickington, she had, at last count, over two thousand garden gnomes in her care—gnomes that she had collected, restored and preserved, or sometimes created from scratch. She even claims to turn her visitors into gnomes.

"You're somebody different, aren't you, when you're a gnome," she observed.

Couldn't argue with that. And what did she think of the company she was keeping (Captain Cutlass et al.)?

"I didn't think any of them was particularly eccentric," she said.

Earlier, I mentioned the couple who moved more than four hundred kilometres across England in search of their lost puppy. There was also a family who moved to the remote Isle of Muck after winning a competition for a house there. But we also talked to a British family who pulled up stakes and moved to *Spain* when their soccer hero, David Beckham, went to play for Real Madrid. I wonder if they've now found a place in Los Angeles.

Perhaps eccentricity is what you're left with when you don't rule the world anymore but your sense of adventure remains undiminished, along with your sense of entitlement and a dollop of individual courage. Ranulph Fiennes—*Sir* Ranulph, actually—raises money for charity by doing things like running seven marathons on six continents in seven days. He did this in 2003 just four months after he'd had heart bypass surgery, and he managed it without once having to use the defibrillator he took along with him, even though in the Falklands he had to run through a minefield, and in Singapore, his running partner (a doctor) got quite ill.

If these adventurous strains have persisted in the British character for hundreds of years, what should dissuade a mere octogenarian from jumping out of a plane for the first time? Georgie Sinclair of Aberdeen, Scotland, didn't foresee any problems. After all, she quite enjoyed ballooning and flying in micro-light airplanes. And of course, she wouldn't be alone; she'd be harnessed to someone who knew what he was doing . . . surely. His instructions about how she should hit the ground were very clear:

"Slide on your bum," he told Georgie.

What neither of them had foreseen was how hard it might be for an 81-year-old lady to keep her legs high in the air while plummeting downward. Georgie's right leg hit the ground first, and she broke her ankle. Probably wouldn't jump again, she admitted, but when her cast came off, she wouldn't mind going for another spin in that micro-light.

Just as well Mrs. Sinclair wasn't wearing an ironing board when she went skyward, which is how Peter Sergeant of Derbyshire went flying one day. That is, he fixed his ironing board to a glider and went up two and a half thousand feet to do his housework. Extreme ironing, he dubbed it. But it wasn't so amazing, really—the iron wasn't plugged in.

The Bear Suit Man aside—and King Robert of Redonda, who was born in Canada—we didn't come across a lot of Canadian eccentrics while I was doing *As It Happens*. Perhaps living in Canada is eccentric enough all by itself, especially in

February. But an encounter with a slightly eccentric Scotsman led us to an ex-Canadian eccentric (as in ex-parrot, *deceased*)—a man known in his day as the "Cheese Poet." Stay tuned.

NINE

Verse and Worse

Honk if you love radio.

⌒

Celebrating the *worst* of something was always one of our missions at *As It Happens*. According to the people of Dundee, Scotland, the World's Worst Poet was one of their own. Here's a sample of his work:

> Beautiful Railway Bridge of the Silv'ry Tay
> Alas! I am very sorry to say
> That ninety lives have been taken away
> On the last Sabbath day of 1879,
> Which will be remembered for a very long time.

We heard about William Topaz McGonagall from Mervyn Rolfe of the McGonagall Appreciation Society, when he came on the radio to tell us about a plaque they were unveiling in honour of their favourite son. It was to go in the ground beside the "silv'ry Tay" and would be inscribed with the opening words of the poem that was mainly responsible for propelling McGonagall to stardom. The event he was writing about was the collapse, in December 1879, of the River Tay bridge.

Mr. Rolfe gave us several more examples of the art that has brought Mr. McGonagall such enduring fame, like the verse he composed on the death of the Earl of Dalhousie. It begins:

Alas! Lord and Lady Dalhousie are dead, and
buried at last,
Which causes many people to feel a little downcast;
And both lie side by side in one grave,
But I hope God in His Goodness their souls
will save.

William McGonagall had hoped that his poetic muse
might recommend him for the position of British Poet Laure-
ate, and he went so far as to walk to Balmoral Castle in an
attempt to make his case directly to the Queen, but he was
not successful. Still, Mr. Rolfe told us, as the world has
decried McGonagall's poetry for more than a hundred years
now, why not build a memorial to him?

It wasn't as though the Scottish bard had gone totally
unrecognized until then. The City of Dundee had already
instituted an annual dinner in McGonagall's honour. On this
happy occasion, the main thing is to do everything back-
wards. They start with dessert and wind up with the hors
d'oeuvres, listening to the welcome address as they exit. No
doubt you've heard a few welcome addresses that made you
want to exit right away, so you'll probably agree that this was
a good innovation.

The Wikipedia folk, by the way, tell us that Mr. McGonagall also fancied himself an actor but that the theatre where
he worked would let him perform the title role in *Macbeth*
only if he paid for the privilege in advance. Apparently, his
Macbeth refused to die at the end. They also note that
J.K. Rowling named her character Minerva McGonagall after
William. Since it's Wikipedia, I've no idea whether any of this
is true, but if you know J.K., you could ask her.

⌐

The interview about William McGonagall naturally prompted our listeners to put forward their own candidates for the title of Worst Poet. One caller, for example, read to us from the work of Theophile Marzials, another 19th-century British poet and a librarian. It went something like this:

> Death!
> Plop.
> The barges down in the river flop.
> Flop, plop,
> Above, beneath,
> From the slimy branches the grey drips drop
> To the oozy waters, that lounge and flop . . .
> And my head shrieks—Stop!
> And my heart shrieks—Die.

There was more—but *my* head shrieks *Stop!*

And here's where our Canadian Cheese Poet comes in, because another listener insisted that the World's Worst Poet title rightly belonged to James McIntyre, a furniture maker from Ingersoll, Ontario, who had a thing for big cheeses. Since we at *As It Happens* were also partial to big cheeses, Barbara did not have to be coaxed to recite McIntyre's "Ode on the Mammoth Cheese Weighing over 7,000 Pounds" for our pleasure.

> We have seen the Queen of cheese,
> Laying quietly at your ease,
> Gently fanned by evening breeze—
> Thy fair form no flies dare seize.
>
> All gaily dressed soon you'll go
> To the great Provincial Show,

To be admired by many a beau
In the city of Toronto.

Cows numerous as a swarm of bees,
Or as the leaves upon the trees,
It did require to make thee please,
And stand unrivalled, Queen of Cheese.

May you not receive a scar as
We have heard that Mr. Harris
Intends to send you off as far as
The great world's show at Paris.

Of the youth beware of these
For some of them might rudely squeeze
And bite your cheek, then songs or glees
We could not sing, oh! queen of cheese.

Wert thou suspended from balloon,
You'd cast a shade even at noon,
Folks would think it was the moon
About to fall and crush them soon.

Some people, on reading this, might be reminded of Sarah Binks, the "sweet songstress of Saskatchewan," but I feel that McIntyre—who, like William McGonagall, was bred in Scotland—is closer to McGonagall in his sense of rhythm and his attraction to dark themes. Note how his "Ode on a Mammoth Cheese" starts out as a tribute, but then you have those swarms of bees, scars, rude youth biting its cheek and, of course, the image of folks being crushed to death by the mammoth cheese as it falls from the balloon.

But I ask you: is this not championship material?

Incidentally, if you can't get enough of bad poetry, there's a helpful little book put together by Kathryn and Ross Petras called *Very Bad Poetry* (Vintage Press, 1997), which is where I found the full text of Theophile Marzials' poem ("Death! Plop . . ."), and now there's a website by the same name where you can sample the work of some of today's worst poets, submitted, apparently, by the poets themselves. This one's called "Underground":

> Under water grottos, caverns
> Filled with apes
> That eat figs.
> Stepping on the figs
> That the apes
> Eat, they crunch.
> The apes howl, bare
> Their fangs, dance,
> Tumble in the
> Rushing water,
> Musty, wet pelts
> Glistening in the blue.

You may be surprised to learn, as I was, that the man who penned this little gem is Barack Obama. Yes, the very one— there's a picture of him and everything! I know, I know, it's the Internet, and I had my doubts at first. But then I came across this passage in Obama's book *Dreams from My Father,* which certainly was written by him, where he's describing his move to New York City and Columbia University, and the effect the move had on him:

I stopped getting high. I ran three miles a day and fasted on Sundays. For the first time in years, I applied myself to

my studies and started keeping a journal of daily reflec-
tions and writing very bad poetry *[stress mine].*

I rest my case.

When it comes to poetry, good and bad, the members of
our audience are no slouches, and for some reason, haiku in
particular set people to sharpening their pencils. For anyone
not familiar with haiku, it's a form of Japanese verse, usually
17 syllables long, usually broken into three lines of 5, 7 and 5
syllables, respectively. When we offered people an excuse to
compose haiku on an *automotive* theme—well, it just made
their day, and ours.

It all started when Aaron Naparstek got tired of the noise
outside his apartment in Brooklyn, New York.

ML: Mr. Naparstek, when did you decide you'd had
enough of honking in the neighbourhood?

AN: Well, it was right before Christmastime of this year.
I'd just started working out of my house and was
spending a lot more time at home during the day than I
had in the past. And also, you know, Christmastime in
New York, things get really hectic. Specifically, there was
this one—there's always been a lot of honking on this corner that I live on that I've just sort of had to deal with—

ML: Why was it so bad that day?

AN: You know, I've actually studied the honking
problem on my corner in some detail, and it has a lot to
do with the way the lights are timed, and it also has a lot
to do with the fact that they're selling Christmas trees a
block north of my house and it creates a lot of extra
congestion—and people were just going nuts!

ML: Cars get stuck and they start leaning on their horn.

AN: Exactly, exactly. And there was this one guy and he was right in front of my window. I live in this little block—it's generally called "Brownstone Brooklyn," little three-storey brownstone apartment houses—really beautiful block, but what it does is it creates this canyon sort of echo effect, this river of raging honking flowing right in front of our house, and this one guy was just leaning on the horn, just non-stop—not like a *toot-toot, toot-toot-toot*, please move kind of thing, but just a *BAAAAAAHHHHHN!!! BAAAHHHN!!!* Non-stop, *non-stop* leaning on the horn.

ML: So what did you do?

AN: So basically, this guy is leaning on the horn right in front of my window. I've got him in my sights. I decided that if he was still leaning on his horn by the time I got back from the refrigerator with a carton of eggs, then he was going to get some eggs on his windshield. And I was really set on it, too. I mean, it was kind of insane. I was very focused. It was like, keep-leaning-on-horn equals eggs-on-windshield. So I got back to the window with the eggs, and I even have double windows—I've got storm windows because of all the honking—so I opened the first window and I opened the second window and he's still down there—*BAAAAHHHHHN!!!*—just leaning on the horn—and I chucked the first egg.

It wasn't very accurate: it hit the back of his car. Then I took the second egg and hit the top of his car. And it's like, no, I want *windshield* . . . and by the time the third egg did hit his windshield, he was getting out of his car and he saw me, you know, leaning out the window, throwing eggs at him—and he just went insane. He went ballistic. He's screaming at me, he's saying, "I'm going to come back tonight, I'm gonna *kill* you! I know where you live."

ML: Oh dear.

AN: He did! He knew where I lived! I was leaning out my window. People started blasting their horns at him, and he's still ranting in the middle of the street and he finally drives off. I got his licence plate and everything and it's like, okay, if he kills me, I have the licence plate.

ML: You'll leave a note for the police.

AN: Lot of good that's going to do me. But basically, it was at that moment that I decided, *Okay, throwing eggs at the honkers is not the right response.* Like, that did not work.

ML: No. This is when you decided on poetry as a solution?

AN: Exactly. I decided that I needed a different approach, and I sat down and started writing these little haiku poems about honking—I called them *honku*. And at first, that was it. I was just writing these little poems and I didn't really have any big plans for them. And a few weeks later, like in the second or third week of January, I printed up 50 *honkus*—the same poem 50 times—and I went out and posted it on lampposts throughout the neighbourhood.

ML: What did it say?

AN: It said:

> You from New Jersey
> honking in front of my house
> in your SUV.

ML: Complete the sentence. Right. They're all from New Jersey, of course.

AN: Actually, they're mostly not. That first *honku* was very specifically aimed at rallying support in the neighbourhood against two easy targets—people from New Jersey and SUVs.

ML: Right.

AN: A little bit of a cheap shot, but I thought, *Okay, I want to rally support here*, so I went after two easy ones.

ML: Did the honking stop?

AN: Didn't solve the problem.

ML: Oh.

AN: Two weeks later I went out and posted a second *honku*.

ML: And this said . . . ?

AN: Oh, forget Enron.
       The problem around here
       is all the damn honking.

And then, a couple of weeks later, I go out to post my third one and . . . First of all, the very first one I started taping up, this woman walked by and she's like, "Ah. You're the Poet of Clinton Street. I love your work!"

And I was like, *Okay, that was interesting. That's kinda cool.* And then I started walking down the street and posting more, and I noticed that other people had started posting their own on lampposts, you know. And they were copying the format and they were like, "*Honku Number 3*"—and there were a lot of them!

ML: Isn't New York wonderful!

AN: It is wonderful.

ML: Has the honking problem abated at all?

AN: Not at all. The one result, we were able to get the police out here—there's a sign right on the corner that says "No Honking. Penalty $125." The cops came out and enforced it for one day.

ML: Did they. Is there a fine for putting *honku* on lampposts?

AN: Yeah, I discovered there is.

ML: Uh-oh.

AN: And I was pulled over by the police as well.

ML: *You* were pulled over?

AN: I was, I was. I was stopped from posting *honkus* a couple of weeks ago and, uh, I don't remember what the specific fine was but I remember I tallied it up, and if I posted 50 poems, each poem could get fined five times in the course of a day, and it came out to $10,000. So I could be fined a maximum of $10,000 a day for posting 50 *honkus* on lampposts.

ML: And the fine for honking is $100?

AN: $125. It never gets enforced.

ML: Dear me.

Odds are it's not much quieter on that street in Brooklyn today, especially in the lead-up to Christmas, but in the wake of that conversation with Aaron Naparstek, we all had a nice time making up our own little verses about rude drivers, stupid SUVs and the like.

The honking won't stop
but it's not trucks, vans or cars.
Damned Canada geese!
—Cindy Sears, D.C. suburb

You'll wake the baby
with random night-time honking.
Patience is hard-earned.
—Steve from North Bay, Ontario

Rural Alberta:
moose, gravel and chipped glass—
What is a horn for?
—Peter MacKay, Fairview, Alberta

Take a lesson from
quiet town in New Jersey:
slow down and stay home.
—Barbara Jones Warwick, London, Ontario

On this Yukon road
only the moose are horny;
blaring antler'd bulls.
—Rod Jacob, Whitehorse, Yukon

Finally, we heard from Michael Lee in Halifax, Nova Scotia, who said he played in a band, and when they were talking about the show and the *honku* story, the band members had suddenly realized that every verse of the song "Moonlight in Vermont" was, in fact, a haiku. I didn't know that, did you? But look—he's right!

Pennies in a stream,
rippling leaves, a sycamore—
Moonlight in Vermont.

"Wasn't that peaceful?" asked Michael Lee. Peaceful, yes— and so different from the noisy, blaring street in Brooklyn that was the genesis of all this creative writing and thinking. I guess you just never know where or how inspiration will strike.

A year later, Villard Books published Aaron Naparstek's *Honku: The Zen Antidote to Road Rage,* a collection of poems on an automotive theme, and Aaron was kind enough to mention Barbara Budd and me in the Acknowledgments.

TEN

Runaway Chevy

Road-tested radio

〜

How's this for a *honku?*

> Honking runaway
> Chevy truck, out of control
> on the L.I.E.

That could have been Elizabeth Jordan's contribution to
Aaron Naparstek's collection after a really scary ride she had
one morning in May 2002 on the LIE (Long Island Expressway). We first heard about it in the office when *As It Happens* producer Mark Ulster played us the tape recorded by
the 911 emergency dispatcher when Ms. Jordan called in on
her cellphone.

> EJ: I'm on the LIE and I've lost my brakes and I can't
> stop.
>
> DP: Eastbound or westbound?
>
> EJ: I'm going westbound.
>
> DP: What kind of vehicle are you in?
>
> EJ: I'm in a black Blazer, '94, four-door—it's an older
> style. I have my emergency brake on. I tried to go into
> Neutral. Should I try to get it into Park?

DP: Uh, I don't know, ma'am. I can't advise you on that. Um . . .

EJ: I—I'm pressing on my brakes and I just can't stop.

DP: Are you pumping the brakes?

EJ: I'm pumping the brakes. I mean it slowed it a tiny, tiny bit. I'm going about 40 right now.

DP: Okay. Are you in the right lane?

EJ: No, I'm in the left lane right now. Should I move over or stay put?

DP: Well, you don't want to stop in the left lane if you stop. Can you try to get over? . . . How you makin' out?

EJ: It's not stopping. If I hold my foot really hard on the brake, it slows down, but even with the e-brake, it's not stopping. I can smell my brakes going. Should I take it off the brake, see what happens? . . .

DP: Are you—you should be coming to that uphill section soon?

EJ: I just went up a teeny hill. I'm going to . . . the shoulder—

DP: [to someone else] She's going to go for the shoulder.

EJ: . . . because I can't stop! [very heavy breathing heard]

DP: Ma'am, don't breathe like that. You'll hyperventilate.

EJ: I know. I know. I know.

DP: Don't want you hyperventilating.

[horn blast]

EJ: Oh my god!

DP: You've got it in Neutral, right?

EJ: No. Shall I put it into Neutral? Shall I try that?

DP: Will you downshift it?

EJ: You mean—downshift it into what? I'm a female, sorry. [panting now]

DP: You have a second gear?

EJ: Yeah.

DP: Try downshifting it into Second.

EJ: Nothing.

DP: Nothing. Where are you now, hon?

EJ: I'm coming up to [incomprehensible] . . . and the traffic is stopped ahead again.

DP: Are you still on the right shoulder?

EJ: No, I'm not. I'm in the traffic lane.

DP: There should be a police officer right up ahead.

EJ: Yes, I think I see him. [horn beeping steadily]

DP: What lane are you in, ma'am?

EJ: I'm on the shoulder and the right lane. And there are cars in front of me and I'm going to hit them! I'm going to hit someone!

Our hearts were in our mouths as we listened to this, I can tell you. Amazingly, Elizabeth Jordan survived, and a couple of days later, she came on the radio to tell us all about it.

ML: Ms. Jordan, how are you today?

EJ: Aah. Tired, frazzled. Still in shock.

ML: You must be. What a hair-raising experience. Listening to the tape, my throat is constricted.

EJ: Yeah.

ML: Where were you—for us foreigners—where were you when you got into trouble?

EJ: I was on the Long Island Expressway, around Exit 52, 53, somewhere in there—I'm not a hundred percent sure—and I was in the left-hand lane and I had just passed someone and all of a sudden my car sped up to 85 miles an hour—

ML: It sped up!

EJ: The speed limit there is 55, so I'm, *Whoa, I'm going a little too fast here,* and I applied the brakes and the brakes wouldn't work. Tried it again, still didn't work. I tried lifting the gas pedal, I put my foot underneath it, tried pushing it up. Nothing worked. So I shifted into Neutral, and the engine made horrible sounds. I thought it was going to explode or something, so I went back into Drive, and I put my hazards on and decided to put the emergency brake on. The emergency brake went down like Jell-O, though. There was no resistance or anything, but it did slow me down to about 50, which was a manageable speed. And at that point, I knew . . . I wasn't going to stop, and I picked up my cellphone and I called 911. I got a terrific operator, luckily.

ML: You did, didn't you?

EJ: Yes, I did. Good thing. And she asked me, "Did I try this? Did I try that?" And we tried a couple of things together but nothing worked.

At one point, I came to an overpass which cut into the roadway and made the lanes smaller, and the traffic was stopped underneath, and I said to her, "I'm going to hit someone." But I happen to be an emergency medical technician here and I have a light that I use to respond to the ambulance—I turned my light on, hoping that someone would see it and get out of the way and I started honking my horn and there was a Jeep Cherokee and he got halfway out of the lane, just enough for me to squeeze by. I still don't remember going through the underpass; I think I shut my eyes.

ML: And then she said, "There's a police car—the police car's going to get in front of you and it's going to slow you down. It's okay if you hit him."

EJ: "Yep," I said. "I see the police car." . . .

She said, "Just line up behind him, and it's okay if you hit him."

And he sped up some to match my speed. Then he slowed down and we hit twice. He braked—he used his emergency brake—and after about a quarter of a mile, he was able to stop us.

ML: You were pushing him along.

EJ: Yes. And by the time we got out, my tires were all smoking and everything, and I was scared to death.

ML: How did you keep from falling completely to pieces, I wonder.

EJ: I think part of it was my training. Being an EMT for seven years . . . we're supposed to keep our composure.

ML: What happened when you got out of the car?

EJ: I just started crying. And I was just, you know, I thanked him and thanked him and thanked him. I just started making phone calls, calling my friends, calling my family, saying, I love you. You know? And of course, they're like, oh my god, are you okay? What happened?

ML: Where's your car now?

EJ: It's outside of my house.

ML: Did you find out why all of that went wrong?

EJ: Well, I've talked to some mechanics, and a mechanic who's a friend of mine came and checked it. They feel that both the accelerator got stuck and the brakes wouldn't work, so that it was twofold. And I'd just had my brakes done about three weeks ago, so we're a little concerned about that.

ML: What an experience.

EJ: I'm just happy I didn't get hurt and happy I didn't have to hurt anyone.

ML: Yeah, we're happy, too. Thank you.

It was a story we could all relate to, and with an outcome that made everyone feel good.

Well, almost everyone. No sooner had we aired Elizabeth Jordan's dramatic tale than folks were on the phone, on email, sending us their reactions to the runaway Chevy Blazer, and what most of them were saying was, "For heaven's sake, why didn't she just turn off the engine!"

Most, but not all. Some were saying, "For heaven's sake, why didn't she put it into Neutral?"

I guess they'd missed the part where Ms. Jordan said she'd tried that and her engine sounded as though it was going to explode. After we aired those reactions on Talkback, more people called to argue with the first callers. Some of these people worried that if you turned off your engine, your steering would lock, and then where would you be?

The argument raged on, outside the CBC and in, because there is nothing like car talk for getting everyone involved. But no one had a definite answer to this question: how *do* you stop a runaway SUV?

Mark decided we should put it to the experts, so he hit the phones and started calling around. First he called the police in Suffolk, Long Island. *Did they know about the runaway 1994 Chevy Blazer?* They did. *And could they tell us, please, what* should *you do if your car is out of control like that?*

"That's a good question," they said. They'd get back to us after they'd finished reviewing the case.

Next, he phoned Young Drivers of Canada and asked them what they would advise in a situation like this. Young Drivers said you should get the car into Neutral and then use your brakes.

"She had no brakes," said Mark.

"Wow, that's not very good."

Don McKnight of the Ontario Provincial Police said you should first take the power away by putting the car in Neutral, then turn the engine off. Don't try to take the key out of the ignition, he said; just turn it back one notch. That way you'll slow the car down and still have your steering.

Bobby Ore, who trains police bodyguards and stunt drivers, agreed.

"Turn the ignition back one position and/or put the car in Neutral," he advised. Better for the engine to explode than to run into a telephone pole or another car.

Brian Holmes of the Canadian Automobile Association said all you needed to do was turn the ignition off. You couldn't remove the key anyway unless the car was in Park, and you couldn't put it in Park if it was still moving. He also advised against trying to use the emergency brakes. Elizabeth had tried and they didn't work, but Brian said if they had, she might have locked her back wheels and spun out of control.

So the consensus seemed to be: first cut power to the engine. Even better: avoid getting into such a fix in the first place.

Six years later, I tracked Elizabeth Jordan down again. She told me she'd got herself a nursing degree, got married and was working in obstetrics in New York. I asked her if they ever found out what went wrong with the Chevy Blazer. She said that, as far as she could remember, a piece of the air intake valve had got stuck in the throttle, probably when her car had been worked on a few days earlier. She was sorry to report that Edwin Hernandez, the police officer who'd saved her life, had since been killed in a car accident.

By the way, Elizabeth Jordan was still driving a Chevy— basically the same as she had before, she said, but newer.

Here's another good little car story. It's May 2005. Andreas Bolga of Cologne, Germany, is driving down the autobahn in his Smart Car (I told you it was a *little* car story) when a huge tractor trailer suddenly starts to move over into his lane . . . where he *is*. The truck driver does not see the little car that's already occupying the space he's trying to move into, nor does he notice anything when he hooks the car onto the front of his truck. He does sense an extra bit of drag, which he thinks might be a flat tire, so eventually he pulls over to the side of the road to have a look-see. To say that he was surprised when he saw what was causing the drag is, I gather, some-thing of an understatement.

Luckily, no one got hurt in that adventure either, although the little Smart Car was quite bent. Andreas said he was going to get it fixed up and keep it, though, because his Smart Car was now his Lucky Car.

At *As It Happens*, we were pretty impressed with how Elizabeth Jordan and Andreas Bolga kept their heads in the bizarre and terrifying circumstances they found themselves in, but Mike Brady may have earned himself the title King of Cool when he and his wheels met with a mishap, and not only because the temperature was hovering around minus 22 degrees Celsius at the time.

Mike, a basketball coach in Regina, was on his way home from visiting friends in Hodgeville, Saskatchewan, when the accident happened. He lost control of his van on a lonely country road around 10:00 p.m. just after Christmas 2002. He had no cellphone. And there was no question of getting out of the van and striking out on foot, because Mike Brady also happened to be in a wheelchair—he doesn't have the use of his legs.

How Mike managed to survive the next 41 hours is a story that rivals Ignacio Siberio's and was the subject of a conversation we had on the radio a couple of days later. First I wanted to know how come he hadn't frozen to death.

> MB: I stayed with my van and I had half a tank of gas
> and I didn't know how long I'd be there, so I ran the van
> every 2 hours for 15 minutes.
>
> ML: Warmed up the van a bit.
>
> MB: Just warmed me up. And I didn't want to warm
> myself up too much, because then you start to sweat and
> that makes you colder. So I just got the chill off me, and I
> had my two dogs with me and one would lie on my thigh

and she would keep warm herself—she's a smaller dog; the other one's a big fluffy Bouvier, and she was steaming the whole time and if I wanted to warm up my hands, I'd get her up on my lap and cuddle her and pet her and hold her, and she would warm me right up.

ML: That was good. You had nothing to eat or drink?

MB: I had two Christmas suckers that I had put in the pouch of my wheelchair to give to a couple of kids I know and I forgot to give them to them, so I had one for lunch on Monday and one for breakfast on Tuesday morning.

ML: Oh gosh. Now, what was going through your mind?

MB: Well, there's a lot of stuff goes through your mind in a 41-hour period when you're by yourself. There was one point where I wasn't sure anyone would find me, because I didn't know anyone knew I was missing. And when you know there's a possibility that you may not make it through something . . . For me it was easy. I mean, I've had a life that's been a fulfilling life, I've done some things that I'm really proud of and I just knew that if that was the time, then that was the time, and if my time wasn't up, then someone would find me. I didn't wait all the time in the van—

ML: You didn't?

MB: I had made up my mind the night before that if they didn't find me by one o'clock Tuesday afternoon, I was going to try to see how far I could wheel down the road. I had to dismantle my chair to get it out of the van, and I threw it out the door and got it back together. Then I warmed up and jumped in the chair about two o'clock and started to wheel back down the road the way I had come.

ML: Is your wheelchair electric?

MB: No, it's a manual chair.

ML: This is your arms and shoulders doing the work.

MB: I was using my arms the whole time. When I got to a snowdrift, the chair wouldn't go through it. I couldn't get going enough up the hill and through the drift, so I crawled through the snow and dragged my chair, and when I got through the drift, I'd get back in my chair and wheel.

I went through two drifts—and they were anywhere from 20 to 30 feet long—and I looked at the third drift down at the bottom of the next hill that I was coming to, and it was at least 50 feet long.

ML: You must have been crying with frustration.

MB: Well, I was looking at it and I was looking at the hill, and I said, *If the next one is the same as that one and I can't see a house from the top of that hill, I'm going to go back to the van. I'm strong enough that I can make it back.* And I'd just started down that hill—I was about halfway down—when a truck came up behind me.

ML: And he was out looking for you?

MB: He was out looking for me. He'd just started at one o'clock and this was around three, so he had just been out for two hours.

ML: What did you say?

MB: "Am I glad to see you!" I don't know if I said it as much as I cried it.

ML: Yes. Because then all the relief would have come flowing out.

MB: That's when the emotions kicked in that I was okay. I wasn't sure at that time whether I was fully intact, because being a paraplegic, I can't feel anything below my waist, and I wasn't sure if my legs were frozen and my toes were frozen, because I expended all my energy on my upper body, keeping it warm and making sure that it was intact, because I couldn't afford to lose a finger or an arm or anything. But if I was to lose a toe or a foot, to me it's not a big thing, other than cosmetically—I would have an empty spot on my chair.

ML: *Were* you okay?

MB: I was totally fine. I had a scratch on my knee from when I got out of the van, and other than that—I think that the people who were looking for me and didn't know I was okay had a harder go of it than I did.

ML: Your dogs are okay, too?

MB: My dogs are unbelievable. They're here and they're happy. They won't leave me; they're always laying at my feet. That was the hardest thing: when I was in the van and waiting and wasn't sure if I would make it—

ML: You were afraid for the dogs?

MB: I was really afraid for the dogs. And I was in a dilemma: do you leave them locked in the van or do you leave the van door open so . . . they can come and go as they want, and at what point in time do you make that decision to open the door and leave it open or what?

ML: Glad you didn't have to.

MB: You know what, there's a lot of people glad and there's no one gladder than this gentleman right here.

ML: I hope you have a very good year.

MB: You know what, they've all been good years.

With that kind of spirit, you knew that Mike probably *would* have a good 2003, but still, I was surprised, when I had a chance to talk with him again five years later, to hear about all the good things that had happened to him *directly as a result of driving into a ditch on a winter night in Saskatchewan.* The first thing that happened was that he came into some money.

MB: After I got lost, the [Regina] *Leader Post* did a follow-up story on my wheelchair basketball team, and a gentleman here in Regina phoned me up and gave me a cheque for ten grand.

ML: A total stranger?

MB: Never seen him before in my life. He just said, "These kids need it." So with that ten thousand dollars, I kicked in seven thousand dollars of my own money and I bought eight brand-new wheelchairs, and that kicked off our wheelchair basketball programme. It got it into the next phase that it had to go, and now these kids that I started with are all in Grade 12 and just graduated.

One of my kids was in Grade 10 and he had a 63 average—one of the smartest kids on my team. And I talked to him. He went from 63 in Grade 10 to 93 in Grade 11. He quit smoking and he's looking at going to the University of Chicago. He did his SATs this weekend.

ML: You must be so proud.

MB: He's looking at playing basketball for the University of Chicago and actually getting an education, from me getting lost in the snowbank. It's such a stupid story; a stupid act on my part gave all these kids a whole different opportunity.

ML: What's your team called?

MB: The Paratroopers. And they're a really cool bunch of kids. . . . Way back when, three weeks after I got lost—I coached a young girls' team and my Paratroopers—we played a basketball game between my able-bodied girls and my disabled kids. They had a great time and I thought, *That was pretty cool*—and then my phone started ringing.

"I heard you played a game. . . . Will you play my team?"

"Will you play *my* team?"

We played seven weeks in a row!

ML: How did your team do in those games?

MB: I was the referee so I cheated a little bit, just because you want everyone involved to have fun. And I also wanted my kids to learn, so as their skills developed, I called it harder.

But the head of the league—they found out that I was doing these exhibition games—he came to me and asked me to join the league the next year. A wheelchair team in an able-bodied league!

ML: Really. Is that the first time that's happened?

MB: First time in the world. . . . We're still playing. That programme is still going on six years later. Just three weeks ago, I went out and bought more new chairs, so I had ten good ones, five on each team.

Now I go to schools with all these chairs and do talks.
I talk about getting lost in the snowstorm.

ML: You just never know, do you?

I said to Mike that it seemed to me that he must have
restored hope to a lot of broken lives, and I wondered what
had happened in his life to restore hope after he got hurt.

MB: I'll probably cry here. I had huge family support,
and that's one thing that happened to me this year: my
dad passed away. That's why it's hard . . .
   When I got hurt, my dad was almost the same age I
am now, so he walked in and he was a brick. He never
showed that it bothered him. I found out later he almost
lost his business, he was so emotionally stressed. We were
building a workshop and he had just installed the
windows, and he ripped one out and lowered it so I'd be
able to see.
   My coaching is my dad, too; he started me coaching.
He said, "You're going to coach your little brother."
   And I did that as a 15-year-old. And my little brother,
who was 12 when I got hurt, now works with the disabled
community; that's his job.

ML: What a difference you've made.

MB: The only way we can pass on a legacy to people is
through our coaching, through our lifestyle, through our
living. . . . What kind of people did you help develop on
your path through life? I'm passing on the legacy of my
dad and my grandfather and his dad before him. . . .
There's two times in my life that I thought I was going to
die. When I had my accident as a 20-year-old, and I
hadn't lived, I was scared about losing my life. When I got

stuck in the snowbank and I left my van to wheel, I didn't think I would make it when I left. But when I left that day, I wasn't scared. I'd lived a life. I did all that I thought I was going to accomplish.

Obviously, some higher power than me decided that these young kids needed someone to be their role model still.

Seems to me that Mike Brady could be a role model for us all.

When I'd first talked to Mike Brady, after he got rescued in the snowstorm back in 2003, the first words I actually spoke to him were, "Aren't *you* the luckiest guy in the world." This to a guy in a wheelchair! I wanted to cut my tongue out, I felt like such an idiot. I was referring to the rescue, of course, but *still*.

But now I think, okay, maybe not *the* luckiest guy in the world—no denying he's had some bad luck here and there—but here's a man who knows who he is and what he can do and what life's all about, and as he says, he has a great family and good friends, and he's made a difference . . . that's pretty lucky, don't you think?

ELEVEN

This Is the Dance Portion

Radio with a good beat

⌐

Like any team effort, *As It Happens* is at its best when the team are all pulling in the same direction, but it's just as vital to have people whose tastes and skills complement each other. It's very useful, for instance, to have people with good musical taste in your midst, as well as interviewers, writers and chase producers. And we did, though you wouldn't always think so if you heard some of the stuff we played—I'm thinking disco, techno, hip hop, ABBA and almost anything that makes it into the annual Eurovision music competition, which is notable not only for its, ahem, music but also for the fact that the winning song one year was performed by an Israeli transsexual.

Mainly, though, we liked to play blues, jazz, rock, country, swing or something glorious from the classical repertoire. Barbara Budd fancies that she has a good singing voice and likes to sing along when the occasion calls for it, but as I mentioned earlier, she thinks I'm tone-deaf and she always greatly preferred that I not join her. I will admit to being somewhat underdeveloped, musically speaking, but I like to think I can spot great talent when it comes along—Feist, for example. She swept the Juno Awards in 2008 and high time, too.

Also, I can tell when a composer is insane.

After suffering through hours and hours of Olympic skating on TV the year that everyone was dancing to *Bolero*, I was pretty sure that Ravel must have been suffering from something himself when he wrote it. As it turns out, British psychologist Eve Sobolska had come to the same conclusion. In 1997 she decided to look into the matter, and we were eager to hear the result of her research.

ML: Dr. Sobolska, I'm going to go way out on a limb here and say that it comes as no surprise to me that *Bolero* may be the product of a diseased mind. Is that how you got connected to this story?

ES: Yes. I used to get very irritated by the piece, and I wondered why. And at the time, I had my niece who is a musicologist, who studies theory of music. She was staying with me and I asked her, "Monica, why is it so irritating? So repetitive. I can't stand it."

And then we acquired a score, and she produced some evidence that actually the very same theme is repeated, almost without any alteration, I think it's 18 times in 17 minutes.

. . .

ML: I guess that's what it is that drives everyone crazy.

ES: Absolutely.

ML: So you got to thinking, why would a talented musician produce such a work?

ES: Yes.

ML: And what did you learn?

ES: Well, I then started to read his biographies, and I had remembered that he had dementia. But I didn't know until I started to study this particular piece of music in relation to his other [work], and I started to study the pattern of his creativity—I didn't realize it was one of his last pieces. And I didn't realize that a year before he composed *Bolero,* he already showed signs of disorientation and, one might say, dementia.

ML: What signs?

ES: A year before he composed *Bolero,* he became disoriented during a performance of his music— unusually so.

ML: And what happened?

ES: He just got lost while conducting a piece of music.

ML: And there were other episodes later on?

ES: Yes, later on. And then he somehow collected himself and then he composed *Bolero* in summer 1928, and then there were some further episodes of confusion, and then, amazingly, he managed to produce his two masterpieces, the Concerto in G Major and the Concerto for the Left Hand.

ML: So what do you think the problem was? Alzheimer's?

ES: No, no. Alzheimer's is unlikely to go hand in hand with creativity; it's a very uncreative condition. I think he had influx in his brain, and this condition can fluctuate indeed.

ML: Can you explain that to me?

ES: Well, for instance, somebody who has blood pressure—and he may have had high blood pressure. He had an enlarged heart, for instance, and on this account, he was protected from military service—somebody who has high blood pressure can have small hemorrhages in his brain. Small ones, not necessarily large ones. And there is usually a swelling around the hemorrhage, which can then subside, and therefore the whole picture can fluctuate, and the person can improve, and he did.

ML: So you just get these episodes, during one of which we assume he composed *Bolero.*

ES: Yes. During his lighter moments, yes, absolutely. But on the other hand, this is my hypothesis and it might be completely wrong. But I think already some damage to his brain must have been done, and the *Bolero,* I argue, is a piece of musical perseveration, which means repetitiveness.

ML: What did your musical niece think of your theory?

ES: Well, she disowned me a bit. She said, "Well, I'm not having anything to do with you." But on the other hand, she agreed with me that it was extremely repetitive and very unusual in classical music.

ML: Is it true that Ravel himself didn't like *Bolero?*

ES: That's what I have read. He was quite irritated [about] how instantly famous it became.

ML: Poor man!

ES: Yes. Well, I think, no doubt he was a genius, and like many geniuses, they have great emotional insight into their conditions, and I think this is the tragedy almost. I think he somehow knew; he knew something was amiss.

So there you have it, I thought. *Mystery solved. Bolero is the product of a diseased mind.*

Our audience, I have to say, were not of one mind about Dr. Sobolska's theory.

Hello, this is Emmanuel from London, Ontario. This is my diagnosis: the good doctor seems to be suffering from a condition peculiar to psychiatrists, I think—namely, an irrepressible desire to construct psychological profiles of people who are long dead or whom they've never met. The only known treatment is a strong dose of ridicule.

This is another Eva calling from Toronto. . . . Ultimately, the reason why he wrote it was so that Jayne Torvill and Christopher Dean could perform it on ice. I saw them do that at the Montreal Forum many years ago. It was an event of such magic as I will never forget.

Hi. This is Brian Murrow calling from Brampton. There's a story about the first performance of Ravel's Bolero. *At the end of the performance, a woman in the audience supposedly yelled out, "He's mad! He's mad!"*

To which Ravel replied, "She's the only one who understands."

My name is Gilles Losier. I'm calling from Montreal. Now, about Ravel's Bolero: *I think it's a misunderstood piece of music. It's a musician's piece of music. It's a mantra, and I really feel that only people that have good ears can understand this music, and I pooh-pooh the psychiatrist.*

This is Edith Matheson calling from Alberta. Thank God someone has finally attempted to explain the frenzied phenomenon of Ravel's Bolero. *I must admit that, not only does it irritate me, but it makes me feel absolutely unhinged. If it's played when I'm at the symphony, the first thing I want to do is plug my ears and run screaming out of the auditorium.*

*This is Ben Metcalfe at Shawnigan Lake. Somewhere in
there one of you mentioned that Ravel was reputed to have
disliked Bolero after he wrote it. I can give you his exact
quote about that. He said, "I only made two serious mis-
takes in my life: one was a woman in the south of France
and the other was Bolero."*

We had a lot of fun with the *Bolero* brouhaha, which happened during my first month of hosting, and for me it was an
early indication of how easy it would be to weave the lighter
stories in amongst the more serious ones on *As It Happens*—
and how much the audience loved it when we did. I was
determined to make the most of it, and in this ambition, I
found that Barbara was always a ready ally. Indeed, she was
usually the first to become aware of the situation when we
crammed the show too full of serious or depressing stuff and
forgot to sprinkle a bit of fun around.

Barbara Budd, in case you don't know, is also an actor of
some repute, having trod the boards at Stratford with people
like William Hutt and Maggie Smith. So she was well
equipped to carry on the fine storytelling traditions begun by
Al Maitland. Her readings of *How the Grinch Stole Christmas*
and *Bone Button Borscht,* among others, have become as
much a part of the show's seasonal fare as Al's *Shepherd* and
The Gift of the Magi. Combine this with her own flair for writing, and you have someone who can and does frequently take
an unremarkable script and bring it to life on the air. Barbara's talents weren't always sufficiently appreciated, though;
we did take her for granted at times. And then she would go
away for a while, and we'd become aware that the show wasn't
sounding quite the way it ought to—like the time she frac-
tured her leg during March Break.

She was showing her son and a friend around the Brock Monument on the Niagara Escarpment, the site of the Battle of Queenston Heights during the War of 1812, when a piece of ice sent her crashing to the ground. Heroically, she managed to get them all back to the car and then back to Toronto before taking herself off to Emergency to have her bones set. None of this was public knowledge, though, and when she didn't come back to the show as expected, some of our listeners began to get a bit agitated. "Where is Barbara?" they wanted to know.

So one fine day, we rang her up.

ML: Barbara!

BB: Mary Lou, how are you?

ML: I'm fine. How are you?

BB: It's so nice to talk to you on the phone. I listen to you every night.

ML: More to the point, *where* are you? Because, you know, people have been asking. I mean, they think, okay, so you went away on March Break—that's been over for weeks. All I've been able to tell them is we haven't seen you.

BB: I think it's so nice people even care that I'm away. I'm in . . .

Where do you think any *As It Happens* girl would be when you called her?

ML: Well, you'd be in Reading, of course.

BB: That's exactly where I am.

ML: You're not! What are you doing in Reading?

BB: You know what, I'm on a Canada Council grant and I'm travelling around to all the places—now, Reading, of course, is very special, and actually, it doesn't quite fit into my proposal with the Canada Council—but what they gave me licence to do was to go to a lot of the places where I've mispronounced the name.

ML: You never mispronounce a name.

BB: Yeah, right.

ML: Well, there was Nyack [New York]. But you know—

BB: You know what? Unfortunately, I have to end my trip in Nyack, because just before I went on this trip, I called Nyack *gnakk* [sounding like one syllable].

But it's really sort of a Canadian goodwill thing, so I thought, *I'll start in Canada.* I'll start on the west coast and—remember that time we did the interview about the whale songs?

ML: Yes.

BB: And you know, I'm not from B.C. . . . I mispronounced Juan de Fuca.

ML: What did you call it?

BB: Well, I don't want to say it again—I'll just get into more trouble—but it was close to being very bad, and I got letters from people upbraiding me for not knowing how to pronounce it, that I should really put the *FEW-kah* in it. . . .

So I started out in Sidney, British Columbia. You know, other people have mispronounced their names, I guess, but people on the west coast are pretty possessive about the Strait of Juan de Fuca. They got het up about that. I'm here now in Reading. But I'm going on to Wales.

ML: Is Reading lovely?

BB: Ye-es.

ML: There was a little hesitation in there. Just a bit.

BB: Well, you know, it was a very, very famous industrial town. . . . But you know what? It's lovelier because of us, I'm told. Because they love the fact that Canadian broadcasters talk about Reading frequently, and they've had a lot of tourism because of *As It Happens*.

ML: How did you get a Canada Council grant to do this? I mean, is it a sort of art thing? Are you going to put a CD out when you're finished or weave the names into a tapestry or something?

BB: Well . . . a quilt, perhaps. Including the Welsh names. . . .

ML: Look, nobody can pronounce any name in Wales except the Welsh. It's their revenge on the rest of the world.

BB: True enough. I'm just sorry I never mispronounced the name Prague. I'd love to go to Prague but I have no reason to. . . .

The Canada Council does marvellous work, though. They do artists-in-residence and writing plays and writing music but they also—over the years, I've noticed they give out grants to some pretty wacky projects. . . .

And I thought, *Well, I'm going to apply. I'm going to just see whether or not I can do some good work, spreading goodwill from Canada to some of these far-off places.*

And, by George, I got a Canada Council, Mary Lou.

ML: Well, that's fantastic.

BB: And I'll be a better pronouncer when I come back, I'm sure. . . .

ML: You're great on radio, and I can't wait to hear you again, right here beside me.

BB: Well, aren't we lucky that when I am away on something as wonderful as this—what a lucky *break* for me, eh?

ML: It *is* a lucky break—

Russ Germain (who was subbing for Barbara) *extro*'d the interview:

Barbara Budd is the regular co-host of As It Happens. *We reached her at the Broken Bone Tavern in Reeding, er, Redding, England.*

Russ, by the way, with his sexy baritone and his own dry wit, happens to be an announcer from the old days, when radio announcers were hired for their language and elocution skills and the way they sounded; consequently, he also did a brilliant job co-hosting *As It Happens*. I confess we didn't miss Barbara quite so much when he was filling in for her.

Anyway, Barbara and I had our conversation about her Canada Council grant on April 1, 2004. Here's what Talkback had to say the next day. Names have been removed to protect the gullible.

Hello, my name is BR. I'm about 50 kilometres west of Saskatoon. I've been a great fan of CBC for many decades and a fan of As It Happens *for equally many decades, but tonight I am just totally disillusioned and disappointed with Budd's gloating over how she scored a Canada Council grant to visit many places around the world that she has mispronounced the name of. I think you've got to be more responsible with the taxpayers' money, Miss Budd. Please clean up your act. Bye-bye.*

GR calling from High River, Alberta. Wow, I mispronounce names all the time; I think I should get a Canada Council grant also. If there was ever a reason why we should just ban the Canada Council totally and severely restrict the funding the CBC gets . . .

Hello, As It Happens. *This is MK in Syracuse, New York, and I have to say, "Barbara, way to go with the Canada Council grant!" Proof that you can get money to do the most amazing things. Thanks for a wonderful show, and Barbara, have a safe trip.*

Hi, this is K. calling from Vancouver. I'm really happy that Canada does things like this, that they hand out grants for what many people in these days of fiscal conservatism would consider are very frivolous activities because—well, you know what, why not?

Among the various catcalls and hurrahs, there were a couple of people who twigged to the fact that we might have been up to something fishy the day before.

Hello, Mary Lou and Russ and Barbara. It's Paul Coyle calling. I just thoroughly enjoyed your interview with Barbara, explaining where she's been. You really had me going. And suddenly, it dawned on me that today is the first of the month of April. That was classic, absolutely classic.

Hello, Barbara, this is Wendy Zilka calling from Edmon-ton, and I was just listening to your charming little seg-ment, supposedly in Reading, and if this is an April Fool's joke, then I hope that you will come clean.

And then, as so often happens with Talkback, we got a suggestion for some music and picked up a nugget of new information, too.

It's Bill Shaw phoning from Bedford, Nova Scotia. If, in fact, Barbara Budd did fall and injure herself at Queen-ston, how could you resist playing Stan Rogers' "MacDon-nell on the Heights"?

The song is about MacDonnell, who essentially took up the banner and continued the charge after Major General Sir Isaac William Brock was shot dead and, for better or for worse, kept Canada from becoming part of the wealth-iest and most influential place in the universe.

Just to get us started on the right note, Mr. Shaw himself intoned the first verse to us over the phone:

> *Too thin the line that charged the Heights*
> *And scrabbled in the clay,*
> *Too thin the Eastern Township Scot*
> *Who showed them all the way.*
> *And perhaps had you not fallen*
> *You might be what Brock became,*
> *But not one in ten thousand knows your name.*

Major MacDonnell (or Macdonell or Macdonald . . . first name unknown) fought and died with Brock, and his body also lies buried under the Brock Monument.

This is so typical of the way our listeners enrich the show through their emails and phone messages and their composing and singing—and their *dogs'* singing. (Does anyone remember Pickles, the poodle who sings along to the *As It Happens* theme?) I know I've mentioned it before, but it's impossible to overstate the extent to which we depended on the wit and humour of our audience. Look what happened, for instance, when someone brought up the subject of wacky warning labels. We did the interview, we heard a few examples and then the listeners posted these:

A sign seen on a wheelbarrow: *Not for use on highway.*

A sign on a paper towel dispenser on a B.C. ferry: *Do not hang from towel. Misuse could be fateful.*

On a septic tank cover: *Do not enter.*

On a hair dryer: *Do not use while sleeping.*

On a hair dryer in a Japanese hotel: *This appliance is to be used for drying hair only. Not for the other purpose.*

On a woodstove: *Caution—hot when in use.*

On an electrical appliance: *For indoor or outdoor use ONLY.*

On an electric recliner: *Do not use in shower or swimming pool.*

On a children's cold medicine: *Avoid alcohol beverages, driving a vehicle and operating machinery when taking this medication.*

On a package of Japanese steak knives: *Do not leave in children.*

On a room deodorizer: *Avoid being eaten by children.*

On the Hoover Tower, San Francisco: *In case of an earthquake, duck.*

In a parking lot in Banff, Alberta: *No skiing on pavement.*

And my personal favourite:

On a car windshield sunshade: *Do not drive while this is in place.*

The scary thing, as many have pointed out, is that you know these signs are probably there for a reason.

Over the years, our listeners have also found more things to do with duct tape than you could have imagined—and with Spam. They send recipes for roast turkey and shortbread cookies and other goodies when they're in season. (No haggis recipes needed, thank you.) But as we've seen, their real strength lies in playing with words and naming things: things like runaway pigs and Canadian political factions and, on one occasion, smallish pieces of land surrounded by water—or what we used to call "islands" before the European Union (EU) got hold of them.

The EU is a very effective trade bloc, of course, but it also supports a vast and overbearing bureaucracy who have to keep busy somehow. Passing regulations governing the proper size of leeks, the official shape of a banana, what you're allowed to put in cheese and so on is one way they keep busy. And also—as it happens—provide much fodder for ridicule.

One day in January 2003, Ian Gillis of the Scottish Islands Network was called on to explain to us the new requirements for islands. An EU island wasn't an island any longer, he said, if it had a fixed link (a bridge) to the mainland or if it was longer than four kilometres or if there were too few people or if it had a capital.

What would we call the Isle of Skye then? I wondered. *Or the British Isles, for that matter?*

And why was the EU doing this?

Mr. Gillis couldn't enlighten us there, but he said that on the Isle of Muck, they were considering having themselves reclassified as a shipping hazard.

On what to call a non-island, though, our listeners were not at all stranded. Van Boyd in Haliburton, Ontario, had a whole archipelago of suggestions:

No man's land.
You-land.
We-land.
The we'll of Skye.

According to this scheme, said Mr. Boyd, Prince Edward Island would become Prince Edward We-land. And just think of the employment opportunities: the maps that would need changing, the road signs and so on.

John Wallenberg of Montreal said that, logically, an island which is no longer an island should be a *was-land.* John Myers of Toronto said an isle that wasn't an isle must be an *ex-isle.* Peter, in Mississauga, suggested calling them *den-isles,* and Clare Neufeld offered *in-continents.*

Vivian Hemsley of Bolton, Ontario, said if the island had a causeway, it could be called a *hi-land,* because it might be an island—or it might not be. Or you could spell that *by-land,* since you get there by land. If it had a population under 50, you could call it a *buy-land,* because more people would have to buy land there to have it qualify as an island.

Nicholas Wade of Lethbridge, Alberta, said that if Prince Edward Island no longer qualified as an island, it should be renamed *Prince Edward Object.*

Finally, Amy Langstaff from Montreal called to say, "I hope I haven't missed the boat on the topic. The request was for a name for an island that is no longer an island. It seems clear to me that that would be an *erstwhile-land.*"

Oh, you think you're so clever, don't you?

To return to the subject of April Fool's jokes . . . I know people are always accusing the Press of making things up. We don't usually. For the most part, we try very hard to get the facts straight and to dig up all the relevant facts, and the CBC, I think, does a pretty good job of it.

But when the occasion calls for it, we can and do tell some pretty big whoppers. A good April Fool's joke should be outlandish but not so outlandish that it might not be true. Years ago, when I lived in Ottawa, someone ran a story on April 1st about how they were going to replace the old clock on Parliament Hill with a digital clock. More recently on *As It Happens,* the producers pretended that the Canadian Mint was going to pull five-dollar bills out of circulation and release a new three-dollar coin to go along with the loonie (one-dollar coin) and the toonie, perhaps to be called a threenie.

When I worked on the show *Sunday Morning,* we presented an entire documentary about a fictitious "stan" (as in Turkistan, Kazakhstan, Uzbekistan). It was shortly after the break-up of the Soviet Union, so we figured no one would be too surprised to learn that there was a "stan" they'd never heard of before.

But my favourite AIH April Fool's joke before the one about Barbara and her "Canada Council grant" was the one

we cooked up concerning a new financial deal that CBC
Radio had struck with the Disney Corporation. We wondered
if we could persuade the then President of the CBC to play
along, and to our delight, he agreed. So here is CBC President Perrin Beatty explaining to me why there would be nothing wrong with Disney and the CBC getting into bed
together. He did it without a script, and except for the premise, without any input whatsoever from us.

ML: Mr. Beatty, I can't believe this. You're not serious
about joining CBC Radio to Disney!

PB: Mary Lou, times are tough. We've just had two very
expensive labour settlements. We've been through 400
million dollars' worth of productions. You have to find
some way to make ends meet.

ML: But this—I mean, not only is it a noncommercial
network, but it's a *Canadian* one. I mean, I can't—

PB: Well, Mary Lou, what's the choice? Do you want
commercials back on CBC Radio? We're not asking for
anything outrageous. Disney simply wants a tag at the
end of the programme, indicating their involvement
in the programme and an association with CBC. It
enables them to make a real contribution to Canadian
taxpayers.

ML: At the end of every programme.

PB: Yes. For the sort of money that they're looking at, I
think it's reasonable that there be some recognition. But
you know, it's not our intention to run ads, to be running
Kleenex ads or car ads—that's what we used to have on
CBC Radio. All we're asking for here is the opportunity
to get an infusion of a little bit of money and some

recognition for people who are being very good corporate citizens.

ML: It's an American company!

PB: Well, Mary Lou, we heard the same argument when the RCMP did their deal with Disney.

ML: Exactly.

PB: You heard the same thing: the world was going to come to an end. This was a Canadian institution that shouldn't be allowed to have an American company helping to publicize it.

Well, it's worked very well. It's generated revenue for the RCMP. What is more quintessentially Canadian than the RCMP? I don't think anybody believes they've become an American institution. Nobody will believe that we are either, because they know that we're committed to Canada.

ML: But even if it worked well in terms of revenue . . . I mean, you remember the outrage of people when the RCMP deal was announced. You don't think they'll be outraged about *this?*

PB: Well, there'll be people who will be hesitant about it and have some questions, I suppose, but there were in the case of the RCMP, too. But when was the last time you saw a letter to the editor of the paper complaining about the deal with Disney and the RCMP? Change requires that people open their minds and look at things that are fresh.

ML: How much is Disney proposing to give us?

PB: Well, it's major. That's what makes it so attractive as a recognition of their ability to have some connection with French and English radio. We're looking at $250 million. This is real money.

ML: They'd essentially buy the whole thing. They'd own it.

PB: No, not own it. It's a partnership. And if you look at our strategic plan, we're talking about doing more partnerships with the private sector, and when you get a good corporate citizen like this . . . We've done business with Disney over the years. Every Sunday night since I was a boy, we've had Disney on, and Canadians have tuned into it and have felt it was an important part of our schedules.

ML: Now, does this have anything to do with the fact that just the other day, we heard Minister [Sheila] Copps throwing cold water on all your ideas—your strategic plan—the plans for the new channels that you were hoping to get licences for this year?

PB: Mary Lou, you've got to balance the books at the end of the day. Either government writes a cheque or else you have to get it from advertising or else you have to look for some imaginative new way to get an infusion of new money. If the government isn't prepared to hand over more money and if those of us like you and me don't believe we should be commercializing CBC Radio and putting in car ads, then you have to look for something else that will allow us to get the money that we need to do the job.

ML: Are you saying we'd go off the air if we didn't have a deal like this?

PB: Somebody's got to pay the Hydro bills.

ML: Money can't be found anywhere else in the corporation for CBC Radio?

PB: Well, Mary Lou, unless you're prepared to give up some of your salary . . . But we just signed two very expensive collective agreements, and we've got to find ways of paying for that and of providing new programming and of serving Canadians with the standard of programming that they have a right to expect. And here you have a partner of high quality—indisputably.

ML: You think this will get through the House? Past the government?

PB: Well, what makes you think we need government approval on something like this? It's a partnership, as opposed to a change in legislation.

ML: Have you had any conversations with the Minister about this or with Mr. Chrétien [the Prime Minister]?

PB: Well, as you know, there's an arm's-length relationship between government and the CBC, and it's important for us to have our own plans and not to go to government and to ask them for permission in advance for everything that we're doing. If it makes sense for the corporation and it's good for our audiences, then it makes sense for us to move ahead.

ML: So if this goes through, we'll be saying, "*As It Happens* was brought to you by Walt Disney" at the end of every programme.

PB: It's just a little to ask for something which will help us to have an infusion of new money that we need to do an even better job.

ML: Thank you very much, Mr. Beatty.

PB: Thanks, Mary Lou, for having me.

This story, like the one about Barbara's Canada Council grant, raised the dander of a few listeners. Around the office, some people were shocked about how plausible Mr. Beatty made it all sound. They even worried for a time about whether we had accidentally stumbled on a plan that might turn out to be true. It *was* true that the RCMP had given Disney control over who'd be allowed to use the Mountie image around the world.

In the end, there was no deal between the CBC and Disney—but maybe there should have been. Constant budget cuts and failing ratings and ad revenues (CBC Television does carry commercials) and the neglect, benign or otherwise, of successive governments have left the corporation cash-strapped and stressed. I hope it survives these trying times as it has survived challenges in the past, because it's hard to imagine Canada without the CBC and impossible to imagine it without *As It Happens*.

TWELVE

The Wrath of Grapes

Radio that gets into the corners

 ⬅

This is the transcript of a conversation between me and Don Cherry, CBC TV hockey commentator and hockey coach, on the day in December 2001 that the *Toronto Star* ran a big story about the ailing fortunes of his AAA hockey team. The Mississauga IceDogs were dead last in the Ontario Hockey League, and their centre had just quit. The interview started off all right.

ML: Mr. Cherry? Hello?

DC: There used to be a nice song called "Mary Lou."

ML: Would you like to sing it?

DC: [singing] "Mary Lou, I love you." I remember my mother had a record. "Mary Lou . . ." Anyhow . . .

ML: Hmm. But listen, you're ducking the issue here.

DC: All right.

ML: What's with the IceDogs?

DC: IceDogs are doing all right. We're in the top third of the draft and we draw over 2,300 and, uh, we've lost ten games by one goal, and we're doin' all right. We got twice as many wins as we had last year. Some people are upset that some kid—three-goal scorer—goes home and we get headline sports.

ML: You said you're top third of the draft. That's because you're last again this year. Right?

DC: Right. Well, not this year; last year.

ML: Last year, right. But twice as many wins this year?

DC: Right.

ML: And how many is that?

DC: Five.

ML: And how many losses?

DC: Twenty.

ML: It's not great, is it?

DC: No, it's not great.

ML: And you finished last, last year?

DC: We finished last.

ML: And what about the year before that?

DC: Last.

ML: Before that?

DC: Yeah.

ML: [laughing] Well, what is wrong with your team?

DC: Well, we're a franchise. We're goin' along, we're doing the best we can and we're fightin' our way out of it, and everybody likes to see that. When a celebrity's having a tough time, they like to jump on him. It's like picking wings off flies, and they have a great time bringing up the record and that.

ML: Yeah.

DC: That's the kind of people we are in Canada. Anytime there's a celebrity having a tough time, it's great news for people. Why, you get on the front page of the *Toronto Star* and you get on CBC Radio—

ML: Yeah.

DC: If we had've been in first place, would you have called me?

ML: Sure, I would've.

DC: Oh sure, you would've.

ML: But listen, Don—

DC: Sure, you would've. You would've called me for sure. You're like one of those investigative journalists: [whispering now] "Let's phone Don Cherry, let's phone Don Cherry. He's having a tough time; he was on the front page. Let's do it."

ML: [laughing] Listen, you go on TV—and you know everything, right?

DC: Absolutely.

ML: You know everything there is to know about hockey.

DC: Absolutely.

ML: But you can't win a game!

DC: I have to go on CBC to pay your salary, because nobody listens to you on the radio.

ML: Oh, are you sure?

DC: Nobody watches the sex life of a bumblebee or the rest of the programmes, so I have to go on the most-watched thing in Canada. Now, what do you have to say about that?

ML: You might hear from the people who don't listen to us.

DC: I'll hear from all three of them, right?

ML: But listen: do you know anything about hockey or not?

DC: I know a lot about hockey. I was Coach of the Year in the American League and I was Coach of the Year in the National League, and I know a little bit about hockey and I'm doing the best I can.

ML: But why can't you win a game?

DC: Well, it's the same thing as you. Now, you're a good reporter and you're a good announcer and look at you: you're on in the middle of the afternoon. I mean, who is really listening at ten to two? Sometimes circumstances are that way. You get stuck in a role like you're in, that I'm in, and you have to fight your way out of it. I'm sure you're trying to get into prime time, like about drive time—about four or five—but here you are, stuck at two o'clock.

ML: Do you know as much about hockey as you do about radio?

DC: Well, I know I'm at two o'clock and there's nobody listening, I'll tell you that.

ML: Could be because we're actually on the air at six-thirty.

DC: Oh, you're on the air at six-thirty! So this is taped!

ML: Yeah, it is.

DC: So this is taped, so you can edit out—you can edit what you want. You don't really have the—what do we say?—to go on live, eh?

ML: We're not going to edit at all!

DC: I don't want to say what you don't have to go on live. I got it. So you're going to edit all this out. I got it.

ML: It must be your good manners and charm that brought your team along to the place where it is now.

DC: Well, I don't know what it is. I'm the most watched thing in Canada, and when somebody asks me questions like this, they open themselves up for what you're gonna get. Now you can edit this down any way you want.

A couple of things to note here. One: we did not edit so much as a snicker from that exchange with Don Cherry. Why would we? Two: Don Cherry—also known as "Grapes"—was perfectly correct about his celebrity. As the coach on "Coach's Corner," he was, and is, the most-watched figure on CBC and probably all of Canadian television, both delighting and repelling people with his opinions, his political incorrectness and his sports jackets (the word *wild* doesn't do them justice). I could always tell when Don was about to make new headlines—conducting his contract negotiations in public, say, or referring to French-Canadian hockey players as sissies— from the harried expression on the face of my friend Ruth-Ellen Soles, because it was her job as Corporate Spokesperson to assure Cherry's legions of fans that the CBC was certainly not going to fire him and to explain to his critics why not. For sure, though, the money he brought into the CBC coffers helped pay my salary and hers.

Three: we did have a great story, as one or two of our listeners hastened to tell us. Some prefaced their remarks by saying things like, "I'm driving along the 401 with my husband listening to your interview with Don Cherry, so I guess we're two of your three listeners." One man said how tickled he was to have his two favourite broadcasters on air together and getting on so well, more or less.

What is it about hockey, though, that makes people just want to throw down their gloves and fight? One of Barbara Frum's more memorable interviews—along with the Big Cabbage— featured a tussle with Harold Ballard, former owner of the Toronto Maple Leafs and Maple Leaf Gardens, who told her that women had no business on the radio. And then there are the hockey parents! Not as crazy as soccer fans perhaps, but the parents of kids' league players are notorious for hurling abuse at referees, coaches and opposing teams, suing over their kids' failure to win coveted positions and, on occasion, even exchanging blows with the parents of other players.

We can't even agree about where the game originated. Was it in Windsor, Nova Scotia, around 1800; in Dartmouth in 1827; or in Halifax in 1870? Many sources say that the *first recorded* game was played in Montreal in 1875, but in February 2004, the Director of the Art Gallery of Nova Scotia told us that he had a lithograph in front of him showing a hockey game that was played in Dartmouth in 1867, which puts it eight years ahead of the Montreal game. Jeffrey Spalding admitted that the print belonged to a series entitled *Curling on Lakes in Nova Scotia,* but there's no doubt, he said, that what they're doing in his picture is playing hockey: the players are on ice, they're wearing skates and they have curved sticks in their hands. To clinch it, he cites a Halifax newspaper story from the same time that describes a "hockey match between the Garrison and the Fleet" on Oathill Lake in Dartmouth. This doesn't necessarily make Dartmouth the birthplace of hockey, says Spalding, but it is proof that Montreal's game was not the first to be recorded.

The Montreal game, incidentally, was played by the McGill *Football* Club, which may help explain why the game in North America is so physical. It ended—as did the Army-Navy game in Dartmouth—in a fight.

Hockey players can't even set up a backyard rink without getting into a brawl with someone. At least that's what happened in Kanata, a suburb of Ottawa, a few years ago. Neighbourhood parents had laid out a rink, watered it and strung up lights so the kids could play after dark, which in Ottawa in January comes at around 4:30 in the afternoon. The bureaucrats thought the electrical cords in the trees posed a major safety hazard *(and playing hockey doesn't?)* and ordered the lights taken down, which earned them a very public flogging in the media. I don't need to tell you what happened when they tried to ban *street* hockey in Ottawa.

The most abuse I've ever heard directed at the CBC—from outside the halls of Mother Corp herself—was during a technicians' strike in the 1970s that caused the Saturday night hockey broadcast to be cancelled. I was working in Ottawa at the time, and I saw the pages and pages of virulence contained in the records of phone calls from enraged fans, all dutifully reproduced by the poor receptionist at CBOT—and that was just one station. You can imagine how frustrated the fans were when the National Hockey League bosses themselves locked out their players for the 2004/05 season and the fans couldn't blame the CBC.

In fact, some of us at the CBC did our best to get a Stanley Cup series going *without* the NHL. It was a couple of guys in Edmonton who got things started, when they set up a website to "Free Stanley." They argued that the Stanley Cup didn't actually belong to the NHL; Lord Stanley of Preston, a former Governor General, had indicated, when he gave the Cup to Canada, that he intended it to be awarded annually to the best *amateur* hockey team in the Dominion. In 1926 it became the *de facto* trophy of the NHL, but if the NHL wasn't going to play a championship series that year, the Cup's trustees should allow non-NHL teams to compete for it.

That was the line from the "Free Stanley" boys, and we at *As It Happens* thought it made sense, so we jumped on their bandwagon—or, rather, I did. In retrospect, I wonder if all our producers quite had their hearts in it, but it was nice while it lasted. We faced off with Brian O'Neill, one of the Stanley Cup trustees, who insisted that the Stanley Cup was now, officially and contractually, the property of the National Hockey League. He had no desire to muddy the waters by trying to pry it loose. Rod Payne, lawyer for the "Free Stanley" movement, countered with an argument for why, legally, the trustees had had no business in 1947 trying to delegate control of the Cup to the NHL. Mr. Payne thought that, if any hockey team were to issue a formal challenge for the Stanley Cup that year, the trustees were bound in law to consider it.

Then we got some really big firepower:

ML: Your Excellency, you think the Stanley Cup should go to a women's team this year, do you?

Governor General Adrienne Clarkson (GG): Well, it's not exactly the way I would put it; the way I would put it is that the Stanley Cup should not have a year where it is not awarded. The reason I think that is that I feel some responsibility towards the Stanley Cup, as it was first given for excellence in hockey by my British predecessor, Lord Stanley, in 1908/09, and since it came out under that aegis, as I watched what was happening to our regular hockey season, I began to think, really, Canadians don't want to be without the Stanley Cup for a year. It means more than just a trophy. The Stanley Cup is a symbol of our national identity through hockey. . . .

Its basic premise is excellence in hockey, so we have to say, "Okay, who's excellent?" Everybody else who's excellent has a Cup. There's the Allen Cup, there's the Memorial Cup, but Women's League hockey does not have a Cup, and I think this year would be the time to say, "Women could do this."

ML: This is a fabulous idea. I mean, those lads in Edmonton who started the campaign "Free Stanley" will be thrilled to have you onside!

GG: Well, I am onside because I feel that we have to make sure that this Cup is given, so that the standard of excellence in hockey is not dropped. And who could save the day? The women could save the day!

ML: As always.

GG: [laughing] *You* said that!

ML: I know. But let me ask you something: Clearly, you've been having people doing the research about the Cups and everything—

GG: Yes.

ML:—and we're clear about what Lord Stanley's wishes were—that it go to the best team of the year?

GG: Excellence of amateur hockey.

ML: It was amateur in the beginning.

GG: Yes, amateur, and the reason why the Cup was installed—and there's documentation about this between the trustees and Lord Stanley's secretary, about the fact that they really wanted to recognize the best in *amateur* hockey, because professionalism was beginning to take hold and they wanted to say this is the best in amateur hockey.

ML: Now, we spoke to one of the trustees yesterday, and I must say, he seemed a little reluctant to consider awarding the Stanley Cup to anybody else or making it available and, I mean, that's to put it mildly. I don't know how—I mean, if *you* asked for it, surely he couldn't refuse *you!*

GG: Well, I would like him to listen to what the Canadian people are thinking. I'm only representing them, you know. I represent all Canadians and I think I represent them in this particular case, because I'm saying, "I don't want to see No Stanley Cup!" . . .

It's not about legal technicalities; it's about the psyche. . . .

You know, hockey is one of those things that everybody grows up with in Canada—everybody! And even in the days when girls didn't play, sometimes they snuck out with their brothers. . . . I think even the Americans understand that it's a part of our psyche, that it isn't a part of their psyche. They play it and everything, but it's *us;* it's our real being.

ML: So you're saying it should go to a Canadian team?

GG: No. No, I think you have to—it's just like the NHL—

ML: Canada and the U.S.

GG: The Canadian Women's League would play to the East and West finals, and then they would play each other and then play the States.

ML: Would you go to the finals?

GG: I certainly would. I'd go to more than the finals.

ML: Really.

GG: I certainly would. I like watching hockey—in real life. I'm not that keen on watching it on television. . . . [On TV] sometimes I can't follow the puck, you know. I suggested once to somebody, "Why don't we light the puck?"

ML: Oh! You know they did that for a while in the States.

GG: Did they?

ML: I think so. They had a little—it was sort of a purple dot on the screen, and I dunno, they were laughed out of town, I think, for doing that. You know, most of the Canadians said, "What's the matter? You can't *see* a hockey puck!"

GG: Well, I just—I want to see where this goes, because you know, public opinion should decide what they want. I'm just putting my Governor General's worth into it.

ML: Should be worth something. Thank you, Your Excellency.

. . .

Barbara Budd [*extro*]: Well, get a load of that! Adrienne Clarkson is Governor General of Canada. She's not only the Voice of the People—she's the Voice of the Queen, for crying out loud.

The public opinion we were hearing was running about twenty to one in favour of giving the Stanley Cup to *somebody* in 2005, although one immigrant from England let us know she took exception to the GG's claim that we all grew up with hockey. Another woman said she loved the idea that female hockey champions should have a Cup of their own, but she wasn't sure they needed a "cast-off." What about a *new* trophy from the Governor General—a "Clarkson Cup"?

Our listeners had various ideas about whom Stanley should be awarded to. One caller said it should be awarded to the Toronto Maple Leafs, because they'd never win it playing hockey. But most agreed that the Cup ought to be freed from the "sole grasp of Big Business and millionaire bullies," as one caller put it.

Neither the voice of the people nor the voice of the Queen proved enough to win the day, however—at least, not that day. The Stanley Cup remained unawarded that season. But apparently there was a legal challenge lodged with the Ontario Superior Court because a year or so later the NHL caved in and agreed that, in future, if they weren't going to be using the Stanley Cup one year, they would graciously allow someone else to claim it—temporarily, of course.

Oh, and the GG's office did buy a new trophy. It's called the Clarkson Cup, and it will be awarded every year to the best women's team in the Dominion.

To get back to Don Cherry: He was right, of course, when he said that we probably wouldn't have called him if his team had been winning. I mean, where would be the fun in that? It's not true that we wanted to humiliate him, though; we just knew he'd make for some great radio. And while we love to salute the best—we talked to Junior Hockey Coach Brian Kilrea, for instance, when he was inducted into the Hockey Hall of Fame (he's won more than a thousand games with the Ottawa 67s)—where is it written that we shouldn't tip our hats occasionally to those who achieve another sort of distinction?

I remember a conversation we had with an American basketball coach after her team suffered a resounding defeat of 103–0. Jennifer Marks never got a bit testy. Perhaps the fact that they were from Texas and were called the *Lady Chaparrals* had something to do with her good manners. When I asked her if they'd considered playing baseball instead, she laughed good-naturedly. Ms. Marks did admit that they'd had a hard time just getting enough girls who wanted to play basketball to make up a team, but she hoped that in a few years they would be more competitive.

The Sheffield and District Junior Sunday League in England, on the other hand, were not at all amused when the *Derbyshire Times* described a 29–nil result at one of their soccer games as a "comprehensive trouncing." League chairman Matthew Harman seemed to think the losing team would feel worse about seeing the result depicted in that way than they would about the actual loss, so he had issued a kind of edict against talking to the Press and declared that anyone who defied his rule would be subject to disciplinary action.

And then there are folk who make a virtue out of losing. Not only Canadian ice skaters (*just kidding!*) but, well, I'm thinking again of the aptly named Zippy Chippy—aptly named, that is, if you think of "zip" as standing for "zero" and not speed. Notwithstanding that Zippy is the grandson of Canadian racing champion Northern Dancer, at the time we caught up to him (so to speak), he had just lost his 85th race and was tied for *the most losses for a thoroughbred in American racing history*. Lost handsomely, too—by 37 ½ lengths. Here's part of my conversation with Zippy Chippy's owner and trainer, Felix Monserrate.

ML: Mr. Monserrate, Zippy Chippy has the right pedigree. Why can't he win a race?

FM: I don't know. Sometime I try to ask him, but he don't give me no answer. He try to run, he try to win but . . .

ML: Oh now, is he really trying?

FM: Yes, he try to catch the front runners, but they run more than him.

ML: What about this problem of, when the gate opens, he just stands there?

FM: It's hard to explain, because you know, I try to find what is the problem. He trained perfectly in the morning—he was pretty fantastic—but last two, three times, he just breaks slow.

ML: When you say "breaks slow," what do you mean? What happens, actually, at the gate?

FM: They break, the horses start running, and when he sees the horses in front of him, that's when he goes.

ML: When they're *all* in front of him.

FM: Right.

ML: Has he ever won you any money?

FM: To me, yes. He pays his own way.

ML: He does! How does he do that?

FM: Well, at the beginning of the year, he got two or three seconds—I'm making money. He finishes fourth or third and there's a little money to pay his own dinner, his own food.

ML: So you want to keep racing him.

FM: I hope I can keep racing him, yes.

ML: Because if he's going to be the losing-est horse ever, he might as well go for the record, I guess, huh?

FM: Well, I cannot say that, because if he run again and he wins, you know . . . I'm not going to tell him *not* to win! If he can win, why not?

ML: Yeah, why not?

FM: Right. I think one of those days, he will come up and say, *Hell, let me run!* and do what he's doing best—running. To me, he's a winner every time he runs.

ML: How long has he been racing?

FM: Hmm . . . He's seven years old—the last five years.

ML: Maybe he thinks it's time to go to the stud farm.

FM: Nah, he cannot be that: he's a gelding. He'll have to keep earning a living running.

ML: Oh dear. Does he know that?

FM: Well, I think he knows, here's a guy, a good father, right here that's not going to let him down. Whatever he do, it will be okay for me. If he don't run, he will be in my barn like a pony. I will keep him no matter what. He's like part of my family here. He will stay.

ML: Is he a pretty horse?

FM: Um . . . They say he's ugly.

ML: They say he's *ugly?*

FM: He's ugly—and he's a little mean. But it's okay for me. He's just a big show-off. He don't do nothin'.

ML: You love him.

FM: Yeah. He try to bite, but he don't bite. He try to kick, but he don't kick.

ML: He tries to run, but he don't run!

FM: Right. He try to run as hard as he can, but he cannot catch the front runner.

ML: Has he ever won a race?

FM: No, no. It's amazing.

ML: Never!

FM: Never.

ML: His record is 85–zip.

FM: No zip! He got 85 [losses] and he got a couple of seconds and thirds. No *wins*, but he shows a little bit sometimes he can run.

ML: Well, you let us know when he runs again, and we'll be rooting for him, one way or the other.

Felix Monserrate *said* that he wanted his horse to win, but I wonder. Zippy Chippy—who, incidentally, made *People* magazine's 2000 list of "most interesting personalities"—did go on running, if that's the word and, er, celebrated his hundredth loss on September 11, 2004, in Northampton, Massachussetts. Felix tells me Zippy Chippy retired that December because they were going to make a movie about him, so of course, he had to be well rested and looking his best. Last I heard, the movie deal was still on, as soon as they could get the financing and all.

And by the way, Zippy Chippy did eventually win a race, although not against another horse. In August 2001, he came first in a 120-foot race against a minor league baseball player. Then he won another—which still only makes him 2 for 3 against humans, because back in August 2000, he lost a 40-yard race to Rochester Red Wings outfielder Jose Herrera.

I don't know how the Lady Chaparrals are faring, but I've since learned that there are fewer than 150 students at their school, the Christway Academy in Duncanville, Texas, and that's counting all grades—kindergarten to Grade 12, boys and girls. So I have a new appreciation for the difficulties they face in trying to form a girls' basketball team, never mind a winning one. Sadly, their good-natured former coach, Jennifer Marks, died in March 2008 giving birth to her second child. She was 32.

As for our dear Mississauga IceDogs, they had some success, too: they got to the finals in 2004 and came first in their division in the 2004/05 season. In 2006/07, they had their best year ever in terms of wins (43), but the team got sold and moved to St. Catharines, so they're now the *Niagara* IceDogs. I wish them all the luck in the world. You, too, Grapes.

THIRTEEN

The Maple Leaf Forever

Radio that carries all the way to the back benches

⤳

Hockey isn't Canada's only national sport; the other one is politics. Some people think it's lacrosse, but they're wrong. Politics commands way more attention, although not necessarily from all our listeners. I remember a call from an American listener pleading with us not to talk so much about Canadian politics, because it was so boring. Never mind that we weren't actually making the show for an American audience—although we love to have them on board—the man had a point: when you compare Canada to Poland, say, where identical twins can hold the jobs of Prime Minister and President, respectively, or the Balkans or Russia or even Nepal, our politics might seem not only trivial in the stakes department but also wholly lacking in entertainment value. But it's not true.

Granted, you won't likely find people clinging to the edges of their seats over the outcome of a federal-provincial conference or even a federal election, and our issues are not like the issues they have in the Middle East. But as Stephen Leacock and other humorists have demonstrated, if you can't find something funny about what's going on in Ottawa, St. John's or Moose Jaw, you're just not paying attention.

I mean, this is a country where a party that advocates destroying the country (the Bloc Québécois) not only elects members to Parliament and may be called Her Majesty's

Loyal Opposition, but thanks to an overhaul of the *Elections Act* by Prime Minister Jean Chrétien, is supported with *federal* tax dollars. Even Canadians who couldn't vote for the Bloc if they wanted to, because they don't live in Quebec, are required to help finance the separatists.

This is a country with two official languages, English and French, but English signs may be outlawed—and a person can become Prime Minister without speaking either of them. Just ask Jean Chrétien.

This is a country whose premiers have sported names like "Wacky" Bennett and "Wacky Junior" and where a big-city mayor (Toronto's Mel Lastman) shakes hands with the Hell's Angels and welcomes them to town.

The New Democratic Party, believing itself to be the conscience of the country, is humorous only in its sincere belief that it speaks for *all* Canadians while regularly attracting about 15 percent of the vote, but the Progressive Conservative Party—which spawned the Bloc Québécois and the Reform Party, which then became the Canadian Alliance, which then re-merged with the Progressive Conservatives to become the Conservative Party (non-progressive)—has provided more than enough material for levity, especially during Stockwell Day's term as Leader. Apart from holding his first press conference as a federal MP wearing a wetsuit and sitting astride a Jet Ski on the shores of Lake Okanagan, Stock made quite a splash when it was revealed that the world as he knew it was no more than six thousand years old. He also believed that the Niagara River ran from north to south (which would, presumably, mean that Niagara Falls falls *up*).

Needless to say, Stock quickly became a media darling, and when his Canadian Alliance Party decided to find a new name, we had a field day. The *National Post* thought the new party should be called the Canadian Reform Alliance Party, or CRAP. Comedian Rick Mercer started a campaign to get Stockwell Day to change *his* name to Doris.

Our listeners lobbied Talkback with their own suggestions for what to call the new Canadian Alliance:

> *The Reform Party*
> *Stock on the Rocks*
> *The New Alliance Party (NAP)*
> *The Day Old*
> *The Liberalized Progressive Reform Alliance Party*
> *The Twilight Zone ("It comes at the end of the day, and there's an eerie sense of otherworldly danger.")*
> *Misalliance*
> *Stock Option*
> *Day Care ("They're all a bunch of babies.")*
> *The Party Formerly Known as Alliance Formerly Known as Reform Formerly Known as Tory*
> *PITA, or Pain in the Alliance Party*

When he wasn't casting about for a new name, Stockwell Day was doing things like apparently spying on the Prime Minister. To be fair, I don't actually know if he was spying on the PM, because the story got a bit mixed up, as things tended to do when Stock was around. But here's the story as *Globe and Mail* reporter Andrew Mitrovica related it to us in April 2001.

A meeting had taken place in the Centre Block on Parliament Hill with Day and his Chief of Staff and two Alliance MPs—and a private investigator whom the party was thinking of hiring to try to dig up some dirt on the Prime Minister in connection with a golf club in Shawinigan, Quebec. Day at first confirmed that the meeting had taken place, but a bit later, he said that after checking his daytimer, he realized he had never met the man in question; he only *thought* he had, because he'd read it in the *Globe and Mail*. And they weren't looking to spy on the PM; they wanted more information on organized crime.

Perhaps Stock was distracted by the lawsuit he got tangled up in after one of his constituents accused him of slander. Mr. Day was the Alberta Treasurer when he questioned the integrity of Red Deer lawyer Lorne Goddard, who was defending a convicted pedophile in court. In the end, Day settled the suit at a cost of $792,000—and the bill was covered by Alberta taxpayers.

But I wouldn't want you to think that Stock was the only guy who ever got a bit confused breathing in the heady air of Parliament Hill. What about poor old Dennis Mills, the Liberal MP who graciously consented to give us an interview in the same month about the new committee he was going to chair on bulk water exports (speaking of heady substances)? The government, we thought, had already announced that it wasn't going to allow bulk water exports. Why set up a committee?

"The whole issue of water is not crystal clear," said Mr. Mills. "We want to make sure we have our position on water in a solid state."

He should be a writer for As It Happens, I thought.
But I said:

ML: Well, is there *any* possibility in your view that the government will move to allow the export of bulk water?

DM: There is absolutely no chance that the Government of Canada will take any other position than the one we've always articulated. Minister of Foreign Affairs John Manley reasserted that position today in the House of Commons—that it's final.

But we could say something in the House of Commons, and if it's in conflict with a trade agreement, the trade agreement is paramount. That's why we must have these hearings and why we must have this debate as Canadians, so we reaffirm our position as a nation. I think it's linked to our sovereignty, Mary Lou.

ML: So in terms of this committee, you are not interested in trying to decide whether or not to export bulk water but only how to stop it.

DM: Well, when you're chairing a committee of the House of Commons and it's all-party, we have a duty to listen to people on all sides of the debate. And we now have a democratically elected Premier in Newfoundland [Roger Grimes] who has a different view. It's not unlike the health care situation, Mary Lou. If a particular party in Canada started a private health care system, that essentially opens the floodgates right across the country under the Free Trade Agreement terms.

Call me dense, but I did feel that the situation was less than "crystal clear," and it was about to get murkier still, because before this interview got to air, our Editorial Desk learned that the Prime Minister's Office, when questioned, had refused to confirm Mr. Mills' appointment as Committee Chair. In fact, the PMO refused to confirm that there even was a committee *to* chair.

We called Dennis Mills back.

ML: Mr. Mills, since we spoke earlier, we've been talking to the Prime Minister's Office—

DM: Yes?

ML: And they're saying there is no water committee.

DM: No, what they're saying is the committee has not been struck—and I think I said to you we wouldn't be starting our hearings until August. But the letters of support from all the Opposition parties I have in my possession—so does our House Leader—so we're now just sort of working out the technical details, and when those details are in place, then we should start our hearings. In August.

ML: So you have no doubt that this committee is going to be set up?

DM: Well, the Prime Minister has named me Chair of the Committee. I have the Opposition letters—not physically in my possession at this moment, but I have them in my possession. And unless somebody from the Opposition goes against their own letter—and I mean, I doubt that—everything's proceeding.

ML: No, it seems to be somebody in the Prime Minister's Office that's saying—

DM: No, no. I talked to Francie Ducros about this just moments ago. The actual striking of the Committee hasn't happened, but the machinery is done for putting the Committee in motion.

ML: And the Prime Minister has asked you to chair it.

DM: Yes, he has. He announced it in caucus yesterday.

ML: Why do you think the PMO wouldn't confirm that?

DM: Well, I'll tell you why. When you have a special committee of the House of Commons, there is a technical thing that has to be done—you have to have the support of all parties—and the Prime Minister was not aware that we had it in writing, the support of all the Opposition parties.

ML: As of now, they're just denying any knowledge of this.

DM: No, I think if you speak to Francie Ducros *now,* she would acknowledge that they have the letters of support, which she didn't have earlier and was unaware of.

But the PMO refused to come to Dennis Mills' rescue. The most they would concede was that while there was no committee at present, they saw "no reason why there should not be a committee at some time in the future." Sadly for Mr. Mills, the Prime Minister never quite got around to striking this very important special committee. I wonder if it had anything to do with Mr. Mills having been so agreeable as to talk to us that day.

Incidentally, Madame Ducros's own career in the PMO was cut short, when, speaking to a reporter, she referred to George W. Bush as a moron.

A number of public figures preferred not to talk to *As It Happens* for some reason—or to any media. I never had the pleasure of interviewing Alberta Premier Ralph Klein, for instance, no matter how nicely or how often we asked. Prime Minister Stephen Harper talked to us a number of times before he got the top job, not afterwards. Politicians covet the free air time when there's an election campaign on, of course—unless they're so assured of victory they don't need it. Then, sometimes, they'd rather not risk an unscripted encounter where they might say something to derail their campaign.

Some politicians are so afraid of their own mouths—so wedded to the script—that they probably wouldn't sound natural talking to their own mothers, in which case we didn't particularly want to talk to *them*.

Speaking of programmed responses always makes me think of one of the earliest interviews of my career, when I was co-hosting a daily TV show in Ottawa called *Four for the Road*. Our brief was to roam around Ottawa and the Ottawa Valley, from Pembroke to Hawkesbury and Kapuskasing to Smiths Falls, looking for people and stories. The show was broadcast live from the studio two or three days a week, and we taped the other shows from the field, using a remote studio—basically, a control room in a truck.

One day I was scheduled to talk to a chef—call him Etienne Lebrun—who had made a name for himself in a little country restaurant north of the city. Our bilingual researcher, always happy to have an opportunity to practise her French, did the whole pre-interview with M. Lebrun in his native language. One of the questions she forgot to ask him was whether he could, in fact, speak English. As it turned out, he could not, and the interview went something like this:

ML: So M. Lebrun, you've made quite a reputation for yourself up here. What makes your cooking so appealing?

EL: Vell, ve haf verry good, very fresh food. Our *terrine de faisan* is excellent.

ML: And what brought you to this part of the world?

EL: [pause] Our *terrine de faisan* is excellent.

ML: It is indeed. We've just sampled it. Very, very good.

But you did not study here, did you? Where did you learn to cook?

EL: [another pause] Also, our *confit de canard Sarladais* veet *aubergine farcie . . .*

And so it went until, mercifully, my allotted eight minutes were up. Since that time, whenever I've overheard a researcher practising his French or Spanish or Russian on a prospective interview subject, I've made sure to lean over and whisper, "Please be sure they understand that the interview will be in *English* before you book them."

A corollary of that might be, "Make sure the guest's English is good enough to be understood by someone listening to the interview on a car radio in traffic or in the kitchen with three kids yelling." Listening to someone talking on the radio on a cellphone from the other side of the world can be taxing enough without throwing an impenetrable accent into the mix.

But getting back to politics . . . In my experience, the people who were hardest to pry loose from their prepared media responses were often, I'm sorry to say, female Members of Parliament. I think it must have stemmed from a lack of confidence. Talking to some of them in public was like trying to have a conversation with a slot machine. No matter what you asked them, you'd get one of the pre-scripted responses or "talking points" that their media advisors had prepared for them.

That said, there's no shortage of male public figures who are careful to a fault, and there are plenty of women who are far from shrinking violets: Conservative Senators Pat Carney and Elsie Wayne come to mind, as well as former Liberal MP Sheila Copps and the straight-shooting Deborah Grey. Grey, an Alberta woman who suited up in leather and rode around the capital on a Honda Goldwing, made a name for herself as the country's first Reform Party MP, and went on to become Deputy Leader and Acting Leader of the Reform Party and its various successors and incarnations before retiring in 2005. She once brought a pig into the House of Commons to protest against a Liberal motion to increase MPs' salaries. In his recent memoir, *My Years as Prime Minister,* Jean Chrétien says he regarded Grey as a "feisty and effective opponent," and he had a lot of admiration for her.

Three of the four women I've just mentioned hail from the west or the far east of the country (Newfoundland), so maybe it's where you grow up that determines whether you'll be frank and outspoken or careful and timid. Pat Carney certainly falls into the former category. Once I made the mistake on air of appearing to treat the Canada-U.S. salmon wars too lightly— I think I referred to them as "the fish thing"—and Senator Carney went ballistic. Or pretended to. As a veteran pol, she knew how to exploit a situation to her advantage, and she got the attention she wanted for what was, admittedly, a very serious issue in her constituency. Steaming or not, Carney was always good value on the air, and I enjoyed talking to her.

Of course, it's not hard to figure out why people in the public eye are afraid to speak frankly. In an age of instant, universal communication, to say nothing of political correctness, you have to walk on eggshells sometimes in order not to end up with egg on your face. The smallest slip might spell the end of your public career; adversaries will take your words out of context and beat you up with them, and the media will be howling with glee.

We can't help it; scandal and controversy are as mother's milk to us. Which brings us back to the Conservative Party's forerunner (and successor), the Alliance. Not surprisingly,

Stockwell Day's style eventually spawned a revolt from within his own party led by, among others, Chuck Strahl and our old friend Deb Grey. For a while, the eight renegades called themselves the Independent Alliance Caucus (IAC). Then they became the Democratic Representative Caucus (DRC), which formed a coalition with the old Progressive Conservative Party (PC) to become the PC-DRC.

And again Talkback wanted to help out with the naming of the new (breakaway) party:

> *More CRAP*
> *The Block Stock—or BS—Party*
> *The Dissident Original Reformers in Segregation—*
> *or DORIS—Party*
> *Eight Days in the Stock-ade*
> *The Regressive Conservatives*
> *The Day-nouement Party*
> *The Annual Party (You just assign a number to it, so*
> *it might be the Fourth Annual Party one year and*
> *the Fifth Annual Party the next year.)*
> *A Giggle ("since all of the Alliance are a laughing*
> *Stock")*
> *Rebels without a Clause*
> *Eight-Point Stock Plunge*
> *Chuck and the Day-Breakers*
> *Octa-gone*
> *A Rabble of Rebels*
> *Day's End*

By this time, people inside Stockwell Day's party were suing *each other. As It Happens,* May 17, 2001:

Barbara Budd: It was a typical day in the life of

the Canadian Alliance: members of the Leader's
office threatened to sue an Alliance MP; the new
Communications Director resigned; and the divisions
within the party grew even deeper. A lawyer representing
Day's Communications Office demanded an apology
from Chuck Strahl, who they say defamed them when he
talked about "dishonest communications" coming from
the Day office. We reached the former Communications
Director, Ezra Levant, in Ottawa.

ML: Hello, Mr. Levant.

EL: Hi, Mary Lou.

ML: Did you resign or were you fired?

EL: I resigned. I offered my resignation voluntarily.

ML: Under what circumstances?

EL: Well, I think it was becoming apparent to me that
my forceful style of politics—an aggressive, loyal style—
was becoming at odds with the new stance of
reconciliation and diplomacy that is required to have
harmonious relations between the Leader and the
caucus. In other words, I was starting to get between
Stock Day and the MPs, and that's totally not what I
wanted to do. So out of loyalty to Stock and the party, I
said, "If I'm getting between you and the MPs, if I'm rub-
bing them the wrong way because I'm such a loyalist, let
me pull myself out of the equation." And so I did.

ML: Was there any discussion of this letter that you sent
to Chuck Strahl?

EL: Ah, that was, uh—

ML: A catalyst?

EL:—a very minor matter in the whole scheme of

things. Essentially, as you know well, the past few weeks and even months have been very challenging for our party. There's been a lot of internecine bickering—it's been unfortunate—and my approach through this time has been a forceful and aggressive one, and this letter to Chuck Strahl was just one example of that.

So I guess my answer is, "Sort of. Yeah."

ML: So you wrote this letter—

EL: No.

ML: What?

EL: My lawyer did.

ML: Okay—and you and three other people signed it, threatening legal action against Chuck Strahl if he didn't apologize for talking about dishonest communications. Have I got that right?

EL: Pretty much right. Again, we didn't sign the letter; it was signed by our lawyer. It's a typical demand letter, basically saying to Chuck, "You said something that was false and defamatory, so please apologize and retract." I actually spoke to Mr. Strahl personally earlier in the day, and I sent him a personal note, asking him the same thing. As you saw, he refused to.

And you know what, it's just unacceptable for a man of Mr. Strahl's stature to go on national TV and make a slur like that, and I believe it was in my interest and in the interest of my shop here—the communications shop—to let Mr. Strahl know that you simply can't go around and defame people.

ML: Same problem Mr. Day had with the Quebec judge, I think.

EL: Well, I'd say it's more analogous to the Goddard matter; here's a case where Mr. Strahl was asked to apologize politely, privately, in advance. Instead, out of pride, Mr. Strahl dug in his heels. He doesn't want to admit that he was wrong. So if he's digging in, I'm afraid he's going to have to face the consequences, and it's a shame that just as Mr. Strahl's little party's getting started, it's embroiled in his own Goddard-style defamation fiasco.

ML: So you're going ahead with this.

EL: Of course.

ML: Did you show the letter to Mr. Day?

EL: No.

ML: You didn't think he should know?

EL: I had gone through other procedures here, you know, in the office. Mr. Day's a busy man. We do hundreds of things a day through our office and not all of them are cleared by the Leader.

ML: Mr. Day, apparently, has seen it now. Did you have a conversation about it subsequently, when it came to light publicly? You leaked it to the paper, right?

EL: Yeah, only in the most glancing way. You're emphasizing this letter as the reason for my resignation. It's only part of a larger picture—my aggressive approach to defending Stockwell Day—

ML: I'm also interested in what Mr. Day's reaction was to the letter, though.

EL: Well, this morning when I met with Mr. Day, the subject of the letter— I mentioned it only in passing when I offered him my resignation. I basically started the discussion with Mr. Day: "Stock, I'm here to help you and the party. I think, given my style and the current situation, since I'm a bit of a pit-bull and you need someone who's a bit more of a diplomat, I'm going to offer you my resignation and my best wishes."

ML: Did he try to talk you out of it?

EL: He reluctantly accepted.

ML: Given that people who have been complaining these past few weeks about the Leader's office, given that much of what they say relates to how the Leader consults or doesn't consult with them, do you think that you've been the problem?

EL: You know, until a couple of weeks ago, the Alliance was actually doing pretty well in the polls; we were still in the 20 percent range. Only when we saw Chuck Strahl's Hamlet *shtick*—"Oh, what do I *do?*"—day after day after day . . .

The damage being done to the party has been done by this "loyal band."

ML: And not at all by you or Stockwell Day.

EL: Well, because it has turned into a civil war, there's been shooting back and forth. But my point is, a modern, professional, disciplined, mature political party keeps that sort of stuff behind closed doors of caucus.

And the other kind of political party is what makes our day—so to speak. The Quebec judge reference, by the way, had to do with Stockwell Day's having criticized a judge in the Shawinigate case, thus leaving himself open to either another lawsuit or a contempt of court charge.

Ah, Shawinigate! Another juicy story about shenanigans in politics, but too complicated to go into here. Enough to say that the story is set in a hotel next to a golf course in

Shawinigan, Quebec, Jean Chrétien's old riding, and the characters include a Prime Minister, a bank President and a convicted felon from Belgium.

Canadian politics boring? Pshaw.

There was, in time, another leadership race in Stockwell Day's party, which Day lost to Stephen Harper, causing the DRC to break away from the PC-DRC coalition and rejoin the Alliance. Shortly afterwards, the PCs replaced *their* Leader, Joe Clark, with Peter MacKay, who won a hotly contested leadership race by promising never, ever, ever to join up with the Canadian Alliance—and promptly did just that. They jettisoned the word "progressive," and the newly reunited Tories became known simply as the Conservative Party of Canada (CPC—or is that the Communist Party of Canada?). And that's the story so far except that a rump of the old Progressive Conservative Party, consisting of members who didn't want anything to do with the merger, went to court to try to have it declared null and void. They lost.

Another thing that's fun to watch in Canadian politics is all the switching of partners. Not talking about sexual partnerships here—though, goodness knows, there's enough of that to keep the rumour mills grinding—but about the individuals who for reasons high and low and sometimes rather obscure decide to leave the Liberals and join the Conservatives, or leave the Conservatives and join the Liberals. By sheer coincidence, the switcher often lands a plum job in his new party—a Cabinet post, say—but he makes it clear to everyone that his switch was a matter of conscience.

Switching allegiance is nothing new, of course. People throughout history have found it expedient at some point—or rather a matter of conscience—to change party affiliations,

Winston Churchill being a notable example. And the practice was not unknown in Canada before now. Pierre Trudeau's politics were closer to the NDP's than to the Liberals' before he joined the Liberal Cabinet of Lester Pearson and then became, himself, the Liberal PM. Lucien Bouchard was sympathetic to Quebec's separation before he was appointed Canada's Ambassador to Paris by Conservative Prime Minister Brian Mulroney. Then Mr. Bouchard became a Conservative Cabinet Minister, which was just before he became Leader of the separatist Bloc Québécois, which he co-founded. Jean Charest was the PC Leader in Ottawa before becoming Liberal Premier in Quebec.

But hard as it was to keep track before, the practice seems to be gaining momentum. There were several Alliance MPs who switched to the Liberals when Stephen Harper beat them in the leadership race. Stephen Harper himself once worked for a Progressive Conservative MP, and before that he belonged to a Liberal student club. In the 2006 election, a Liberal candidate in British Columbia who romped to victory while portraying the Conservatives as scurrilous rats more or less found soon afterwards that he'd been sadly mistaken and what he'd meant was that the Conservatives were fine people and he'd be honoured to join them and fill a Cabinet position in the new Conservative government.

Much of the fun seems to have gone out of federal politics for the moment, in part because Prime Minister Harper is a rather humourless and careful man and keeps his ministers on a short leash lest they do or say something embarrassing. There was a funny moment, though, when Gilles Duceppe, Leader of the separatist Bloc Québécois (the party that sits in the Parliament of the country it's sworn to break up), announced that he was stepping down as BQ Leader so as to run for the leadership of the PQ, or Parti Québécois (that's the Quebec *provincial* separatist party for those of you from away), but changed his mind before the print was dry on the newspaper headlines. I can't remember what reason he gave, but the pundits said that when Duceppe realized he wasn't a shoo-in as PQ Leader, he decided to keep the job he had, along with its very handsome salary and pension, rather than risk getting the old heave-ho from Quebec voters. The man he'd thought to replace, by the way, was a young gay guy who had openly admitted to sniffing coke in his youth, which in his case, happened to be while he was already in government—none of which deterred the Parti Québécois from choosing him as their Leader. But when he lost an election, the party decided to turf him.

So it's not as though there's no more humour to be found in the halls of power, and we all know it's just a matter of time before Tory lips start flapping again on the Hill, whether the PM likes it or not. But I think the main reason we are not so amused these days by our Honourable Members is that Canada today is a country at war. The shadow of Afghanistan—Canadian lives lost, our young men and women maimed, the agony of the Afghans themselves—means that we cannot view the political scene with an altogether light heart. Now the stakes *are* high, it *is* a matter of life and death and we really must hope and pray that our government and public servants—and all of us—are up to the new challenges we face. The war has its roots, as far as Canada's concerned anyway, in that second day that will live in infamy—the day we usually refer to simply as 9/11. And what a hell of a shock that was.

FOURTEEN

Millennium Madness

Radio that asks, Why 2K?

⁓

Does anyone remember how the world was going to end when the calendar turned over to January 1, 2000? "Y2K" was the term we adopted for the problem, which had to do with computers and how they weren't programmed, many of them, to recognize any date past 1999 and so would probably go into a big snit, the way computers do, and crash all over the place, ending Western civilization as we knew it. That didn't happen, whether because we put about a million IT guys on the case and updated all the critical software or because it didn't pose that much of a threat in the first place. At any rate, we got past the witching hour of midnight without a catastrophe, and lots of people had a grand party to usher in the new millennium.

Some people pointed out that January 1, 2000, wasn't actually the beginning of the new millennium, only the beginning of the last year of the *old* millennium, and we should wait a year to ring in the new era, but numbers have a magic all their own, and that fresh-looking 2000 was not to be denied recognition. The way I think of the change is that the old millennium ended with one of the best stories I've ever covered, and the new one started with the worst story—both of them in the U.S. I'm referring to the presidential election of November 2000 and the attack on the World Trade Center in September 2001.

It so happened that I was in Washington on election day—November 7, 2000—having been sent there to anchor a news special for CBC Radio. The U.S. being the only superpower left standing after the Cold War and an economic behemoth to boot, elections there are watched with great interest all over the world—but especially in Canada, on the other side of what was at the time "the longest undefended border in the world." Canada is to the United States as a mouse is to an elephant, our geographic expanse notwithstanding: 90 percent of our trade is with the U.S, and as the old adage goes, if someone sneezes in Washington, we get pneumonia, and so on. That's why the CBC decided to mount a radio news special on election night.

Since it was November, however (not the end of the fiscal year, when funds flow like Niagara for a few weeks), they didn't want to spend any money, so the special would consist of me and a couple of guests in our Washington studio and would last just one half-hour, from 9:30 to 10:00 p.m.

"What if the outcome isn't decided by ten o'clock?" I wanted to know.

"Doesn't matter," they said. "We can report later developments in the regular hourly newscasts."

To be honest, with my unerring political instincts, I was more concerned about the possibility of the election results being known well *before* we got to air, thus depriving us of any element of suspense—a ridiculous worry as it turned out.

Shortly after the polls closed on the west coast, the Amnets (American TV networks) projected that George W. Bush would have enough votes to become the next president of the United States, and they declared him the winner. A few minutes later, though, they *un-declared* him, as their computers took Florida *out* of the "Bush" column and put it back under "Undecided," the reason being that George Bush and Al Gore were virtually tied in Florida. In the rest of the country, they had already racked up an equal number of electoral votes, so Florida's votes were critical.

Lack of suspense was not going to be a problem. With Florida "back in play," we now found ourselves smack dab in the middle of the most interesting U.S. election night since Dewey didn't beat Truman. Unfortunately, on CBC Radio, our half-hour was up. I signed off and then hung around the National Press Building for a few more hours, watching late results trickle in and fetching coffee for my colleague Henry Champ, who remained on the air for CBC Newsworld. I was itching to be back on air, but we'd made no provision for a tie vote and there was no more "special" for radio that night. When I finally went to bed the next morning, most people still thought that Bush would prevail, including Al Gore, who phoned Bush to concede. Then Gore, too, did an about-face. When the Washington *papers* went to bed, all they could report was that they had a cliff hanger on their hands.

And what a cliff hanger it turned out to be. My friend Laura Parker, a Washington-based print reporter, was in Seattle for a family funeral the day before the election; the day after the election, her boss called and told her to get herself to Florida—*stat!* She wound up not getting home again for seven weeks, barely finding a moment to buy clean underwear and a cotton shirt during that time.

I went back to Toronto to follow the story from the *As It Happens* studio, where clean shirts were not a problem, although the pace of events sometimes had us sweating more than usual. No one seemed to know how to fix the "Florida problem." Bush's small margin of victory there made a recount in Florida inevitable, but when people started complaining that the voting machines hadn't worked properly, that the process was too complicated for some voters, that ballots had been properly marked but not properly counted, that they'd been counted twice, or not at all, it was clear that a simple re-count wasn't going to settle it. Batteries of lawyers descended on the Sunshine State. Legal challenges, court rulings, hourly press conferences and shifting poll results succeeded one another with dizzying speed. Water-cooler conversation everywhere was of dimpled ballots and hanging chad and pregnant chad. (Chad was what they called the bits of confetti-sized paper that got punched out of a ballot when you voted by machine; if it wasn't completely punched out, it might be hanging or pregnant.)

Some scenarios put Gore ahead by a few votes, others Bush. The story went from Broward County to Dade County, from Miami to Tallahassee, and from Florida to Washington and back. You couldn't take your eyes off CNN or the wires for a second or you'd miss a new turn in the story.

At *As It Happens,* we were having the time of our lives—especially Senior Producer Mark Ulster, who was a close observer of the American zeitgeist. Every night, just as we went to air, or just afterwards, a new judgment would come down from somewhere—*Count! Don't count!*—and a new appeal launched somewhere else. We had to work overtime to keep the show from being dated as it moved across the country to B.C., but it was terrific fun.

This excerpt from a conversation I had with Jeff Greenfield on November 22, 2000, may help you remember what it was like. Jeff was, and is, a political analyst for CNN, and that day he'd used the words "constitutional train wreck" to describe what awaited his country as George Bush appealed to the U.S. Supreme Court to shut down all hand re-counts in Florida, while the Florida Legislature threatened to make hand re-counts irrelevant by naming their own slate to the electoral college.

ML: Mr. Greenfield, on CNN you used words like *nuclear, unbelievable, constitutional train wreck*. Is it getting that bad?

JG: Those were understatements.

ML: You were at a loss for words to describe the situation?

JG: Well, I think what happens is that many of us who, institutionally, don't like to hype stories—try to act restrained in most cases, because there is a tendency on television to bloviate and make everything amazing—really are now looking at the situation, and realism requires that you go to the thesaurus and find some of the more extravagant adjectives. We are getting closer and closer to a situation that this country has not faced since the election of 1876, and that is a humungous, bitter, fundamental clash in the Congress over the identity of the President under rules that literally nobody understands.

So if that's not a train wreck, it'll do until the real thing comes along.

ML: All right. You were speaking also last night about the possibility that the Florida Legislature would name its electoral slate—Republicans—and the Democrats would also send a group of electors to vote. Can that happen?

JG: Well, the last time it happened that meant anything was 1876. In 1960, in Hawaii, two different slates of electors were sent because the vote was so close—Congress ultimately decided it was the Democrats—but in that election, it didn't mean anything.

ML: Right. What happened in 1876?

JG: In 1876—surely we all remember this—Rutherford B. Hayes, the Republican, and Samuel Tilden, the

Democrat, were in a close race. Four different states had
disputed electors; four different states—including
Florida, by the way—sent two slates of electors to
Congress. They formed a special commission—no part
of the Constitution, they just came up with this notion—
and after a great deal of what is largely considered highly
suspect horse trading, the Republicans got *all* of the
contested electoral votes on a party-line vote, and histori-
ans tell us it was in return for promising the South that
Reconstruction would end and that they could go back
to racial supremacy.

With that little historical footnote, it could happen, if
the Florida Legislature decides that this process is either
so mucked-up, so unfair or jeopardizes Florida's electoral
presence in the Congress, that they take it on themselves
to assign electors. They have the power to do this under
federal law, which is taken from the Constitution. Our
system, basically, gives the state legislatures almost total
power over the electoral vote.

ML: Okay, then, flip that around: What would be the
grounds for the Democrats saying, "*Our* electors are the
valid ones"?

JG: If the hand-counts come in and give Gore a plurality
and, say, the state Attorney General says, "As the state's
legal officer, I find this is the right count, and the electors
should be the Democrats," the *two* slates could show up
in Tallahassee. Presumably, the Republicans would meet
in the official state chamber, because the Legislature is
Republican; the Democrats would move over to some
other office and somehow cast their votes. They'd be
transmitted to the Congress, one by the Governor and
Secretary of State, and the other by the Attorney General,

and there you have two slates of electors. And then it's fundamentally up to the Congress to figure out which slate it will accept. The only problem is there does not seem to be anyone who actually knows how this would happen. Presumably, both houses of Congress—

ML: Would vote?

JG: —would vote. That's what happens when electors are challenged.

We have one more wrinkle if you don't think this is enough: If the current vote totals hold up, the *Senate* would be divided 50–50.

ML: Because it's the *new* Congress that would vote?

JG: The new Congress meets January 5th or 6th—they haven't figured that one out either. If you assume a party-line vote, and that's not necessarily the case, the House would narrowly vote for the Republican slate, the Senate would be tied and then—you ask the logical question: "Well, could the Vice-President, who would still be Al Gore, break the tie?" Everyone I've talked to has given me the same answer: We're not sure.

ML: My goodness.

JG: And by the way—

ML: He would not be allowed to vote, surely.

JG: Well, it's not clear. He votes to break ties in every other situation.

ML: But he wouldn't still be— Oh, I guess he *would* still be the Vice-President.

JG: Sure, he would. That's the whole point. The new Congress convenes January 6th; his term expires January 20th. He is the Vice-President; he presides over that joint session that traditionally counts the electoral votes. So he's *there*. But I actually bothered to talk to the historian of the Senate and said, "Well, you know, is this a ministerial function? Is it the kind of function you vote for on ties in legislation? What is it?"

He said, "We don't know. The 19th-century law that was passed after that Hayes-Tilden disaster doesn't make this entirely clear." There's one other thing. Suppose the House says, "Okay, the Republican electors are the ones we recognize," and the other House says, "No, the Democrats." What happens then? We don't know. Negotiation? Compromise?

ML: Okay, now let me ask an up-to-the-minute—I *think*—question.

JG: Have you looked at the TV yet? It could have changed.

ML: Not in the last ten minutes. It's changing by the minute, I know.

Miami-Dade: last time I looked, the canvassing board had decided to stop the hand-count, because it did not believe it could meet the deadline set by the Supreme Court, which was Sunday night. Have I got that right?

JG: Right. As of now, that's right.

ML: Without that vote, presumably Vice-President Gore doesn't have a chance and they couldn't send—

JG: Not so fast.

ML: Okay.

JG: If Palm Beach County counts all those disputed ballots—those now infamous or famous dimpled ballots—and Broward County counts all the dimpled ballots, the Gore people think they just might catch up with those.

ML: Oh, they might still count the dimpled ballots?

JG: Well, we *don't know*. The Supreme Court of Florida did not say yea or nay. They, in effect, said to the county boards, "Count." The opinion that they cited, which comes from another state, seems to indicate—and I'm sorry to be so, you know, evasive, but it's not evasive; this is the ambiguity we're all in—*seems* to suggest you can count them.

My sense is that if they do, that will only further ratchet up what I can only describe as the *fury* that the Republicans feel that this election is being taken from them and further encourage them to go nuclear—which is to say, name their slate of electors based on the state Legislature.

This was more or less the tenor of most of our on-air conversations about the U.S. election. What really made it fun, I think, was the delicious irony of it: the world's only superpower, the greatest democracy, the epitome of know-how and fairness and the rule of law, couldn't figure out how to count votes. People from places like Guatemala and Ukraine were offering to send observers to help the Americans exercise democracy at home.

And it went on and on. Months and even years later, we were still getting reports on the vote result in several Florida counties because some media organizations had got hold of the ballots and were determined to conduct the re-count that the U.S. Supreme Court had halted. We also started to take a look at the sorts of voting machines and systems in use around the country, and we were surprised to learn how many of them were prone to giving inaccurate results. The worst system of all, of course, is one that is entirely electronic, in which there is no paper record to be examined in case of a challenge, and which is susceptible to tampering. Believe it or not, this is the system Florida installed *after* the 2000 election. Maybe they just don't approve of democracy in Florida.

Not only in Florida. I read in the *New York Times* not long ago that about 30 percent of American voters were confronted with paperless electronic voting machines in 2006. Now some Congressmen are working to see that every jurisdiction has some form of paper voting record *before* the 2008 presidential elections. A few American commentators have pointed out that up in Canada, in federal elections, they still use a pencil to mark an "X" on a piece of paper, which they stick in a cardboard box, and this seems to work pretty well. So we do and so it does, but I have no confidence in its lasting: it's too easy and too cheap. It's only a matter of time before someone insists that we replace our simple, inexpensive, accurate system with a fancy, pricey one that doesn't work as well.

When the media did their re-counts in Florida in 2003, Bush did squeeze out a narrow victory—at least, in some cases—which was also the official result when the Supreme Court (stacked with Republican sympathizers, by the way) decided in December 2000 that they would not overrule the Florida Legislature (also Republican, plus the Governor was George Bush's brother Jeb!). This wonderful roller-coaster ride then came to an end. But as Jeff Greenfield had predicted, by that time, neither side was prepared to believe that the other guy could have won fair and square, and it would be some time before Bush's opponents would stop thinking of him as an impostor in the White House. It would be nearly ten months, actually.

By the time I got to the CBC building on September 11, 2001, all regular programming had been suspended and Michael Enright was anchoring the radio network coverage from the news studio, having just taken over from Shelagh Rogers, who had been holding the fort up to that time. Shelagh had been on the air, hosting her own network programme, *This Morning*, when the planes hit the World Trade Center. To everyone's embarrassment, CBC Radio continued with regular programming for more than an hour, although there were brief news bulletins. As I drove downtown to the studio, I was getting all my radio news from a private Toronto station that was carrying the audio feed from CNN. This was how I learned that a third plane had crashed into the Pentagon and there might be another on its way to Washington.

It sounded as if Armageddon was happening and CBC Radio was asleep at the switch. We were told later that the reason for our sluggish response that morning was that Master Control rooms in some parts of the country had been automated to save money, making it difficult for network managers to take control of their stations from coast to coast. Whether this was the root of the problem or not I don't know because several years later when the shuttle *Columbia* disintegrated over Texas, after the problems with Master Control had supposedly been cleared up, we were back in the same fix: private radio beat us to the punch again.

That said, there weren't many facts to report when Radio News finally did take over on September 11th, apart from what you could see with your own eyes—on TV. The burning buildings in New York, the crumpled Pentagon. There were rumours of a fourth plane heading for Capitol Hill or the White House, of buildings on fire in Washington, of a plane crash in Pennsylvania. There were TV images of President Bush being given the news while he was visiting an elementary school in Texas. He spoke a few words into a microphone, then vanished aboard Air Force One, headed for an unnamed destination.

It wasn't clear whether the U.S. Cabinet was in emergency session in the White House or in a bunker or had left the capital altogether. We were all scrambling to find someone who could tell us something of what was going on, and we were having a hard time of it. I don't recall anyone mentioning al Qaeda or Osama bin Laden that day—names that wouldn't have meant much to us anyway at the time. The pictures of the burning towers got worse and worse, and the worst of all were pictures of people, overcome by heat and smoke, jumping *out* of the World Trade Center and falling one hundred storeys to their deaths. In a documentary I saw later, a microphone at ground level had picked up the sound of bodies hitting the pavement. *Thud! Thud! Thud!*

And then the twin towers collapsed.

Later, when she was recalling those terrible images, a friend of mine in Cambridge, Massachusetts, said to me, "I have lived too long." She would have preferred never to have seen such things. But didn't we all feel that way?

Or what did we feel?

For myself, I remember only the shock—and some fear, since no one knew how many more attacks awaited us or where. But mainly I was focused on work. When Michael Enright was ready to be relieved, I moved into the anchor chair, and now it was my turn to talk to whomever the producers could get to a phone, picking up any scraps of information they could provide. Linda Perry and Louis Hammond were in the streets of New York with cellphones. Washington correspondent Frank Koller drove up to New York but couldn't get into Manhattan because all the tunnels and bridges had been closed. He described only what he could see from the Jersey shore. We heard clips from or did interviews with New York Mayor Rudolf Giuliani, New York Governor George Pataki, New York fire chiefs and many others—but no one knew very much.

In Canada, meanwhile, thousands of unexpected visitors from around the world began arriving in Newfoundland and Nova Scotia after the U.S. Federal Aviation Administration closed American borders to incoming air traffic. The FAA also grounded all domestic flights, as did Canada, stranding Prime Minister Jean Chrétien and his Cabinet all over the country. Canadian Transport Minister David Collenette was essentially acting alone when he gave the go-ahead to re-route North Atlantic passenger planes to Canada's east coast. He spoke afterwards of his admiration for the air traffic controllers who got everyone turned around and safely brought into harbour.

The visitors, when they put down, also had to find somewhere to stay and something to eat and drink, and if they were Americans, extra sympathy and understanding. The people in Gander, Newfoundland, and elsewhere delivered. Many new friendships were forged that week, and years later Americans were still finding ways to show their gratitude for the comfort they had found on this darkest of days.

Ultimately, I can't find the words even now to describe the turmoil, horror and grief we witnessed on that terrible day and in the days that followed. The sound of laughter was forgotten. I was shocked one morning as I headed into the Broadcasting Centre to hear two young women giggling merrily. *Who are these unfeeling creatures,* I wondered, *who could laugh at a time like this?* Baseball games were cancelled; the comics on late-night TV were muted. Families clung to each other for security and comfort.

It soon became clear that there were no survivors to be found in the rubble of the twin towers. Pictures of missing fathers and sons, mothers and daughters, lovers and friends had been posted all over Lower Manhattan, but they weren't coming home now. It was a heart-breaking story to cover, but working on the story was easier than *not* working on the story; it gave us an outlet. There was nothing else we could talk about anyway, nothing else we could think about; working for news, at least we didn't have to pretend to be doing something else—we had a licence for our obsession.

When regular programming resumed at the end of the week, it still wasn't *normal* programming; there still was really only one story. As more days passed, we did begin to ease back into something resembling our old habits, but the world *had* shifted, and we would begin to see the outlines of the new world very soon. There was a new emphasis on security, for example. People accustomed to their liberty had to start thinking about how much freedom they could trade off for security. Citizens and neighbours with a Middle Eastern cast were regarded with suspicion.

There was fresh panic when someone started mailing samples of deadly anthrax to news anchors and legislators in the United States, fearful speculation about whether this was a new terrorist attack. The anthrax sender has never been identified for certain, but there's a consensus now that it was a disturbed individual—an American—acting alone. Another plane crashed in Rockaway, Long Island, on the outskirts of New York City, but that, too, it transpired, was unrelated to the terrorist attack.

Down at Ground Zero, the clean-up was getting under way. On October 26th, we had a chat with Bart Voorsanger, a New York City architect who was part of a group assembled by the Port Authority to identify and preserve things they might eventually want to include in a memorial before they all got carted off to Staten Island, to a landfill site bearing the eerily apt name Fresh Kills. As he described his grim task, we began to realize the scope of the damage visited on New York on 9/11.

ML: Mr. Voorsanger, what kind of things have you salvaged?

BV: Well, they've really fallen into about four or five categories and the categories keep expanding, but the first major category, of course, is the collapse of the actual buildings, the towers themselves, because they were a unique structure—the perimeter with this very, very heavy steel cage—and it broke into four- and five-storey pieces that were literally hurled through the sky into the adjacent buildings and collapsed into the site itself. These weigh tons and tons and tons—I think everybody has seen the photographs of just the four- or five-storey piece that's remaining at the base. It looks a little bit like a piece of a cathedral. So pieces of this we're saving.

And the second category, the workers and the firemen and policemen, understandably in a very emotional state, have sort of canonized objects and pieces and fragments of what was remaining there. There was a fire engine that was almost totally destroyed, and I think a lot of firemen were killed in that collapse, so they've taken that off. They want to make that into their own memorial. They found a light pole that had been broken off, and when they first started the rescue, they hoisted it up with an enormous

American flag, a little bit like Iwo Jima—the famous iconic image of Iwo Jima. So what we've done is we've taken these sorts of images that have become memorable and emotional and we're trying to store them. There's a cross that's on the site right now made up of part of the structural steel, and we will save that.

The third category is objects that are off-site, damaged, destroyed. There's a fire engine, there's a taxi, police cars—all these things have been destroyed—and the force of the explosion, the force of the destruction was so unbelievable that these have been mangled in an unrecognizable and unique way that would be very memorable, to remind people of the force of the destruction.

Fourth, there would be fine art objects. I mean, there was an Alexander Calder sculpture, a stabile. There was a great Louise Nevelson piece. Juan Miró had a huge tapestry—some of these things are, of course, gone, but they did find pieces of the Calder, so we've recovered that.

And then, lastly, photography is an incredibly important thing, and video.

ML: Taking pictures.

BV: Taking pictures. This is very emotional and very important to people. For example, Bellevue Hospital— many of the families of the survivors came there with photographs of their families, trying to see if they could be found, and so they've formed these sort of memorial walls, and we're offering to save these intact. And I know that St. Vincent's Hospital wish to make their own memorial. This is just the beginning of this effort.

ML: How have you been affected by spending so much time still attached to that dreadful site?

BV: It's—it's a very emotional process. Not only for me and for people working, helping on the site—because every time you go down to Ground Zero you're reminded in a completely different way what a terrible tragedy it was. It reminds me of Berlin in World War II; just unbelievable destruction—literally, 20 blocks of destruction.

And then one day you go down there and the survivors are weeping, surrounding the site. Or you have the firemen digging for body parts. . . . It's a very difficult scene there. I don't think the public really understand the level of devastation. At some point, it will be opened up and I think they're going to be really flabbergasted. I mean, it's just an extraordinary thing.

Even then, weeks after the event, it was not uncommon for people talking to us from New York suddenly to be overcome by emotion and unable to speak. Jan Hoffman was helping to write the *New York Times* obits—their "Portraits of Grief"; she said she often ended up in tears as she interviewed friends and family of the victims of 9/11.

ML: Ms. Hoffman, how did this page come about, these Portraits of Grief? Did you decide right away that every single victim was going to be remembered?

JH: A few days after the disaster, a number of reporters and editors were sitting around trying to figure out what we could do to commemorate the victims, and . . . finally consensus was achieved that we would try to do little almost jewel boxes about as many victims as we possibly could.

ML: How did you start to collect the names?

JH: We started in a very crude fashion, by sending reporters and interns out to look at flyers on bulletin boards all over the city. Then, as we began to publish some of the portraits, corporations would contact us, unions would contact us. We combed the Internet, where a lot of people had posted the loved ones they were seeking, and we began to collate this vast list.

ML: Is there an official list now?

JH: It keeps floating up and down; it's not really nailed down. We have the *New York Times* list that we've been working from.

ML: Yes. And how many names are on your list now?

JH: Right now we have, I would say, about 2,700.

ML: When you have a name and a contact number, who writes the stories?

JH: There are a team of reporters who are given a series of these. I'll be given the name of a victim, and often just a phone number, so I'll have no idea whether I'm calling a mother, a son, a cousin, a friend—literally, it's a blind phone call.

ML: Right.

JH: And it can be extraordinarily awkward, particularly if I think I'm calling about a man and I find out it's a woman. I've reached children unknowingly, elderly parents—I'll say, "Hello, this is Jan Hoffman from the *New York Times*," and I'll just launch into my tentative speech, hoping that I have not hurt somebody inadvertently.

ML: And what do you tell them?

JH: I tell them the truth, which is, we're trying to write an appreciation of as many victims as possible, and I want to know if they have a few minutes to speak with me to share some of their thoughts about someone they loved . . . and a lot of people don't want to talk.

ML: They just can't bear to talk about it?

JH: They can't bear it. More people do, but a lot of people don't want to talk. . . . And I don't want to press them, because this is obviously not a traditional news story. If I feel that it's just not the right time, I may make a phone call a week later, and in some of those situations, it's been more successful. Particularly in one instance, when I called a woman—it turned out to be a mother— and she said they were still looking for her daughter. I thought that she clearly had not come to terms with what had happened, and so I waited a week and talked to her again and got a full story.

ML: They're heartbreaking to read.

JH: Yes.

ML: They must be very difficult do.

JH: It's true, but I keep remembering that I don't have the hard job, because I don't have to live with the memories and the nightmare. And I have to tell you that more often than not, I end up weeping on the phone with people. It's chilling, it's heartbreaking, it's sad.

It's also quite beautiful. And I also feel honoured to be doing it, to help to celebrate some of these wonderful people.

Part of the problem with the job is that some people are articulate and some people are not. There are sometimes language barriers. So what I try to do is figure out—if I can't get a full sense of someone from the person I'm interviewing, I gently inquire if I can speak with somebody else, if there's a friend or another family member . . . someone from the business. I remember once I asked, "Well, is there someone from the business that I can speak to about your husband?"

And the woman said, "They're all dead."

ML: That was [financial frim] Cantor Fitzgerald probably.

JH: Right. And so I do the best I can. My goal is to try to get a sharp and distinct sense of the person as an individual.

ML: Are there any that have stood out particularly in your mind?

JH: . . . There's one man—when I heard about him from his brother, I couldn't stop crying. He was a very quiet, unassuming man who was Jamaican-born, in his late 30s, divorced—and he lived all of his life, unbeknownst to his family, working with African-American underprivileged youth. They did not know.

He would leave his work, twice a week, in Manhattan, and drive out to Queens to counsel young men, get them jobs and drive all the way back home to New Jersey—I mean this was quite an extensive commute. And at his memorial service, more than 30 young men came up to the family to say how the victim had graced their lives.

ML: And they had no idea.

JH: They had no idea. They knew that he coached inner-city basketball, that he had coached football—they knew a lot of stuff about him, but this kind of thing they had no idea about. . . . And all the man really wanted in his life was to be married again and have children of his own. So I just wept as his brother described that to me.

This particular man was also the neatest person on the planet. He had his closet organized by length of shirt sleeves; his khakis were organized by shade of khaki. You know it's all these kind of wonderful details that make people come alive.

ML: Yes. Sometimes people are making an impact, obviously, that has nothing to do with their position or how they are seen by those people.

JH: I have to say, one of the ironies of doing this is I've learned that almost nobody, in speaking of the dead, speaks of their work. They speak of their connections to others. We hear small, wonderful, intimate moments—what someone did for someone else, what they did for the community at large—but I almost never hear, "You know, he really did a good day's work" or "He was brilliant at achieving such and such." It really makes you pause and think about what you'll be remembered for . . . and what's important.

No one should forget the frightful cost of September 11, 2001. As Jan Hoffman said, the numbers don't begin to reveal the true cost—but the numbers are terrible all the same. Cantor Fitzgerald, the firm that had occupied the top floors of Number One, World Trade Center, lost 658 of their people—more than two-thirds of the company. When all the bodies, and parts of bodies, were counted, the number of people killed in the attack on New York came to 2,750, including 343 firefighters, 23 policemen and 24 Canadians.

That was just New York. Another 184 people died at the Pentagon, and 40 people were killed when United Flight 93 crashed in a field in Pennsylvania. Flight 93 is presumed to have been heading for the White House or the U.S. Capitol Building until some passengers foiled the attempt. They all died anyway.

In November, Kathie Scobee Fulgham came on *As It Happens* to tell us about a public letter she'd written to the children who lost their parents on 9/11. Dying in such a public way, she told us, creates special problems for the ones who are left behind. She spoke from experience: Kathie was 25 in January 1986, when her father, Dick, flew the space shuttle *Challenger* on its last, fatal mission.

> . . . *It should have been a moment of private grief, but instead it turned into a very public torture. We couldn't turn on the television for weeks afterward, because we were afraid we would see the gruesome spectacle of the* Challenger *coming apart a mile up in the sky.* . . .
> *My father died a hundred times a day on televisions all across the country. And since it happened so publicly, everyone in the country felt like it happened to them, too. And it did. The* Challenger *explosion was a national tragedy. Everyone saw it, everyone hurt, everyone grieved, everyone wanted to help. But that did not make it any easier for me. They wanted to say good-bye to American heroes. I just wanted to say good-bye to my Daddy.*

I asked Kathie Scobee how she got through finally. She didn't get any grief counselling, she said; she didn't accept that anyone else could understand what she was going through. But every time someone called or wrote to express sympathy, she asked them for a story about her dad so that the memories of how he *lived* might gradually supplant the all-too-vivid images of how he died. In her letter to the children of 9/11 victims, she suggested they do the same.

> *You need stories about your Mom or Dad from their friends, co-workers and your family. These stories will keep*

your Mom or Dad alive and real in your heart and mind
for the rest of your life. Listen carefully to the stories. Tell
them. Write them. Record them. Post them online. The
stories will help you remember. The stories will help you
make the decisions about your life—help you become the
person you were meant to be.

"There are still hard times," Kathie told us. "It's been 15 years and I still miss him, but the grief is not as raw."

Eight months after the terrorist attacks on Washington and New York, we learned about a strange little offshoot of the disaster: David Travis, an atmospheric scientist at the University of Wisconsin, told us that as a result of there being no planes in the air over the United States in the days following September 11, 2001, scientists observed that temperature differences between night and day had increased. The reason for this, they surmised, was that the contrails of the thousands of aircraft normally in the sky tend to moderate temperature differences by blocking out the sun during the day and blocking the radiation of heat from the earth's surface at night.

Six years after 9/11, Al Gore has helped put climate change, *aka* global warming, near the top of the agenda for many national and international institutions and got himself a Nobel Prize to boot (though not for science), so he's gone some way to ensure that when they write the whole history of this time and place, he'll be remembered for more than just being the failed presidential candidate of the beginning of this chapter. It's too early to say how President George W. Bush will be remembered; much depends on how things turn out in Afghanistan and Iraq.

FIFTEEN

Air India

⤳

I regret to advise you that one of our aircraft, VTEFO, Flight 182, of June 22, 1985, from Toronto and Montreal to Delhi and Bombay via London, was reported lost at sea off the coast of Ireland in the early hours of the morning.

It was Air India's early morning announcement on June 23, 1985, that alerted the world to the loss of 329 lives in an airplane accident in the North Atlantic. Only it was not an accident; it was a deliberate act of terrorism.

Every *As It Happens* producer is a generalist, dipping into many and varied subjects every day, five days a week. Each of them also has favourite stories, or stories that haunt him or her. Mark Ulster loves American politics and culture. Robin Smythe keeps an eye on health and science matters (and Don Cherry). The problems of Vancouver's Downtown East Side would not have got the scrutiny they did without the nagging of Max Paris. Meagan Perry had a passion for Japan, Sarah Martin for France—and Datejie Green spent more hours than we had any right to expect trying to get decent phone lines to Kenya.

After the dramatic events of September 11, 2001, I developed a kind of obsession with the Air India debacle. My interest was a bit late coming. Air India Flight 182, en route from Toronto and Montreal to Delhi, disappeared from radar screens off the coast of Ireland early in the morning of June 23, 1985. There's never been a worse act of terrorism involving Canadians—prior to 9/11 there had never been a worse act of aviation terrorism *anywhere*—and yet we seem never to have taken it seriously enough. The investigation of the crime took nearly twenty years. The trial, when it finally occurred, was an exercise in frustration. Worst of all, the surveillance of at least two of the people involved *prior* to the bombing failed to see what, in retrospect, were clear signals that an attack was in the offing. In other words, with better police work, this tragedy might have been averted.

For many Canadians, it's hard to escape the suspicion that there would have been a greater outcry over these lapses had the victims been more, um, *Caucasian*-looking. The victims were mostly Canadians, but Canadians of Indian descent.

I don't plead any special case for myself here. When Air India went down, I was packing up the house in preparation for a year at Harvard as a Nieman Fellow, taking a leave from the CBC TV programme *The Journal*. Air India barely registered in my consciousness. Of course, I was shocked when I heard the news. I grieved for the victims and their families—and then I moved on. Which is what most everyone else seems to have done, too.

Whatever lies at the root of our failure to give Air India the attention it deserved, there's no denying we failed. For example, Indian officials, up to and including Prime Minister Indira Gandhi, warned Canadian officials on numerous occasions that Sikh extremists in Canada were plotting and sponsoring criminal acts against India and, very likely, against Air India, but they were left at liberty to scheme away.

Talwinder Parmar was one of the extremists. Parmar came to Canada in 1970 and founded the organization Babbar Khalsa, which was dedicated to the establishment of an independent Sikh state in the Punjab. In 1982 Gandhi tried to extradite him from Germany in order to try him for the murder of two policemen in India, but the Germans only sent him back to Canada. In October 1984, four months after the Indian army's raid on the Sikhs' Golden Temple in Amritsar, Gandhi herself was assassinated by her own bodyguards, who were Sikhs. Gandhi's assassination provoked widespread killings of Sikhs and Hindus in India, further inflaming passions on all sides. Parmar, too, was later murdered in India— but not before playing a leading role in the bombing of Air India Flight 182.

Another man who merited watching was Inderjit Singh Reyat. Born in India, Reyat apparently found his fervour for the Sikh religion when he was growing up in England and brought it with him to Canada in 1974. He worked as a mechanic for Auto Marine Electric in Kamloops, British Columbia, and later in Duncan, on Vancouver Island. It was Reyat, we now know, who procured materials used in assembling the bombs that blew up the Air India plane and killed two baggage handlers at Narita Airport in Tokyo the same day.

And there was Ajaib Singh Bagri, who'd immigrated to Canada in 1971 and worked as a forklift operator at a sawmill near Kamloops. Bagri was another outspoken advocate for Khalistan, the Sikh state they wanted to found. After the Indian army's raid on the Golden Temple, Bagri addressed a crowd in Madison Square Garden in New York, promising them, "We will kill fifty thousand Hindus."

Canada didn't ignore the warnings exactly, but the response was inadequate. The newly formed Canadian Security Intelligence Service (CSIS) was tasked with keeping an eye on Sikh agitators in British Columbia, and it did; in 1985 CSIS installed wiretaps and put Talwinder Parmar under surveillance. But when CSIS agents followed Parmar to a meeting with Inderjit Singh Reyat in Duncan one day and then followed them both into the woods, where they heard a loud bang, it didn't occur to them, apparently, that someone might be testing a bomb. They later told the RCMP that they thought it was a gunshot they'd heard.

This happened on June 4, 1985, two weeks before Flight 182 was attacked.

Later it transpired that the wiretaps were not as useful as they might have been either, since the phone conversations CSIS was listening to were in a language no one at CSIS could understand, and having them translated was a slow business. And then—unbelievably—most of the tapes got erased. And CSIS was erasing wiretap material linked to Sikh terrorists even *after* the Air India explosion. The agency claims that the erased tapes held no relevant information, but RCMP spokesmen have since remarked that having the tapes intact might have led to a successful criminal prosecution.

In the event, Mr. Justice I. B. Josephson, who presided over the Air India trial when it eventually occurred, did say that authorities had violated the Charter rights of one of the suspects on three occasions—one of them being the destruction of the wiretap evidence. And Reid Morden, the man chosen to head CSIS after the Air India debacle, told CBC News that he believed the agency had dropped the ball.

In 2006 the federal government finally established a commission of inquiry into the Air India disaster, but why did it take so long to do so? One reason was that no one wanted to jeopardize the criminal investigation—which made the outcome of that investigation 20 years later all the more frustrating.

Canadian police and security agents weren't the only ones asleep at the switch, though. One wonders, for instance, how two men named Singh got their bags checked through on separate flights to Delhi and Tokyo when neither man ever boarded a plane. Both tickets had been bought with cash the day before. Both bags carried bombs.

Air India and the RCMP, we later heard, were not entirely in agreement over who should be paying for the extra security Canada was supposed to be providing to Air India operations in Canada, but it was being provided—up to a point. On June 22, 1985, the X-ray machine used to check the bags being loaded onto the Air India flight out of Pearson International Airport in Toronto broke down and was replaced by a hand-held sniffing device. People testified later that when the device beeped, the security agents ignored it, and the agents themselves claimed it didn't work very well.

There was to be a further baggage check when the plane took on new passengers at Mirabel Airport near Montreal, but that didn't happen either. Air India 182 was now running almost two hours behind schedule, and the flight took off before the bags were rechecked. Were the pilots more concerned with the schedule than with their own safety? Did they realize the bags hadn't been properly examined? Were they aware of the level of threat that terrorists posed to Air India?

In hindsight, given all the warnings and the preparations, the Air India disaster should never have occurred. Hindsight, of course, is always 20/20, so we must make allowances. But how do we explain Canada's actions *after* the disaster, which were no more adequate than its attempts to avert it?

Early in 2002, the Air India investigation was entering its 18th year and no one had yet been tried in connection with the worst act of terrorism in Canadian history. Inderjit Singh Reyat was serving a ten-year sentence in connection with the bomb at Narita Airport. It was assumed that he was also involved with the Air India bomb, but the physical evidence tying him to the bomb on Flight 182 was still lying somewhere on the bottom of the Atlantic Ocean. It wasn't until February 2003 that Reyat eventually pleaded guilty to providing materials for the Air India bomb, and in a deal that CBC's Rex Murphy dubbed a Boxing Day sale of Canadian justice, received an additional five years in prison. We made that out to be about five *days'* imprisonment for every man, woman and child who went down on Flight 182. But in the spring of 2002, even that sorry excuse for justice had yet to be delivered, and the whole case seemed to have fallen off the radar screen. So we at *As It Happens* set about preparing a special programme to air on June 21st, the eve of the Air India anniversary. We wanted to remind people that the murderers were still at large, that their victims were still awaiting justice. On that show, Salim Jiwa, the author of *The Death of Air India Flight 182*, told us about the ongoing agony of the victims' families.

"People have been overcome to the point of devastation," he said. "They can never get over the picture of what happened to them."

People died of heart attacks, he said, and their families believed the strain of Air India was responsible. Others carried on somehow, as they did after the 1988 explosion of Pan Am Flight 103 over Lockerbie, Scotland, but the way victims' families were treated after Lockerbie bore no resemblance to how Air India families had been treated. American families of Lockerbie victims received condolence messages from the White House; they were invited to Washington. Air India families said they'd been kept in the dark by both the RCMP and the Government of Canada. The Prime Minister conveyed his sympathy to *India*. Canada just hadn't rallied round the Air India victims, Salim said.

"We have failed these people as a nation."

Vancouver Sun reporter Kim Bolan, who had covered the Air India case from the beginning, brought us up to speed on the criminal investigation. The RCMP had made two arrests finally, and the trial process was beginning to creep forward. Charged with 329 counts of murder and conspiracy were Ajaib Singh Bagri, the forklift operator from Kamloops and Ripudaman Singh Malik, a businessman and prominent member of the Vancouver Sikh community. Also charged was our old friend Inderjit Singh Reyat, who was already serving time in connection with the bombing at Narita Airport. Bolan informed us that the reason it had taken so long to lay charges was that a lot of potential witnesses were too afraid to testify. Many in the community, Kim said, were also doubtful that they'd ever be able to put this case behind them—a statement that proved sadly prescient when the verdicts came down nearly three years later.

In our special, we also spoke to two survivors who, although devastated by their loss, had managed to build something from the wreckage of their lives. Because we had time, producer Robin Smythe and I decided to interview them in person rather than over the phone, which was our usual custom.

One of the people we talked to was Lata Pada, the founder and Artistic Director of the Sampradaya dance company based in Mississauga, Ontario. She was also an acclaimed choreographer and performer of Bharata Natyam, a classical dance form originating in southern India. Lata Pada recounted for us how in early spring of 1985, she had travelled to Bombay to rehearse for an upcoming performance, expecting to be joined by her husband, Vishnu, and her daughters, Brinda and Arati, when their school year ended. Instead, she got a phone call from Air India—and life as she had known it suddenly ended.

Now, 17 years later, Lata Pada had remarried and was living with her second husband in a suburb of Toronto. She had recently premiered a multimedia stage performance based on the explosion of Air India. After 1985, all Pada's work had been informed by the loss she suffered when Air India Flight 182 went down; an earlier creation had dealt with the unravelling of her personal identity, which is what happened when she lost her roles of wife and mother. But now she was performing the first work to deal directly with the explosion aboard Flight 182, using panels of fiery silk, the sounds of aircraft flying overhead, the sounds of the Air India announcement and of the telephone message her daughter Brinda had left on a friend's answering machine moments before boarding the doomed aircraft.

As Michael Crabb wrote in a review in the *National Post,* Pada's show could have come across as ghoulish, but her art transcended the self-indulgent and conveyed her message with dignity and restraint.

For Pada it was a way of going on, transforming her pain into art. For 15 years, the recording of Brinda's last words had lain untouched on a corner of her desk. She'd never had the strength to listen to it. Now she was hearing it every night, purging her pain with every repetition. Dance had given her solace and comfort, she told us. In the beginning, it was just something to divert her, to keep her from going crazy; now it had brought her to "some level of mental peace."

I am happy now. I have so much to be grateful for. I'm thankful for the 22 years I had with Vishnu, thankful for the 18 years with my daughters, thankful that my art has given me the tools to cope.

But what if you don't have dance to carry you through? Where do you find the strength and the will to go on after such a devastating loss? Anant Anantaraman found salvation in creation, too, but in his case, it was a music scholarship and a school that got created. In 1985 Anant was working for the Department of Defence in Ottawa. Like Lata Pada, he lost his spouse and two daughters on Flight 182. When I met Anant, he told me that the pain of his loss was indescribable. I could well believe it. Every parent's worst nightmare is the loss of a child, but to lose your children and your mate in such a violent way, and not even have a body to bury, must be like being thrust into Dante's ninth circle of Hell.

And so it seemed to Anant. Echoing Lata Pada's description of a self unravelling, Anant recalled that after the tragedy, he didn't know who or what he was. He walked around his empty house, clutching the pillows that his wife and daughters had slept on, because there he could still detect the scent of their bodies. When that was gone, there was nothing. He had no will to live, he said, but he had been raised to believe that suicide was wrong. He had to carry on—but how?

As time passed, he began to consider what the message of Air India might be for him. What was he meant to learn from it? He began to spend more time in India, near his sister-in-law's home in Yercaud in Tamil Nadu—and he saw that people there had a lot of unmet needs. For a while, he helped feed children in an orphanage. Then he thought, *This is not the way to help; if you really want to help these people, you must feed the mind, not the body.* He decided to set up a school for the children of the coffee plantation workers who worked in the hills around Yercaud.

The Bhawani Memorial School, named after Anant's wife, opened in June 1999 on a site that a visitor has described as a bit of God's country.

During our walk, we saw the flowers that he is growing around the school playground. He and his children are

quite a way from the traffic, noise, pollution and the grime
of the cities. The place has fresh cool air, beautiful natural
surroundings and all that is wonderful for the children to
grow up.

In the spring of 2002, when Anant first talked to us, the
school consisted only of a dining hall, a kitchen and a well,
with classes taking place in the dining hall, but it was already
a huge accomplishment. Anant's eyes lit up with joy and pride
as he showed me pictures of his fresh-faced, neatly uniformed
young kindergarten and primary school charges. These were
his girls now—his girls and boys. He had found a new family
to replace the family that had been taken from him.

Every spring Anant returns to Ottawa and Toronto to visit
old friends and do some fundraising for the school and for the
music scholarship he set up to remember his daughters, Rupa
and Aruna, who were both accomplished violinists. In Ottawa
he stays with his friend Claire Heistek, a musician in her own
right, and a member of the Board of Directors of the Bhawani
Anantaraman Memorial Foundation. When Anant arrives, we
work out a place and time to meet for coffee or a bite to eat
and to get caught up. Last year when we met, we talked about
trying to get an Ottawa school to adopt the Bhawani school
as a project, to help collect money and books for it. I think of
it as a small step in the direction of compensating one of the
Air India families for our country's neglect in their regard,
although the debt is vast and ultimately unpayable.

In April 2003, Messrs. Bagri and Malik finally went on trial
for the murder of 329 people aboard Air India Flight 182.
(Reyat, you will remember, had pleaded guilty in February
2003 of supplying materials used to make the bomb that took

down Flight 182.) In March 2005, Justice Ian B. Josephson handed down a verdict that shocked the country: Ajaib Singh Bagri—not guilty on all counts; Ripudaman Singh Malik—not guilty on all counts.

After 20 years and more than $100 million, the longest and most expensive investigation and trial in Canadian history, concerning the worst terrorism case in Canadian history, had failed to find anyone guilty.

Here's some of what Judge Josephson had to say in his six-hundred-page judgment:

Words are incapable of adequately conveying the senseless horror of these crimes. These hundreds of men, women and children were entirely innocent victims of a diabolical act of terrorism unparalleled until recently in aviation history and finding its roots in fanaticism at its basest and most inhumane level.

I began by describing the horrific nature of these cruel acts of terrorism, acts which cry out for justice. Justice is not achieved, however, if persons are convicted on anything less than the requisite standard of proof beyond a reasonable doubt. Despite what appear to have been the best and most earnest of efforts by the police and the Crown, the evidence has fallen markedly short of that standard.

Josephson said he found the credibility of many of the Crown witnesses wholly wanting. One of the witnesses had been paid three hundred thousand dollars by the RCMP. (The police said it was to cover expenses.) Another witness revealed herself to be inconsistent and, apparently, a disappointed lover. One potential witness was dead: the newspaper publisher Tara Singh Hayer. He had been expected to testify about what he knew of the accused and their behaviour in the Indian community, but he'd been killed in 1998. In Josephson's judgment, Reyat's testimony was "intentionally vague and evasive, often bordering on the absurd." He found Reyat to be "an unmitigated liar under oath." And he added: "[Reyat's] hollow expression of remorse must have been a bitter pill for the families of the victims. If he harboured even the slightest degree of genuine remorse, he would have been more forthcoming."

It *was* a bitter pill for the families who were awaiting justice, as were the acquittals of Bagri and Malik. The Air India families still had no one to blame for the deliberate act of terrorism that had taken the lives of their loved ones 20 years earlier. Lata Pada was among those who'd made the trek to Vancouver to hear the verdict. On the air that night, she told us she was devastated.

> *As you can imagine, Mary Lou, this is really a dark day for all of us. It's re-living the tragedy that befell us 20 years ago, and we're feeling as though we're experiencing another tragedy. It's a travesty of justice. The verdict is an indictment against the justice system that we believed in.*

Ms. Pada acknowledged that the case had had holes in it and that some of the witnesses were problematic, but she worried that the "not guilty" verdict would send a message to the world that terrorists could commit terrible acts and get away with them.

Vancouver Sun reporter Kim Bolan told us she was surprised, too; she'd hoped for at least one "guilty" verdict. But since the judge had made it clear that he didn't find any of the key witnesses believable, there seemed to be little ground for appeal.

On our Talkback line, many others expressed their disappointment with the Air India verdict. Perhaps the most thoughtful response, though, came from Joe Young of Lance, Nova Scotia. He said that he'd nearly cried while listening to Lata Pada on the day the verdict was delivered, but all the same, he had never been prouder of our justice system. Judge Josephson, he thought, must have wanted as much as anyone to find someone responsible for the Air India outrage; he must have felt great pressure to deliver the outcome he knew everyone wanted. Other courts in other countries would have made sure to find *someone* guilty. The fact that Josephson could not was proof of his courage and steadfastness in upholding Canadian law, and we should be thankful for it.

For himself, Justice Josephson has never spoken publicly about the Air India case. He said what he needed to say in his judgment, he told me when I approached him—except for one talk he gave to Justice Department lawyers in Ottawa in 2007. In that address, he spoke about the level of security they'd had to install in the courtroom in Vancouver to make the hearing safe for its participants and about the use they'd made of modern technology in the handling and recording of testimony. The only mention he made of the pressure he might have felt came toward the end, and his words echoed those of our Talkback caller:

> *How essential judicial independence is to our judicial system was never made more clear to me. The pressures were significant, but I was free to do exactly what my judicial conscience led me to do.*

⌣

Was justice done where Bagri and Malik were concerned? Who knows? Our system demands the presumption of innocence until proven guilty, and the Court said that the prosecution had failed to prove their case beyond reasonable doubt, so we have to give them the benefit of the doubt.

When I asked Anant Anantaraman for his reaction to the Air India verdict, he told me, "I don't care. It doesn't matter anymore. I don't expect anything. I don't want to hear about it. I don't want to think about it." Even with all he'd accomplished, 20 years after the death of his wife and daughters, the loss was still too painful to think about. But two years later, when I told him I wanted to write about this and about him, he agreed, and when Claire Heistek said that she believed the Air India story would not have been such a cock-up if the victims hadn't been Indo-Canadian, he agreed with that, too. For all our sakes, I hope that we at least learned something from what happened in June 1985.

SIXTEEN

Mike the Headless Chicken

Radio for fur and fowl weather

〜

If you want to talk about endurance, you'd be hard pressed to come up with a more illustrative case than Mike the Headless Chicken. It was Mark Ulster who noticed one day that the good people of Fruta, Colorado, were about to celebrate their second annual Mike the Headless Chicken Festival to honour the memory of a Wyandotte rooster who refused to die even after he'd had his head chopped off. He ran away instead. (Kind of puts old Ignacio Siberio in the shade, doesn't it?)

As Sally Edginton of Fruta's Chamber of Commerce tells the story, it was one Farmer Olsen who did the dirty deed (i.e., the chopping), and he was so impressed by Mike's determination to go on, *sans* head, that he decided to help him stay alive. The Olsens, Mike's would-be executioners, became his guardians and caterers instead, trying to keep him from bumping into things when he ran around and feeding little pellets directly down his—well, throat, I guess.

I know, I know; it's tragic. But Mike pressed on and so did we.

ML: Why didn't they put him out of his misery, if I can use the word?

SE: Well, apparently, Mike really wasn't in that much misery, because he was trying to crow, and from the reports that I've read, he acted just like an ordinary rooster. I assume he thought he was blind.

ML: He didn't know he didn't have a head.

SE: No. He was fed and watered, and he was in the chicken yard and, basically, went on as a chicken.

ML: I know people have said unkind things about chickens' brains, but don't they need *some* brain to operate? To move?

SE: Well, that was my reaction when I heard about this chicken without a head, but they took him to Salt Lake City, and the University of Utah scientists there checked him out and determined that there was enough of his brain stem left for him to function.

ML: Enough in the neck.

SE: Right. The university tried to re-enact Mike with a chicken that they had put under anaesthesia, and it just didn't work. So there was something unique to Mike.

ML: Mike *was* pretty special. Eighteen months he lived?

SE: Eighteen months.

ML: And he went on tour?

SE: He toured the west. I know there are reports out there that he toured all over the nation, but all that I can discover is Salt Lake City south to San Diego and to Long Beach. He travelled around with a two-headed calf.

ML: Oh my gosh.

SE: I know. But he would preen and crow—and sleep with his neck under his wing.

ML: Aw.

SE: I guess he gained weight. "He was a fine specimen of a rooster," to quote Mr. Olsen. "He just didn't happen to have his head."

ML: What did he die of eventually?

SE: Mike choked to death on a kernel of corn [choking sounds heard—mine]. I know. Poor Mike.

Sally Edginton went on to talk about the festival, and I asked her what sort of events they had. She said they started off with a 5K run, which they dubbed "Run Like a Headless Chicken." Then they had chicken dinner and chicken games— egg tosses, egg races—and "Pin the Head on the Chicken."

ML: Ms. Edginton, is any of this true?

SE: Mike is *true!* He really is true. In fact, he was written up by *Life* magazine in the October 22nd issue, 1945. They have photos there, and if you'd like to see a photo of Mike, you can go to the Net.

ML: He won't be standing on his head.

SE: No, as far as I know, he never stood on his head.

Sally assured us that the Mike the Headless Chicken Festival in Fruta was to celebrate Mike's will to live, not his headlessness—and high time, too, I say. But, then, what about Louetta Mallard's little dog Dosha, another unfortunate American animal? Doesn't he deserve a festival or a laurel of some kind, too? Dosha, apparently, stepped out to pee one day and took it into his head to jump the fence and go on a spree instead. Sadly, he was hit by a car and left to die at the side of the road. Luckily, the police came along while Dosha was still alive. Sadly, again, instead of taking Dosha to the vet, they shot him. (Didn't have no time to be going to the vet, apparently.) Then the police took the "carcass" to the Public Works yard, and the people there stuck him in a freezer until the Humane Society could come along and collect the remains. Luckily, the Humane Society folk noticed that Dosha, although well chilled, wasn't actually, technically *dead*—more remaining than remaindered, in a manner of speaking. They set to thawing him out and setting his broken bones, and Dosha and Louetta lived happily ever after.

Not everyone who's hosted *As It Happens* is wild about what people have sometimes called our "stupid animal stories"—or so I've heard. But our four- and six-footed friends, and some with no feet at all, have provided us with hours of diversion, and the audience would seem to share our fondness for them, at home and abroad. Remember Bonnie and Clyde, our ham on the lam in Malmesbury? They developed such a following in England that the BBC made a movie about their escapade. In 2004 Lynn Horsford (not making this up) came on the show to tell us about *The Legend of the Tamworth Two*. She said they had several pigs playing the parts of the two original truants, partly so as not to tire them out and partly because they couldn't find another two pigs that could master all the skills required to re-enact the jumping, running, swimming and so on that the originals had got up to. Bit of a porcine Olympics, really. I haven't seen the final product, but I'm sure it will pop up one day on the Discovery Channel; at least, I hope so.

Probably Ms. Horsford had not then heard about Mouse the Talking Pig, or they might have found a role for *her* in the movie. We didn't hear about her either until November 2005. That's when we spoke to Mike Rees at his farm in Bridgend, Wales.

ML: Mr. Rees, I'm told you have a talking pig.

MR: That's absolutely correct. Mouse is the world's first talking pig.

ML: Is it a mouse or a pig?

MR: No, she's called Mouse.

ML: Your pig is called Mouse.

MR: That's right, the reason being she has a long, long snout, grey and black in colour, and has large ears.

ML: So does she object to her name? Is that why she started talking?

MR: No, no.

ML: What happened? How did you discover she talked?

MR: Oh, 10, 12 days ago, I came out of the shed to feed her—it was dark, quite early in the morning—and I heard someone say, "Hello." In a French accent, believe it or not.

ML: "Hello" in a French accent.

MR: Exactly. And I look around—no one around. Look down—it was Mouse the Pig talking, saying "Hello."

ML: And did you say "Hello" back?

MR: I speak to her every morning. *"Hello."* So whether she's picked it up that way, I'm not sure.

ML: Does she say anything else?

MR: We are working on that one.

ML: Are you.

MR: Yes.

ML: What words are you trying to—

MR: I can't tell you that yet, can't disclose that yet. That's a farm secret until we perfect them—then we'll get back.

ML: Does the "Hello" sound like a . . . grunt?

MR: Right. [He senses skepticism.] I've got TV—they've been up to us four times—and they captured it on TV every time. It's brilliant. I recorded the footage. I can play it on the air for you.

ML: Okay.

MR: You can get the "Hello" quite clearly.

ML: Okay.

[*British female voice*]: *So let's hear it one last time.*

Mouse: *Hello. Hello.* [Or: *Oink. Oink.*]

MR: Whaddya think? Want to have that again?

ML: No, we got it.

MR: Clear enough?

ML: Yeah, that was good. Do you have cows and chickens and horses and things?

MR: We have 14 horses and 3 chickens.

ML: Does any of the horses speak?

MR: Neigh. Of course not.

ML: What about the chickens?

Well, the chickens didn't speak either, but Mouse the Pig was just tremendous, Mr. Rees insisted. Plus, she'd just given birth to eight piglets: four of a cream-and-beige stripey hue and four that were a cross between Tamworth (See? She could've been in the pigs-on-the-lam movie!) and French wild boar—hence the French accent, he said. Of course.

A lot of the animal stories we've done on *As It Happens* have been in a more serious vein but no less interesting for that. A good many of them fell into the category of science or ecology. We reported on the plight of the endangered right whales on the east coast and on Luna, the overly friendly orca who lived in the waters off British Columbia—and, of course, on Willy of "Save Willy" fame, another killer whale. His "real name" was Keiko, and after he became world-famous for being rescued from an aquarium in Mexico, money was raised to have Keiko shipped back to his native waters near Iceland, where he would be free again to live the way whales are supposed to. That was the theory.

It took a while, but Keiko *was* eventually flown home—at huge expense and, no doubt, some discomfort to Keiko—but the whale did not thrive in his natural environment. Apparently, he didn't *want* to swim around in icy water without friends or entertainment. In 2002, while he was still being watched over by human caretakers in a kind of large, open pen in Iceland, he gave his minders the slip and made off for Norway. In September he followed a fishing boat to the Norwegian town of Haka, where he seemed to be inviting people to play with him. He was hungry and had lost weight. He died of pneumonia the following year.

The marmot recovery people on Vancouver Island have been having a bit more luck in their attempts to prop up the population of the native marmot species. It was June 2002 when we first talked to Andrew Bryant, chief scientist of the Marmot Recovery Project in Nanaimo, British Columbia. You may wonder, as I did, whether the marmot really was an endangered species and why we would find it necessary to ensure its survival anyway. A marmot, after all, is just a sort of woodchuck or groundhog—in other words, a *rodent*.

Dr. Bryant had heard it all before. "There's a popular notion out there," he said, "that a marmot is a marmot is a marmot." But nothing could be further from the truth, apparently. There are 14 species of marmots in the world, four of which live in Canada, and one of them is exclusive to Vancouver Island. This is the one on the verge of extinction; they'd counted only 30 marmots emerging from hibernation that year.

The problem, as Dr. Bryant outlined it, is that Vancouver Island marmots live on mountaintops: one family atop one mountain, another family on the next mountain and so on. To propagate in a healthy way (no incest among marmots), the teenagers need to wander off and find suitable mates on a neighbouring mountain, but clearcutting has interrupted this practice, and this is how: clearcut logging has removed the forest cover from the valleys between the mountains. Now, marmots don't like forests, and they love clear, open spaces, so instead of tearing through the forest and rushing up the next mountain to find his soulmate, the errant teenager just settles down in this lovely open valley, where, presumably, he lives happily, albeit celibately, until a cougar comes along and eats him—cougars and wolves being the other elements in the marmot reduction scenario. Poor marmots.

Dr. Bryant's plan for saving his groundhog friends was to breed them in captivity and then ferry them about from mountaintop to mountaintop, to join up with their wild cousins and engage in a little hanky-panky. When we caught up with him again in 2004, he was sad to report that they hadn't made a lot of progress to date. Of the four marmots released by the Marmot Recovery Project the year before, three had immediately become lunch (see above) for bigger fauna. But they were pressing ahead. The marmot savers had been given something of a boost by the B.C. Natural Resources Minister Joyce Murray, who had publicly encouraged local huntsmen to take up arms against the neighbourhood cougars. This call for a cull caused a flurry of negative attention from the anti-hunting community until it was explained that there was no cull as such. The Honourable Ms. Murray was only hoping that hunters would take their full quota of cats and wolves in marmot areas.

Last time I checked with the marmot recovery people, Dr. Bryant's associate Sean Pendergast was pleased to tell me that the marmots were coming along nicely. He said the captive breeding programme in particular was wildly successful; that is, marmots that had been born and raised in captivity were now happily producing many little marmots in captivity. This is occurring, by the way, in zoos all over Canada. Yes, unbeknownst to you and me—until now—marmots are flying hither and yon across the country all the time courtesy of Air Canada (which doesn't want to carry your pet schnauzer anymore, but that's another story).

Anyway, the zoo-bred marmots have been released into the wild in ever-increasing numbers, and their survival rate has steadily improved—nearly half of them survived in 2006. And in 2006 two marmots that had been released a couple of years earlier bore litters—four pups each—and they all emerged successfully from hibernation. This was cause for great celebration in the marmot welfare community, who now see more reason to hope that they will eventually reach their goal of about three hundred wild marmots.

Our introduction to the marmot crisis came a year after we learned about snail sex. Ronald Chase of McGill University was the man who, in June 2001, enlightened us as to the antics snails get up to when mating—namely, shooting darts at each other. Now, in evolutionary terms, when you record a particular—not to say peculiar—behaviour on the part of a plant or animal, you ask yourself how it might promote the animal's long-term survival. (Vancouver Island marmots, for example, might be well advised to become allergic to meadow valleys.) But when it came to snails' arrows, Dr. Chase said, scientists had been distracted by their own species' lore. Immersed as they were in Greek mythology and images of Eros, they thought the arrows might be a device to turn on the opposite sex in order to engage in . . . hanky-panky. As a result, they hadn't bothered to investigate the snail darts business too closely, which left him a nice opening. What he discovered was that when a snail gets hit by a dart, he stores up more sperm; in other words, it may or may not be a turn-on, but it will make the dart receiver more likely to produce little snail babies when he mates.

Here's a wee complication. Snails are hermaphrodites—that is, they are both male and female at the same time. I don't really understand how this works, but there you are; the snails must have sorted it out, because they're not nearing extinction as far as I know.

We've been surprised and delighted and fascinated for more hours than I can count by the many, many scientists—biologists, chemists, oceanographers, astronomers and so on—who have appeared on *As It Happens* and chatted away about their work and shared their excitement about everything from flying snakes and kangaroo rats to moose noses, whale songs, turquoise skies and the science of throwing a baseball. Their enthusiasm is irresistible. Even when they go astray, they're interesting—and it happens all the time in science, of course. It happens in other walks of life, too, only scientists are often quicker to admit their errors than other people. I hope Dan Goldston won't be upset if I remind folk of the time he developed a proof regarding the occurrence of twin primes only to discover, almost as soon as he'd published it, that he'd made a wee mistake somewhere along the way.

A prime number is one that can be divided evenly only by itself and by one: 1, 2, 3, 5, 7, 11, 13, 17, 19, 23, 29 are all prime numbers. *Twin* primes are close together, like 5 and 7, 11 and 13, 17 and 19. As the numbers get higher, the pairs get further and further apart. The question that Dr. Goldston was working on was whether you could say with any certainty that prime numbers occurred close together predictably and infinitely often . . . or something like that.

"We always thought this was true," he said, "but we never proved it before."

Dr. Goldston teaches mathematics at San José State University in California, and he'd been working on this problem for 20 *years,* so you can imagine his jubilation when the breakthrough came—as he told us in March 2003. But then the aforementioned disaster struck. It was one Andrew Granville at the University of Montreal who spoiled the party, Dan told us when we spoke again a few weeks later, by demonstrating that the "approximation we were using to detect primes didn't have all the properties we thought it had." So it was back to square one for Dan. At least he didn't have to find a new problem.

Over the years, *As It Happens* listeners and I have had a lot of free lessons in math and physics and chemistry, sometimes from scientists as young as 11, who have accomplished things like making crackers stay crisp when dunked, demonstrating that it takes but a nanosecond for a dropped gummi bear to pick dirt up off the floor and using probiotics to treat a crippling gastric disorder. These were school projects carried out by Gina Gallant in Prince George, B.C.; Jillian Clarke in Chicago; and Lindsey Edmunds in Nova Scotia. When she wrote up her probiotic results, 17-year-old Lindsey became the youngest person ever to have an article published in the *Canadian Medical Association Journal*. I expect to see all their names in the Nobel lists before too long.

Violet the Very Valuable Chicken also started life as a school project, a classroom lesson on the meaning of life, using chicken hatching as the experiment. When the experiment was over, Violet and her sister Ruby went to live with the Flight family (still not making it up) in Fitchingfield, England. Somehow Violet ran afoul of the parish council there—they wanted to kill her—which was when Paula Flight took out a million-pound insurance policy on her.

We'll let Mrs. Flight pick up the story.

PF: Violet and her sister Ruby used to roam around the village free till one day parish council received a complaint from a resident in the village that Violet was making a mess around the war memorial.

ML: What sort of a mess?

PF: They have tree bark around the bottom of the war memorial to keep down the weeds, and they were accusing Violet of teaching the ducks that live on the pond to go to the war memorial and put this tree bark onto the grass when they were looking for grubs.

ML: Violet *taught the ducks?*

PF: Exactly. That's how bizarre it got.

ML: You don't believe that she was a gang leader.

PF: I, personally, don't believe that she was a gang leader; she was doing what comes naturally to chickens, which is to scratch around, looking for worms and grubs and everything. I don't believe that Violet actually taught the ducks how to do it, but residents in the village did believe that the ducks never ever done it before Violet appeared in the village, and now they done it when she was here.

ML: So what happened then?

PF: So they had a big parish council meeting, and I attended. They didn't know me to look at; they knew my name. And they had this big discussion and read out the letter of complaint and proceeded to discuss how they were going to deal with the complaint. And it was discussed by them how to kill the chicken, which would be the easiest and the cheapest way of removing the problem.

ML: Kill the chicken.

PF: Yes. Wring her neck.

ML: They didn't ask you to put her in a coop or anything?

PF: No.

ML: Oh my.

PF: So I made it clear that she was my daughter's pet, and just like anybody has a dog or a cat or a hamster or a goldfish, this was my daughter's pet and they had no right to kill her. She belonged to us. And the debate just went on. Two weeks after, Violet was in the village and a white transit van was coming along the village and it tried to run her over. It came from its proper side of the road to the other side of the road and ran over her.

ML: Did you see that?

PF: Yes, I did.

ML: Oh dear.

PF: But luckily, she just went straight underneath the van and the wheels never hit her, and she came out the back of the van, feathers flying everywhere. So it was at that point—after my daughter kept saying, "Why do they want to kill my chicken? Why do they want to kill Violet?"—that I decided to take out the insurance policy.

ML: But when you went to insure Violet at Lloyd's, were they not afraid that you—not *you* but somebody—might just go out and wring the chicken's neck to collect the insurance?

PF: They were, but they had clauses in the insurance policy: one was very bizarre, and the other one was the protection for Violet.

ML: What do you mean, "One was very bizarre"?

PF: We would only receive the million pounds if she was abducted and eaten by an alien. That was their policy.

ML: By an *alien?*

PF: By an alien; that's what they put in. And the second clause, which was meant more for us, was that she was never murdered or killed by a parish council member, which was what I wanted.

ML: Does that mean you can't collect?

PF: I don't know. It's with the insurance company at the moment; they're investigating the whole situation.

ML: I see. So . . . Violet did come to a sad end?

PF: She did.

ML: What happened?

PF: Well, when we moved two miles away from the village in July last year, we took Violet's pen with us. We moved back into our house with a large garden—and every night when the sun went down, I used to put Violet away, and every morning at six o'clock, I used to get Violet out. And at the beginning of December, I went out there before my children went to school and found Violet outside her pen, dead.

ML: Aw.

PF: I didn't tell the children before they went to school; I told them when they returned from school. And my daughter said, "Look, I don't want any publicity about Violet, Mom. Can we keep this quiet?"

And we kept it quiet, but it was the local police that found out. Then they told the insurance company, and now the insurance company are investigating it and it's all got out to the media again—so that's how it all came out again.

ML: Do you have any idea who did the foul deed? Sorry; I guess you've heard a lot of bad puns.

PF: I have, but it sounds nicer with a Canadian accent. Um, I haven't got any idea. The only thing that I'm suspicious about is the fact that she was outside of her pen. It would have taken somebody to actually open the pen, unlock it, lift her out and—that's where I found her, outside.

ML: Oh, that's terrible. Was your daughter very upset?

PF: Very distraught she was, yeah. I mean, especially
with all the publicity gained in her short life—that
people did want to kill her [chicken]. She was very upset.

ML: How's Ruby?

PF: Ruby died. Ruby got run over.

ML: By a hit-and-run?

PF: By a hit-and-run, yes.

Not a happy ending for poor Violet or Ruby, but at least the
Flight family had their cat, hamster, goldfish and two dogs to
keep them company.

My own house has provided shelter over the years for two
cats, a rabbit, a turtle, some fish, numerous budgies and a
blue-crowned conure. This last, named Zak, I regarded as the
bane of our existence, eating us out of house and home—I
mean *literally* eating the house, along with the picture
frames, the chairs and a shelf of cherished antique books, all
the while making a fearsome racket and pooping on our
shoulders at every opportunity. He, or more likely *she*—you
can't tell about conures—was my son's bird, and like many
parrots, he/she was fiercely devoted to his/her chosen
human and had only disdain for everyone else. For some reason, I was fond of him. Her. Have you seen the documentary *The Wild Parrots of Telegraph Hill?* If so, perhaps you
can understand how easy it is to fall in love with parrots in
spite of their obnoxious habits.

What I'm building up to here is that my friends at *As It
Happens* knew about my love-hate relationship with parrots, and they rarely missed a chance to get a parrot story
on the air. Over the years we talked to many people who

had gripping stories to tell: their parrots had been lost or stolen, recovered, arrested by customs officials, subpoenaed to give testimony in court. One parrot (English, naturally) had taken up sewing, and more than one had been sent up for using inappropriate language in public places. There was even a parrot named Zak who liked to whistle the *1812 Overture.*

Allegedly.

The thing is, no matter how clever and talented these parrots were or how well they talked, sang, whistled or swore *off* the air, the minute we put them on the radio, they clammed up (so to speak). I was getting a reputation as the interviewer who couldn't coax a sound out of one of the most notoriously chatty creatures on the planet.

Until November 2003. When we were preparing a special 35th anniversary programme in the Glenn Gould Studio in Toronto, Executive Producer Lynn Munkley and the rest of the staff decided to spring a parrot on me as a surprise. I'm not sure whether they'd taken pity on me or they wanted to demonstrate to our "live" audience just how inept I was when it came to interviewing guests of avian persuasion—a bit of both maybe—but right at the end of the programme, Barbara introduced Susan Sherman and her friend Jingle Bell, a magnificent double yellow-headed Amazon parrot (who had only one head, actually).

I said, "Does he talk, Susan?"

"No. Did somebody say he talks?"

Very funny, I thought.

Anyway, Jingle Bell was a real trouper. His best trick was if he (Susan claimed Jingle Bell was a "he") did something wrong, you pointed your finger at him and said *BANG!* and he flipped right over and hung upside down from his perch. It was very cute.

But the best thing Jingle Bell did for me was this: he actually *said something on the radio*. He said, "Hi."

When I—so grateful to him—followed this up with "You're a beautiful parrot," he said, "Beautiful" right back. I have witnesses.

SEVENTEEN

War and Pax

*The opening stages of the disarmament of
the Iraqi regime have begun.*

⌢

With these words, shortly after nine-thirty EST on the
evening of March 19, 2003, White House Press
Spokesman Ari Fleischer announced to the world that the
war to topple Saddam Hussein had begun. This time CBC
Radio was ready. How could we not have been after the
months of sabre rattling and the ultimatums? Radio meetings
had been held, tasks assigned, hotels booked and an around-
the-clock call list drawn up. Fleischer's announcement
occurred on my watch; minutes later I was taking my place in
the news studio alongside Barbara Smith, and our own small
army of news and current affairs producers had started
churning out scripts and updates and dialling up people to
talk to: American military experts, Canadian military experts,
Iraqis, experts on Iraq, diplomatic and political voices from
all over, our own reporters on the ground in Washington,
London, Amman, Kuwait City and Doha, and in Iraq.

My fellow current affairs host Bernard St-Laurent joined
us, Jill Dempsey took over the news updates and the lot
of us held the fort until we were relieved in the wee hours of
the morning. The worst part of that night was staggering to
the hotel across the street around 4:00 a.m. only to find that
I couldn't check in to my room, because I couldn't find the
reception desk, which had disappeared in the chaos of a
major renovation.

It's hard to get a sense of how things are going when you're in the eye of the hurricane, which is how it felt. I think we did a fair job of reporting the scraps of news we got hold of, filling in with some of the background material that we'd all been sucking up for months. But if the first casualty of war is truth, a corollary of that might be: the first people to forget this are journalists. Remember the first Gulf War? All those great videos of—well, they could have been of anything, really— shown to us by the American military in their briefings? All those "smart bombs" zeroing in on their targets? There were no reporters on the ground for that one, not in the beginning anyway. The U.S. Department of Defense had decided after the Vietnam War that reporters were a major pain in the butt and very likely the reason they'd lost that war; they didn't want the Press getting in the way of "Desert Storm."

Eventually, reporters were allowed in to see what was going on in Kuwait in 1991, and a few of them became quite famous as a result—among them, Canadians Bob McKeown, who arrived in Kuwait City with a CBS crew a day before the allied forces did, and Arthur Kent, whose reporting of Scud missile attacks from his base in Dhahram, Saudi Arabia, earned him the moniker Scud Stud—and a lot of marriage proposals, too, it was rumoured. But until the Press were allowed to see things with their own eyes, we had *no idea* what was really going on. After they arrived, you still couldn't be sure what was being struck out of their reports by military censors or what they were holding back. I'm not saying you don't need to control information if you're fighting a war, but it would be best if we could all remember that, until the war is finished, a good deal of what gets told about it, from all sources, is likely to be fiction.

The lack of actual reporting on the Gulf War of 1991 was controversial enough that the Pentagon were persuaded to take the Press along on their next outing. In Iraq in 2003, the media were invited to have their people "embedded" with American divisions as they marched toward Baghdad, filing reports as they went. There was a debate about this, too; some people felt the reporters would be compromised by getting too close to the military. My own feeling was that it was better to get the story from a reporter—even an embedded one—than from a general, or in addition to the general's.

Anyway, there were other stories being filed by reporters who weren't embedded, so the "embedded story" would be just one piece of the greater picture. The main problem with the embedded reports, as I saw it, was that the dramatic visual material they contained would probably get more play on TV than other material, which could in turn give them more weight than they merited. The pictures certainly were dramatic at times—no doubt about that—and in that sense, the Iraq War of 2003 was the first war the world watched live on TV.

Radio, as usual, would provide the context. Or so I hoped. But in the beginning, we in radio were as hungry for the drama of unfolding events as our sisters and brothers in television. And, as usual, hard facts were scarce. So what did we tell people on that first night of the war? We told them that there were about three hundred thousand troops at the ready for operation "Shock and Awe." That the U.S. 101st Airborne and the 82nd Airborne were set to land not only troops but also trucks, tanks and heavy artillery wherever they were needed. We told them that the opening salvo apparently had been directed at a "target of opportunity." We told them that the Kurds could hardly wait for the war to get under way and were hoping to join the fight, and that the Turks were warning the coalition not to arm the Kurds.

Beyond that, we speculated. We speculated about whether the ground war had started yet, whether the paratroopers had landed, how the weather would affect things, why the attack had begun at dawn instead of at night, who or what the so-called target of opportunity might be. Was it Saddam? Did they get him? What would happen to Iraqi resistance if they had got him? What kind of resistance were the coalition forces likely to meet anyway? Would Saddam use chemical or biological weapons? Did he have any?

We talked about how some Iraqi soldiers were said to have defected and how Iraqi State Radio was said to have been jammed or even taken over.

It was CBC reporter Frank Koller who reminded us that night on air that almost everything we were able to report at that point was suspect since we simply did not have enough good information yet, but that hardly gave us pause. This, of course, is the really bad side of 24-hour "news", be it on TV or radio: you have to fill the air with *something*. I wouldn't say we actually got anything wrong that night, but much of the time we were just flapping our jaws.

In reviewing the tape of that evening, I was struck by one comment in particular and who it was that made it: Laurie Milroy, a member of the conservative American Enterprise Institute, predicted that the war to topple Saddam would be a short war and that most of the Iraqi public were either in favour of the invasion or, at worst, neutral, but when I asked her about the *post*-war plan, Dr. Milroy said, "That's an unfortunate question, because it's not as far along as it should be."

As history would soon show us, no truer words were spoken that night.

For a while, though, the war went quite smoothly. The Americans and their allies made steady progress toward Baghdad, encountering little in the way of serious resistance, and our own well-planned campaign to cover the war went just as smoothly. All regular programming had been suspended for the time being, so the whole staff was available to pitch in. My shift settled into a comfortable mid-afternoon to about ten o'clock or midnight, with every once in a while a pee break or a few minutes to eat something. Apart from the fact that it *was* a war, we were having a pretty good time at work. I loved the fact that we were live all the time and I loved having a big story to cover every night.

By the start of the second week, we were easing back into our regular schedule, although it didn't get wholly regular for quite a long time. At *As It Happens,* for example, we never went home before ten while there was still a chance of a major development to cover, and that would be the case for weeks to come. Baghdad was taken and Saddam's statue toppled, Iraqis danced in the streets and George Bush dropped onto an aircraft carrier in the Gulf to declare the war over. I recorded it in my own journal.

We were both a little premature.

Those were days, however, when it was still possible to hope for a good outcome. People who had opposed the war might even have been feeling a bit sheepish; after all, a tyrant had been ousted and a country liberated and it had all been pretty much a walk in the park.

Five years later, Iraq smells more and more like Vietnam, more like a swamp than a park, a victory only for the enemies of peace and the enemies of the United States. Everyone blames the U.S.

But for one young Iraqi in Baghdad, the truth is more complex.

We first talked to Salam Pax (a pseudonym) in September 2003, barely six months after the invasion. He had flown to London to attend to the publication of his book, *The Baghdad*

Blog, which was based on excerpts of a web diary he'd started when it first became apparent that the U.S. was going to invade Iraq. Salam was an architect by training, an engaging writer, a witty and keen observer of his environment—and he spoke excellent English. Above all, he had no known agenda, so he made an excellent witness, and we were hungry for witnesses. I began by asking him how his blog had got started.

SP: Really, it was just something personal, small—just corresponding with my friend who left to Amman, Jordan, to finish his Master's degree in architecture. I just thought, *Instead of sending him emails, I'll put it online.* I didn't expect more than six people to look at this, and then suddenly, I'd have 20 people going in there, asking me questions, sending me emails: "So how is it in Baghdad?"—stuff like that. So it got more and more and more totally out of hand. I had no control.

ML: You were as contemptuous, if I may use the word, of the Americans' plans as you were of Saddam and the Iraqi regime. How did you manage to get it out? I mean, what's the process? How come they didn't track you down or censor you—or kill you?

SP: I was lucky, wasn't I?
No, it's—you see, Internet was very new to Iraq. Someone came and set a firewall up and left, and we had Iraqis who were controlling the service provider, who were very new to this, and we were very new to this—and it was a cat-and-mouse game. Sometimes you'd find ways to go around the firewall undetected and you'd use it and they'd block it, and you'd find another way—and, basically, they had no idea about blogs. . . . There were so

many anti-Saddam, pro-war blogs that were writing all sorts of things about what's happening in Iraq, supposedly, but they blocked none of them, because they had no idea what this was. Between . . . their not being aware of blogging and their being actually pretty stupid in the ways they were controlling the Internet—I just got between this and was able to update my site.

ML: You say there were a number of people blogging from inside Iraq?

SP: No, not from inside Iraq, because before the war, everybody was writing about whether they were pro or anti, how it was supposed to be in Iraq in the future, and there was this one single me writing out of Iraq, and I'd get so much hate mail. . . . You know, if I'm writing, "The coming war is not very good," I'd get hate mail. If I'm writing, "Oh, let the Americans come in," I'd get hate mail. So it's a bit of a funny situation.

ML: Because it was never all that clearcut for you.

SP: No! I mean, it's never black or white, is it? I cannot say, "Yes, let's have war." It's my country! They're going to drop bombs on *my country!*

But then again, it's very clear that we were not going to get rid of that regime, that Saddam would be staying there unless we had some sort of foreign intervention. It's never black and white. It's so complex.

ML: What was the most frightening aspect of the war for you personally—and your family? When were you most in danger?

SP: The first time the bombs started falling on Baghdad, I just couldn't realize—I mean, I never thought that I'd be actually that scared. You think about it and you know that there's no palaces near your house, you have no ministries, no government compound, but still—hearing these sounds, the bombs falling, it's just so incredibly, absolutely frightening, you cannot imagine it.

But the worst thing, actually, was after the war. For some reason, we had 15 rounds of shells from a tank being shot at our neighbourhood. Three houses were destroyed, a couple of houses were burned. Luckily, no one died; a couple of girls were injured. We had no idea what was happening. Suddenly, suddenly, our house was being attacked! It was very, very scary. You cannot imagine. For a week after that, you just cannot sit in a room if you're not sure that you have at least four walls between you and the outdoors. That was the scariest part.

ML: You wrote at one point that the general attitude seemed to be, "To hell with Saddam—and may he be quickly joined by Bush."

What is the attitude now?

SP: You know, it's difficult. They came in promising that everything will be okay in ten weeks or something. It's never like this. They came in with really unrealistic promises, but because daily life has become a little bit more difficult these days, people forget that something absolutely amazing and important has happened: an era has ended.

Something new is coming; you just need patience. You need to keep reminding yourself and the people around you that this is just a process. It's a birth, it's painful and something absolutely wonderful is going to happen in—I don't know—five years ? three years?

ML: Well, would you say there is widespread, general discontent at the moment, then?

SP: You know, people need to feel there is progress, and because what has to be done is so huge, this progress is never going to be fast. Now they don't see anything happening, and they just see it's getting actually worse. You have these bombings now; it's very unsafe on the street. . . . You should make people understand that it is on the right track—it will take time but it is on the right track; just have patience.

ML: Are you back at work? Are you going to become a full-time reporter?

SP: No, no, never a journalist. Of course, I'm an architect. Everybody hopes that the reconstruction phase will begin. There is so much to do, we want to be part of it—building Iraq.

Our next encounter with Salam Pax came in February 2004, 11 months after the Americans had shown up. He was back home in Baghdad, and it was becoming clear that things weren't going very well for the invader/liberators—and not at all well for many Iraqis. For Salam, too, the bloom was off the rose, but he remained hopeful that it would all work out in the end. The main thing was that Saddam was gone and the Iraqi people were free to write their own future. I asked him what had changed in the months since we'd last spoken.

SP: Quite a lot. You know, it's kind of— Whenever something really bad happens, like the last bombing near the Green Zone, you go through a week where you're really down. You think it's never going to get better. But usually, you kind of get over that, and it's great to see people just getting on with their lives and trying to do something. Business is going great. You go through the streets of Baghdad and they're full of merchandise, and people are buying and selling like crazy. And they're seeing so much prosperity and money coming in, it's unbelievable.

So, it's good and bad. Like today, with the bombing— that was really bad. But you know, you deal with it—and it's great to see people going on with their lives.

ML: Do you think the bombing will ever stop, though?

SP: It has to at a point. I mean, look: what happened today, for example. It's clearly to scare people off from joining the new police force, the new Iraqi army. . . .

It's so important for us to see the Iraqi police on the street. They are really, for most Iraqis, heroes at the moment, and you know, there are hundreds of people there at the moment, trying to get into the new police force. When these terrorists see that what they are doing is really not stopping people from trying to rebuild their country . . . it just has to stop. I mean, okay, they might be not the most rational people, these terrorists, but at one point, you kind of see how futile what you're doing is.

ML: Are you back at work?

SP: Actually, yes. The great thing that happened just a week ago is that the firm I used to work with is now back to building the hospital they were building before the war, and they asked me to come and get my job back, which is great! Yes, excellent.

ML: You're very happy about that.

SP: Oh yes, absolutely.

ML: You'll have a salary, for one thing.

SP: [He laughs] Yes.

ML: How are your family, then? Are they all trying to resume their normal lives as well?

SP: Oh yeah, oh yeah. I mean, my mom, at one point after the war, decided she's never going to leave the house. Now, though, she goes out, shops with her sister and goes around the city and everything.

My brother is back to his work. You have to be involved, you have to do things, and part of it is participating in your daily lives, your daily duties, and that's the way everybody brings normal life back to the city. It's been—it's been a year now!

ML: Mm. So are you talking at all about the Iraqi caucuses, about the possibility of a total handover to Iraqis? About elections?

SP: Oh yeah, absolutely. This is the big discussion now, you know: how to do it, when to do it. Does Ali Sistani agree with what people are proposing? Are we ready for elections? This is really the next thing, because we realize that maybe we're not totally ready to do things on our own, but this is the first step. We will have some sort of election to choose representatives who will actually govern the country—because the governing council at the moment can't do much at all. I mean, everybody goes and says, "Why is the governing council not doing anything?" Because they don't have the authority to do anything. We need actually a governing body which has authority. So yeah, absolutely—very excited about this, and everybody's waiting for this to happen.

ML: Why do you say the country maybe isn't ready to completely govern itself?

SP: You know, we've been like this closed room with no windows for 30 years. Now the doors are open and you're blinded with the light; you cannot really find your way. It takes time to realize what sort of representation we need, who to choose for this very important role—leading the country through this very difficult time.

And people in this stage, in this chaos, are so easily influenced by certain figures or people who are very— you know, politicians. I worry about the influence certain parties, political parties, will have on people—whether we will actually have honest elections. Fraud is a huge issue, because how are we going to control all of this? We don't have the personnel to actually deal with this. I don't think we're ready for a one-vote-per-citizen thing; I think it's still too early. We need to go through the process of electing neighbourhood councils who will elect representatives from them—this way everybody gets to learn something.

ML: Your lives have all changed radically, have been changed, for better or worse, by the Americans and the British, notably, and there's a lot of talk in London and Washington now about whether Tony Blair and George Bush were lying or were misled about the weapons of mass destruction. What are your thoughts about that?

SP: Look, this whole discussion about the weapons of mass destruction and whether Saddam actually had them or not—it is so unimportant for Iraqis! I mean, we're very glad that things have changed. We got rid of Saddam and we have hopes for a much better future. Now, the weapons of mass destruction—that's really the problem of the governments of the U.S. and the U.K. I mean, if these people lied, then they have responsibility toward their people. For us Iraqis, we were never sure whether he actually had them or not, and to tell you the truth, most Iraqis would say, "If he had them, he would have used them." Saddam was crazy enough to do it. So when the U.S. and U.K. troops came in and there were none, Iraqis went, "Okay, he doesn't have them—and we're very glad that he's gone."

⌐

While the Iraqis were trying to sort out their future, Western reporters on the ground in Iraq were telling us about infighting among Iraqis, about problems with foreign agitators, with security. And coalition leaders were saying that progress was being made and the day was just around the corner when they'd be able to hand over the reins to the Iraqis and go home . . . although no one should be in too much of a hurry; the main thing was to do it properly.

On the first anniversary of the invasion, we went in search of other Iraqi civilians to talk to, to see how things looked from their point of view. Hopefully, this would give us a clearer picture of what was happening than we were getting from either the military spokesmen or the reporters, who were mostly confined to the Green Zone in Baghdad. Finding these "ordinary Iraqis" wasn't going to be easy—for one thing, the phones still weren't working very well—so we gave the job to Gord Westmacott.

Gord had come to *As It Happens* about the time that Chechen terrorists were storming a theatre in Moscow, taking hundreds of men, women and children hostage. The drama ended when a Russian SWAT team rushed in and gassed everybody, killing all the hostage takers and also a significant number of the people they were supposed to be rescuing. There were difficulties inherent in calling Russia and talking to people who only spoke Russian (Gord didn't, but our technical producer Sinisa Jolic did, so that helped), and then, if you found someone, trying to persuade them to persuade someone in authority to come to the phone and talk to a Canadian about this big mess, in English. But in spite of all this, Gord got his man, and we scored the first interview with someone who was willing to identify the gas they'd used in the assault.

Now we figured that Gord was the man to land us an assortment of Iraqis (phones or no phones), and he did. In early March 2004, we talked to a female French professor, a medical resident at Al-Mansoor Hospital, an electrical engineer and a senior high school student—all in Baghdad. We also interviewed a plastic surgeon in Basra and a telecommunications engineer in Erbil. The interesting thing is that the thrust of what they were saying—most of them—wasn't so very different from what Salam Pax had told us: life was difficult but getting better, and they were really very glad to be rid of Saddam.

Dr. Ali Fadhl Ali Nadawi, for instance, the medical resident, said that on the whole, conditions in his hospital were much better than before the war—better than they had been for a long time. I asked him about the resistance fighters, and he said, "I don't call them resistance fighters; I call them terrorists. I am Sunni and I did not benefit under Saddam." He added that people did not want the U.S. to leave at that moment.

Dr. Nadawi shared Salam Pax's reservations about a rush to democracy.

"We don't have proper parties," he told us, "or political organizations."

He was afraid that too much haste would only produce a weak democracy, like Turkey's.

Zuhair Dhuwaib, the electrical engineer, informed us that the power grid was delivering power to Baghdad residents for about three hours at a time—three hours on, three hours off. The problems, he said, were mainly inherited from "the old Iraq," the result of poor maintenance and the damage done during the 1991 invasion and the fact that they'd built no new generators for the past 10 to 15 years. But there was sabotage as well; people were taking down the transmission towers in order to get their hands on the conducting metals, which they were selling on the black market. I asked him if people were angry about not having power. Some were, some weren't, he said; it depended on your politics.

"What about elections?" I asked Zuhair.

"Impossible," he said. They had no electoral system, no voters' lists, no knowledge about the workings of democracy. It would be very dangerous, he thought, to have elections too soon. It would also be dangerous if the coalition forces left too early; if they left, there would be massacres. But he was optimistic about the long run.

"I'm sure Iraq will be the greatest country in the Middle East. It's just a matter of time. We have the people, the resources, the culture—everything except luck."

North of Baghdad, in Erbil, our Kurdish telecommunications engineer also felt it would take time to rebuild Iraq as a proper country. Iraq was a complicated place, with many religions and many ethnicities. What had happened in the past 35 years would not be undone overnight, he thought. He wasn't plumping for Kurdish independence, because he believed Iraq's neighbours would find this intolerable, but he did want a good deal of autonomy for Kurds within an Iraqi state. The plastic surgeon in Basra told us it was pretty quiet there at the time. He said they were grateful for British help in getting rid of Saddam, but now they should leave. He hoped the new

Iraq would be a more tolerant place; he was Presbyterian himself.

The most pessimistic readings of the situation came from two women. Quitaf Ahmed, our graduating high school student, told us her life was horrible. She dared not go out in the street for fear of being kidnapped. She said she was tired of war, tired of being scared and not at all grateful to the coalition forces for freeing them of Saddam. She wanted the Americans to leave within six months, just as soon as they had fixed everything they'd damaged. Nor did she think things would be better five years down the road. Quitaf said she was hoping to study dentistry at Baghdad University and had no plans to leave the city, but oddly, if she did leave, the place she wanted to go to was the United States!

Our French professor at Baghdad University was equally unhappy with the security situation. The streets were full of common criminals as well as resistance fighters, she said. After nine o'clock at night, it wasn't safe for even the men to go out. She wasn't sad to see Saddam go—she couldn't imagine ever talking to foreign radio and saying what she thought while Saddam was around, she told us—but good as it was, freedom didn't trump security. She was looking to a strong Iraqi government for relief, the sooner the better.

Five years into the war, the pessimists appear to have more grounds for complaint than ever. When CBC's Gillian Findlay interviewed Zuhair Dhuwaib again on March 19, 2008, the electrical engineer in Baghdad told her that he had become convinced that the President of the United States was doing harm to the Iraqi people on purpose. How could it be otherwise? he thought. The people who had replaced Saddam were 20 times worse than Saddam had been. Five years after the invasion, Dhuwaib had no water, no phone line and power for only one hour a day. The area where he lived was surrounded by barbed wire. His 5 children and 11 grandchildren and his wife had all left the country, and he was alone.

Salam Pax was similarly discouraged when I spoke to him again. There was nothing left of his hopes for a better future in Iraq.

> *You know, I sometimes look at some of the television diaries I did for the BBC and I feel so stupid about them now. How could I be so optimistic? But I believed it. I believed that we could do it. You could see things going wrong, but you just think, this is part of the process. I think I bought the whole package of "This is part of the process."*
>
> *I was mistaken, I was wrong, and it just takes a while to be able to admit it. But I can't watch them [the TV diaries]; they are painfully, stupidly optimistic. It's a pity; they were really exciting times. And now . . . it's just very scary.*

They'd had elections, Salam said, and elected the wrong people. They had a new Constitution and it was terrible. The violence in Baghdad had reached the point where most of his family had been forced to abandon their homes and flee.

And the man who, during our earlier interview, had laughed at the notion of becoming a journalist had been making documentaries for the BBC and was now pursuing a Master's degree in journalism at City University in London. Here's part of the conversation we had on the phone one night:

ML: No work in architecture?

SP: Right after the war, a couple of friends of mine, we thought this is going to be very good for our profession as architects—to rebuild—but nothing was built; nothing happened. The three of us ended up doing things for media.

ML: You also told me that your family was scattered to the four corners of the world.

SP: It actually took us quite long to leave Iraq, I think. Lots of people had given up much earlier. We thought it had to turn at one point and get better. But that moment never came, so about a year ago, we all thought, *It's getting really bad.* . . . And it felt like it was time for everyone to leave.

So I ended up here in this course. My mother is in Jordan; my father is working on several policy consultancies based in Beirut; my brother is working in Dubai—so, absolutely, we're sort of in four corners of the world. Getting everybody together takes a lot of planning now.

ML: Do you miss them?

SP: Actually, I miss not just my parents but everyone, the whole family. It has been a really long time, probably since the second year after the war—the second year after the fall of Saddam—we couldn't really get together anymore. And then people started leaving, and we don't really know when we're ever going to be able to be going back. This whole surge thing—"The situation is calming down"—this is just . . . The numbers might drop, but in reality, peoples' lives are just as bad as ever.

ML: So this surge thing [U.S. troop build-up] is not going to solve the problem, you don't think.

SP: No. I've still got an uncle living in Baghdad, and what's happened, apparently, is that they partitioned the city either with brick walls or they subcontracted the protection of certain districts to local militias, basically, so you end up not really being able to go from one street to the next. Because nobody can move around, whoever's going to plan something, it makes it very difficult for them to move to another district—the car bombers or suicide attacks.

But at the same time, [ordinary] people can't move anymore. . . . If you want to shop somewhere else, it's very difficult to move. If you need to go to a job somewhere else, it's very difficult. . . . So it looks better on paper, but if you live there, it's still bad.

You reach the point—you had all your hopes, you kept denying, kept saying, "No, no, it will be okay"—and you hate to admit you were just naïve or foolish. It takes a while to transmit it to yourself first and then to say, "Okay, it's about all we can take," which is really, really hard.

And you're sort of stuck in the middle of a situation where you think, "So if I say this is bad now, would I want it to be as it was before the war?" And you can't answer this question! Of course, you don't want *that,* but then again, you don't want *this* either.

And I get asked this a lot. It's a very difficult question— almost unfair to ask.

ML: So how is it going to end, do you think? I mean, will the country ever be a country again or will it split into three countries or what's going to happen?

SP: I have no idea. There is absolutely no advance on the political project. The whole idea of the surge was to give Iraqi politicians a chance to do something. Unless there is an Iraqi government that really can start the process moving again, I don't see it getting any better. At the

moment, you hear very little news from the southern
provinces that have been handed back to Iraqis. This is
very worrying, because I think if it were going well, you'd
actually have Iraqi reporters there. If there's nothing, it
means that reporters are really scared to go there. It's
very worrying.

A swamp, a morass, a quagmire. This is Iraq today, except for
the people for whom it's a killing field. Salam Pax is an honest witness, I think, and his words fill me with sadness.

Someone once said that we would be sorry when the Cold
War ended, for then we would see how important the threat
of "mutual assured destruction," or MAD, was as a deterrent
to war. I thought at the time that *they* were mad, but it turns
out they were right. When the fear of nuclear war faded and
no one had to worry that a small war might become a totally
annihilating war, people felt free to go at each other again
with renewed vigour. And so they have—in the Balkans, in
the Caucasus, in Africa. A recent report estimates that over 5
million people have died in Congo in the last ten years as a
result, directly and indirectly, of fighting. If those figures are
accurate, that works out to almost one Rwanda genocide
every single year. In Congo alone.

    Nor have our much-vaunted peacekeepers in the U.N. or
in NATO been very successful at stopping the carnage.
There are seventeen thousand U.N.-sanctioned peacekeepers in Congo as I write, and yet there is fighting. NATO went
into Kosovo to keep ethnic Albanians safe from Serbs, and
now the international force can't leave because they're
needed to keep ethnic Serbs safe from Albanians. Bosnians
are safer now than when they were in the process of breaking

away from Yugoslavia, but international forces are still there, propping up the economy, as well as the peace.

And Canadians are no longer just peacekeepers but also peace-*makers*—a much bloodier business. Our efforts to bring some security to the Kandahar region of Afghanistan claim a few more young lives every week. The Manley Report, commissioned by Prime Minister Harper, recommends that we not give up on the people of Afghanistan, but neither should we press on, it warns, unless Canadian troops can be given better equipment from Ottawa and more troop support from NATO allies. It would be wonderful if their efforts to bring peace and security were rewarded in Afghanistan, but those goals, even if achievable, may be many hard years away.

As for Salam Pax, I hope that he and his family will some day be reunited in Baghdad and enjoy peace and prosperity there. And, of course, I hope he gets to play a part in the bricks-and-mortar rebuilding of his country, too, if that's what he wants. For the moment, however, the world may be more in need of his reporting skills than of his drafting skills—so I wish him success there, too.

EIGHTEEN

Mike the Music Man

Radio with a heart the size of Labrador

⌒

Here's a good example of what can happen when you take someone who cares and get him to tell his story on the radio. Photojournalist Ted Ostrowski called the *As It Happens* offices from Goose Bay, Labrador one day in September 2000 to suggest that we have a chat with a musician who had a story to tell about his encounter with some native children in a village called Sheshatshui (pronounced SHESH-a-shee). Harmonica player Mike Stevens was on his way to play for the Canadian Forces in Bosnia, when the tour stopped in Goose Bay to do a few shows there. But why don't we let Mike tell the story in his own words? We reached him at Canadian Forces Base Alert on Ellesmere Island.

ML: Mr. Stevens, where were you when you learned about the gas-sniffing problem at Sheshatshui?

MS: I'd heard probably a week or two before I left. I started to hear stories about it but didn't really geographically put two and two together about how close I would be to Sheshatshui when we were in Goose Bay, Labrador.

ML: So what did you do then?

MS: Well, when I got to Goose Bay, the first thing I did was I went out and got a local newspaper and it all hit home as to how close we really were to where the problem

was going on, and then it seemed to me that if there was
any way possible that I could do anything and—you
know, not that I could do anything. I didn't know what I
could do, but I thought that in the three concerts that we
did there, I would dedicate "Amazing Grace" to those kids,
because music can speak to you sometimes when words
can't. And even if it could create an awareness in the area
and get people thinking about it—who knows?

ML: Their stories had really tugged your heartstrings,
I guess.

MS: Oh boy, I've never seen anything like this in my life.
I think this will change my life.

    After I played in Goose Bay, a journalist up there came
up and he said, "Well, if you have any time off, I'll take
you up there to play for the kids." That kinda doesn't fit
with the regime, because we're on a tour, but by hook or
by crook, I was going to go. So I got up early in the
morning the next day, and Ted came and picked me up
in his four-by-four and took me out to the Sheshatshui
community.

ML: How long did it take you?

MS: I think it took about 45 minutes to get out there.
And along the way, there were these really incredible
monuments they'd built there—they looked like Catholic
kinds of statues—and Ted explained that these were
places where there were either car crashes or possibly
even a suicide and that kind of thing. And as Ted drove
me through the town of Sheshatshui, there were
monuments up there as well, where—well, at one home
that he pointed out, there was a family of five killed
indirectly as a result of the sniffing. Then he talked about
how there was a kid here who had hung himself and a

kid here who had blown his head off—it was terrible. It was eye opening. I didn't feel like I was in Canada anymore. It just was unbelievable.

ML: And then, once you got into the community itself—what then?

MS: When we got into the community, Ted drove around to look for the sniffers. It was about minus 20 [degrees Celsius]. He drove through the houses to this one area—kind of remote, a bush-like area—and there was a trail leading off the road that was littered with what looked like garbage bags and plastic bags, and the stench of gasoline and fuel was really, really strong. We followed this winding trail back in through the bush, and there were running shoes and there was a shirt here and debris, and the smell of fuel was really, really strong.

And we rounded a corner in the bush, and there was a mattress out in the middle of the bush and kind of a lean-to and a tarp beside it, and there just were bags everywhere.

This was apparently where a lot of the kids would sniff until they'd pass out, and they would spend the night there. And this was minus 20. Kids as young as six years old this was happening to. There were no sniffers there then, so we walked back out, and Ted said, "Would you like to see if you can play at the school?"

So he took me over to the school, and they gave us permission and we ended up doing, I guess it was about three one-hour shows for maybe five or six different grades at the school—and it was wonderful. It was incredible. Eyes lit up and there were just tons of questions, and it was really working. It felt like the music was doing its job; it was just the most perfect thing.

So what I'm going to do is—I have a bunch of harmonicas at home, old ones—and what I'm going to do is mail them all to the school, so they'll be making a lot of racket down there when I get back off this tour.

ML: I'll bet they don't get many live musical shows.

MS: I guess they don't; they're so remote. Now, after we left the school, Ted went on another hunt for the sniffers, and sure enough, we were driving around down by the lake and we turned a corner and right there, in broad daylight, in front of everybody, were a group of about, oh, I would say six or eight of them, probably as young as 8 years old, maybe up to 14 or 15. Ted stopped the truck and he got out first—he knows them—just to go talk to them.

Then I got out and got my harmonicas out. You know, it's so cold that a harmonica generally won't even work in that temperature—they freeze up, the reeds don't work—but for some reason, they worked, and I played music for them. I was actually scared at first, and then after about one song, I realized that I had nothing to be scared about.

ML: Why were you scared?

MS: I was scared because it was a vision that I'd never seen before. I've seen crackheads and I've seen addicts, but I had never in my life seen kids or anybody with bags pasted to their faces like this and holding them up, and drool and filth. I just— I've never seen anything like it. It was way too real.

So when I got there and started to play, the first thing that hit me was the stench of the gasoline or the fuel. It was so strong, and they were so close while I was playing that it actually burnt around my lips and underneath my eyes, and I ended up getting a terrible, pounding headache, which I had for about a day afterwards.

I played and then I started to talk to them. I asked them what it was like, what it felt like, what sniffing the fumes did. By this time, they trusted me enough and were opening up enough that we could talk a little bit about it. I asked them if it made you sick. Did you get dizzy? A couple of kids shook their heads, "Oh no, you don't get dizzy." And someone else said, "Yeah, you do get really, really dizzy."

And I asked another if you get terrible, pounding headaches, because I just wanted to see where they were at, to try and understand it. And they all shook their heads like, "No, no, you never get a headache."

And another fellow who was standing there, who was a sniffer, told me that they do get horrible, horrible headaches, the worst you could ever imagine. It's like, how could anybody have things so bad in their life that they would go through that just as an escape? It was unbelievable.

But after we'd played a while and talked, they started to put the bags down. There was one tune in particular, "Amazing Grace," where they broke out into big smiles and then put the bags down. It seemed to touch them, even for a few seconds. Who knows? But it was just really incredible.

I just hope and pray that there's a way that musicians or artists can find a way to either send them things or get out there and make a difference. Someone going without their hand out or without their agenda, without any strings attached, just to go maybe play music or to show them that you care a little bit, because I really believe it'll make a difference. I mean, even for a second, it *did.*

ML: Just to show that somebody cared.

MS: That's what it was: just showing that somebody cared and knew they were there and knew what they were going through. I've never seen anything like it. I think it'll change my life. I just have a totally different opinion on human rights in Canada now. I'll never feel the same way about it ever again.

ML: Have you got your harmonica?

MS: Yeah, I got a harmonica with me.

ML: Can you play a little bit?

MS: Want me to play a number for you?

ML: Sure.

MS: All right. I'll get the Sergeant to hold the phone here.

Then Mike played "Amazing Grace" for all of us, and there wasn't a dry eye in the house.

Ted Ostrowski told me later that Mike Stevens was the first person he'd met in Labrador who seemed genuinely moved by the plight of these children, who wasn't using them to advance his own causes. He seemed genuinely to want to help. I think that's what moved us, too, when we heard him.

As it turned out, we weren't the only ones who were moved as we learned three years later, when Mike Stevens joined us on stage in the Glenn Gould Studio for our 35th-anniversary show.

We had a stellar lineup that day. Former host Michael Enright joined us again, as did former producers Mark Starowicz and George Jamieson. Pam Wallin, who in 2003 was the Canadian Consul in New York, joined us by phone as did Irish peace broker and Nobel Prize winner John Hume and American radio star Garrison Keillor. We even had a live band with us on stage, led by the great Doug Riley (now the late, great Doug Riley, sadly).

But the guest I was most looking forward to talking to again was Mike Stevens. I wanted to let him know he made a lasting impression on us back in 2000, and was curious about what he'd been up to since. He picked up the story again from Bosnia, where he'd gone after talking to us from Ellesmere Island.

When he got to Bosnia, he phoned his wife to tell her he'd arrived safely, and she told him, "You've got about three hundred emails here. It's all over the news. What's happening?"

What was happening was that people all over the country who had heard Mike's story on the radio wanted to know what they could do to help the children in Sheshatshui. Mike told them that if they had any old musical instruments lying around that they didn't need anymore, they should leave their phone numbers with him and he personally would arrange to come and collect them and he would see that the instruments got to the kids in Sheshatshui. In no time, he had a house full of musical instruments and was planning another trip to Labrador. And this is how ArtsCan Circle was born.

ArtsCan Circle grew like Topsy. Today it sends musical instruments not only to Sheshatshui but also to other native communities—like Natuashish in Labrador, Pikangikum in northern Ontario and Kugluktuk at the mouth of the Coppermine River in western Nunavut. Instruments and performers, too—people like David Anderson and Bruce McGregor (*aka* Magoo) and Mike's musical partner, Raymond McLain. On their first trip to Kugluktuk in January 2006, they took four used guitars, eight *new* guitars, a saxophone, an assortment of percussion instruments, some accordions and a complete 24-track Mackie hard-drive recording system. Magoo says they played music and taught music and juggling and helped the kids dramatize their stories. They also set up the recording gear and taught teachers and community leaders how to use it, hoping it would serve as a way to record Kugluktuk's music, stories and history and also share them with people in the south. The temperature, with wind chill, was a brisk minus 47 degrees, but the reception was very warm.

Naturally, it hasn't all been smooth sailing. Sometimes the instruments are destroyed almost as soon as they show up. At one place, Mike was told that all the instruments he'd delivered had been stolen, but then it turned out that some kids had taken them home from school in order to set up their own band, which was just fine with Mike. That's the kind of thing he was hoping would happen.

During our conversation in the Glenn Gould Studio in November 2003, Mike took a harmonica out of his pocket and gave us another demonstration of his musical virtuosity. Did I mention that he's played the Grand Ole Opry over three hundred times? Let me just take a moment to toot his horn, as it were.

Mike's performing has earned him a pile of honours, including being named Entertainer of the Year for five consecutive years at the Central Canadian Bluegrass Awards. *Country Music News* called him "the best harmonica player in country/bluegrass music today." And if you don't care for bluegrass, he can give you jazz or rock. So I was curious about exactly what kind of stuff he was playing now for the native kids he was calling on. This is what he told us:

> One tune in particular is called Fox Chase. . . . It gets the kids' attention. What I'll do is, I'll load myself up with harmonicas and I'll go out into the bush in the middle of the night in fly-in communities—because I can get the kids at the school but I can't always get the kids who don't go to school, and a lot of times they're in the bush at night—and I play this song.
>
> So, envision what happens when the kids hear it. Basically, when they hear this tune, they come out laughing at me, and I hand them harmonicas and we start talking. I've actually got hugs from these kids who are supposed to be so hard-core.
>
> I'll play the tune.

So he played for us again. This time it was brilliant and very funny. The audience roared their approval, and in my mind I could hear the laughter of hundreds of little kids from Labrador to the western Arctic, and I thought, *Aren't they lucky to have met Mike Stevens? Aren't we all?*

The last time we spoke, Mike was about to leave for another visit to Sheshatshui, and this time he was taking his son Colin with him. They were going to drive all the way from Brights Grove, Ontario (near Sarnia)—a very long car trip, especially when you consider that the last thousand-mile stretch, from Baie Comeau to Goose Bay, is all *gravel*.

"This is something you *want* to do?" I asked.

Yes, he did—and so did Colin. Mike's son had been about seven when the whole Sheshatshui project started. He'd driven around the country with his dad, collecting instruments; he'd sipped tea with the donors and heard their stories; and now Colin was really eager to go to Labrador and share that part of the adventure, too.

I said I wished we could do another interview on the radio, and Mike said that documentary filmmaker Brian White was going on this trip with him, so he hoped the story would be kept alive.

I believe it will.

NINETEEN

It's All about *Ubuntu*

Spirited radio

⌒

O n my very last day at *As It Happens,* November 30, 2005, my producers and co-host presented me—live on air— with a sort of *This Is Your Life* package that they had assembled from bits and pieces of my 35 years in broadcasting—TV and radio. There were clips from my earliest television interviews and some memorable *As It Happens* bits. There were comments and toasts—and a few lies—from former colleagues like Paul Soles and Mark Starowicz. My colleagues had gone so far as to track down the man who'd given me my very first job at the CBC, Rod Holmes. (*Thank you,* Rod.) They'd even cajoled three former prime ministers to record a goodbye; maybe some of the PMs had wished me gone a long time ago, but they were kind enough not to say so.

It was hilarious in some spots, touching in others. To tell you the truth, at times it felt a little like an obituary; I kept pinching myself to make sure I was still alive.

Mike Stevens was there again. And so was Feist.

It's funny how Feist came to be on the show. In the weeks leading up to my departure, I was given carte blanche to interview a few of the people I'd always wanted to talk to but hadn't. So they booked interviews for me with writers David Mitchell and Yann Martel; with Pinchas Zukerman, the violinist and conductor of the National Arts Centre Orchestra in Ottawa; with comedian and actor Bob Newhart. I even got to flirt a bit with Ted Koppel, who happened to be stepping down from his perch at ABC's *Nightline* at around the same time.

Sometime during that last month, producer Sarah Martin asked me about my favourite music. Sarah, by the way, is a megatalented lady: she speaks English, French and *Vietnamese,* and she served as our "fixer" in Vietnam when we took the show there in the year 2000. Sarah used her language skills and her charm to cut some very good deals on hotels there, the same way she charmed former French President Valéry Giscard d'Estaing into appearing on the show—speaking English, too.

Now Sarah and writer Chris Howden—one of the funniest people I've ever met—were sharing the job of organizing and producing my exit. So when Sarah asked me about music, I assumed she was thinking about preparing a few special musical interludes for November 30th. I told her I loved Mozart, Paul Desmond, Gershwin, Piaf and the Beatles. She took some notes and went away.

The next day Sarah came back with her music list and said sweetly, "Excuse me, but are there any musicians you like who are still, um, *alive?*"

Poor Sarah. It came to me then that she was trying to book a Musical Guest for me; she wasn't going to just spin a disk or two. *Ronnie Hawkins would be fun,* I thought, but how would we get a whole band into our little crawl space? Yo-Yo Ma was probably tied up. And that's when I remembered that my son, David, had just given me a CD by a young Canadian singer/songwriter called Feist, and she was *awesome.* I told Sarah. It's a credit to both Sarah and the singer that we did get Leslie Feist into our studio to record some talk and music on such short notice.

As we rolled through my broadcasting career on that November night in 2005, I was hard pressed not to shed a few tears at times. In fact, by the end of the programme, Barbara and I were misty-eyed. Then our handsome young intern Kevin Ball burst into the studio wearing a kilt and playing *Bolero* on the bagpipes, and we turned to laughing again.

Kevin was very sweet and he showed great promise as a producer, but I gather he was a bit reluctant to barge in on us, to say nothing of playing *Bolero*. Mark Ulster told me later they'd had to threaten to never let him work there again if he didn't get into his kilt and perform. Kevin must have wondered at the time if working at *As It Happens* was worth the cost, but he finally agreed. The result was spectacular in every way.

But suddenly, I found myself wondering if *not* working there was what I wanted to do. Was I ready to retire, really?

At times I still wonder. There are days when I miss it a lot— the stories, the laughter, the daily chase, the wit and good nature and even the bad grammar of the producers, sparring with Barbara, watching everyone's kids grow up. There were a *lot* of babies born into the *As It Happens* family in the last few years; I guess those producers weren't working *all* the time, whatever they pretended.

And there's the "unfinished business": the ongoing stories, stories I'd covered for 30 years, some of them, and whose outcomes were still in question. What will happen, I wonder, in the Middle East, in Africa, in China, in the Arctic and the Antarctic, in space? What about Somalia and Zimbabwe, Kosovo and Haiti and Cuba? Will the Americans have a black president? How will Canada fare in the 21st century? Will the Toronto Maple Leafs ever win the Stanley Cup?

What will happen in Darfur?

༄

The first mention I find of Darfur in our logs is April 3, 2004. We spoke that day to Jan Egeland, Undersecretary General for Humanitarian Affairs at the U.N., about the ongoing conflict in Sudan. Nothing surprising there: the Sudanese had been going at each other for decades—north against south. But Mr. Egeland was talking now about fighting in an area we weren't so familiar with, in the west of the country. In Darfur. There was a tragedy unfolding there, he told us, and he hoped the world would become aware of it and maybe do something to keep it from becoming a full-blown disaster.

In other words, we should try to keep it from becoming another Rwanda. In those days, just ten years after the Rwandan genocide, "never again" was a phrase that cropped up again and again in international congresses: *never again* a Srebrenica (the Bosnian massacre); *never again* a Rwanda. Just as, after the Second World War, the world had promised, *never again* another Holocaust.

Not long ago, I came across a story told by a survivor of the Rwandan massacre. He said that on the day that the movie *Schindler's List* was sweeping the Academy Awards in Hollywood, the massacre of more than half a million Rwandan Tutsis was just two weeks away. In other words, at the very moment that the world was solemnly promising never again to permit another genocide, hundreds of thousands of men, women and children were about to be hacked to death in their homes by their neighbours. We did nothing to prevent it.

But who, apart from Canadian General Roméo Dallaire and a handful of others, knew what was going on in Rwanda? Most of us had no inkling until the killing had reached hideous proportions. That was our excuse in Rwanda. I thought we shouldn't have that excuse again, so we kept an

eye on Darfur. When U.N. people or other NGOs sent someone to investigate, we sought them out. When U.N. High
Commissioner for Human Rights Louise Arbour went in to
see what was going on, we interviewed her. We spoke to
Canadian Parliamentarians and members of the Arab
League. I even broke down and interviewed Mia Farrow
about Darfur. I usually avoid movie stars who act like foreign
affairs experts, but Mia did a great job of reporting the misery
she was witnessing.

As It Happens wasn't alone, of course, in trying to draw
attention to this poor, beleaguered region, and today everybody knows where Darfur is. And what's all this attention
done for Darfur? You guessed it. Four years of shedding light
on Darfur have brought countless truces signed and broken,
thousands more rapes and murders, continuing misery for
hundreds of thousands of displaced people and growing fric-
tion between Sudan and all its neighbours. There are seven
thousand peacekeepers there now, many of them under-
equipped and ill-trained and all of them undermined by the
government in Khartoum and its proxies in Darfur. The U.N.
promises seventeen thousand by next year—if Khartoum
agrees.

Barbara Frum wouldn't be surprised. In 1978, when I was
interviewing Frum about her time on *As It Happens,* I had
asked her if there was ever a sense of crusading on her show,
if she'd won any victories for her causes:

*Well, my big victory story happened at the very beginning—
the best thing that ever happened to me. The first story I
ever did was supposed to be an exposé and I was supposed
to be a crusader, and the cause that I went after raised a
third more money the year after I went after them than
they did the year before. It taught me a good lesson about*

journalism: it's a very slow drip on a very big rock and if you get a little too pretentious about what you're doing, you're dooming yourself to all kinds of disappointment.

Darfur has been a steady disappointment. Not that the media coverage has garnered support for the Janjaweed, of course, but neither has it put a dent in their murderous activity. And here's a really scary thought: what if all the media attention has only encouraged the Sudanese rebels to go on fighting a hopeless fight in the mistaken belief that the forces of righteousness—or anyway, NATO and the U.N.—will eventually join the fight on the side of the underdogs, the way they did in Bosnia and Kosovo? What if the media attention has been an *obstacle* in the way of a ceasefire? I don't think that's the case in Darfur, but it's something to be wary of in the way we cover conflict—another reason to feel humble.

In any case, it will be up to other people to tell this story now, as well as all the others. History leads me not to expect much progress on any front very soon. But history is also full of pleasant surprises, like the fall of the Berlin Wall, peace in Northern Ireland and the election of Nelson Mandela as President of South Africa.

It was quite near the beginning of my tenure at *As It Happens* that South Africa's Truth and Reconciliation Commission completed its work and the Commission's head, Anglican Bishop Desmond Tutu, agreed to talk to us about his work there. It had been gruelling, he said, hearing about the particular cases of injustice, cruelty and torture that had been inflicted on black South Africans by their white brothers during the apartheid regime. He felt great compassion for them.

But Tutu said he also felt sorry for the torturers, because they did not emerge unscathed. They were broken men. And it was important to remember that the men who had committed evil acts were not themselves evil, he said; they were capable of redemption. It was this aspect of redemption, Tutu thought, that had persuaded Nelson Mandela to look for a man of the cloth to chair the Truth and Reconciliation hearings.

Bishop Tutu was a great admirer of President Mandela. He marvelled that the former prisoner could have gone through what he had and come out of it a noble man, not a bitter one. But Tutu went on to say that he thought forgiveness was more in keeping with an African's nature than seeking revenge:

> Part of the reason why so many come out in this particular kind of way that we have found so astonishing is that in our African worldview, there is a thing called ubuntu. A person is called ubuntu, and ubuntu is the essence of being human. Ubuntu is compassion, ubuntu is hospitality, ubuntu is warmth, ubuntu is sharing, ubuntu is caring.
>
> And because of our sense that I am because you are, because we say a person is a person through other persons, my humanity is caught up in your humanity. If I want to enhance my humanity, it is by the process of enhancing yours. If I de-humanize you, whether I like it or not, inexorably my humanity is diminished.
>
> And so, in part, it is a form of self-interest, this thing of not wanting to revenge, because revenge, anger, bitterness—all of these are corrosive of ubuntu, of the harmony that is for the summum bonum, the great good. And so, in a sense, I am not paying back to you, I do not

settle scores with you, because the anger is dissipated, and
you become a better person, and in that process, I become
a better person, too.

Ubuntu. The essence of being human. *This is what it*
means to be human. When you get right down to it, isn't that
what all our stories are about? All the ones I've written about
here and all the ones I haven't, the ones we've shared on *As It*
Happens and the ones yet to be told?

This is what I will miss most of all: the chance to speak to
people like Desmond Tutu and to share the conversation
with the rest of the country and the world. The chance to
speak to all kinds of people every day, with all kinds of stories.

But Bishop Tutu would be very familiar with this adage,
too: to everything there is a season. I had a wonderful time
hosting *As It Happens,* and now that season is over. It's a relief
to know that the show is in safe hands, with Carol Off and
Barbara Budd hosting and a splendid production crew. Happily, I can still be a listener, which I was before and which has
always been a rewarding pastime. The conversation will go
on, I hope, for many years to come—the conversation, the
music, the laughs, the goofs, the scoops and the nuts.

Happy 40th anniversary, *As It Happens!* Here's wishing you
40 more.

Acknowledgments

The great fear one has when giving thanks is that at least one important name will be omitted, especially when the debt owed is as large as mine. There are, for instance, the legion of producers, production assistants and technicians whose hard work is reflected in every interview and every story contained in the book, and the interview subjects themselves. Without them, there is no show, nor any book. I've put the producers' credits elsewhere with the list of interviews they produced and which I excerpted for the book. Special thanks are due to: Howard Bernstein, who lured me to radio in 1988, Jeffrey Dworkin, who first planted the idea of hosting *As It Happens* in my mind, Alex Frame, who gave me the job, Linda Groen, who guided me through the first years, and Barbara Budd, who made it fun. I am very grateful to George Jamieson and Mark Ulster for reading the manuscript in its early stages and bringing it more in line with the way things really happened and to John Perry for his help tracking down elusive subjects. Thanks also to Barbara Brown for putting the CBC's resources behind me, and to Ken Puley and Brent Michaluk for giving me room in the radio archives and retrieving all the tapes I wanted to listen to again.

I am grateful to Ariel Rogers and Fogarty's Cove Music for granting me permission to quote from Stan Rogers' song "MacDonnell on the Heights," to the Gourds for granting me permission to use "Rugged Roses," and to Michael H. Goldsen, Inc., for the right to reproduce the first verse of "Moonlight in Vermont," written by Karl Suessdorf and John Blackburn. Kim Bolan's and Salim Jiwa's books on Air India were helpful in reconstructing the events surrounding that tragedy.

Many friends and family members have held my hand when the going got rough and otherwise provided support and occasional escape, and I would like to thank them here, among them Tom Axworthy, George and Brenda Berry, Keith and Aileen Coates, John Coates and Catherine Graham, Sheila Crutchlow, Eva Czigler and Peter Herrndorf, John and Lynn Diamond-Nigh, Matthew Hart, Shira Herzog, Carole McDougall, Colleen Orr, Karen Saunders, Joanne Simpson and Paul Mader, Ruth-Ellen Soles, and Wendy Trueman. Val Ross, even as she was struggling to complete her own book and fighting cancer, was helpful and encouraging to me. Mel Bryan, Philip Lewicki, Craig Lockhart, Renzo Galleno and Lirio Peck kept me fed and watered.

To my dear and supremely literate friends Russ Germain and Joan Donaldson, to Wendy Germain and my son David McDougall, who were also prevailed on to read the work in progress, and whose suggestions I found in every case to be an improvement on what I gave them, my heartfelt thanks. I owe an additional debt to David for all the other kinds of support and diversion he has provided throughout the writing of the book and while I was working on the radio show before that.

It was Cynthia Good who first persuaded me that this book should be written and she has steadfastly guided me through its every phase, giving unlimited encouragement, advice and the necessary connections, up to and including my agent Margaret Hart and my contract with Knopf Canada. I thank Cynthia and thank Margaret for following through.

Thanks, finally, to Louise Dennys, Diane Martin, Sharon Klein, Deirdre Molina, Michelle MacAleese, Brad Martin, Duncan Shields, Scott Richardson and all the good people at Knopf Canada and Random House of Canada for taking a chance on me, for finding in my rough proposal the makings of a book and getting it to market. I am especially grateful to Kathryn Dean for her unflagging attention to detail in the writing. And thanks to Gillian Watts for proofreading.

As always, I must remind readers that any errors or omissions that remain in the text are mine alone.

Above all, many thanks are due to my hugely patient, wise and agreeable editor, Michael Schellenberg. I have always known the importance of good editing on the radio and in television and film, and now I am filled with admiration for the transformative power of a skilled book editor. I am indebted to Michael for his gentle poking and prodding, his judicious cutting and re-arranging, and because he made me believe in this project and kept everything on a positive plane from beginning to end.

As It Happens Interview Credits

Chapter Two
Dame Barbara Cartland   1 September 1997

Chapter Three
Big Cabbage   31 December 1976

Chapter Four
Colin Angus   31 May 2004
Derek Lundy   18 September 1998
David Hempleman-Adams   4 May 1998
Derek Hatfield   10 March 2003

Chapter Six
Greg Kelly   2 December 2002
Neil Morrison   2 December 2002

Chapter Seven
Troy Hurtubise   29 November 2001
10 December 2001

Chapter Eight
King of Redonda   29 May 1998

Chapter Nine
Aaron Naparstek   26 March 2002

Chapter Ten
Elizabeth Jordan   31 May 2002
Mike Brady   2 Jan 2003

Chapter Eleven
Eva Sobolska   19 September 1997
Barbara Budd   1 April 2004
Perrin Beatty   1 April 1999

Chapter Twelve
Don Cherry   13 December 2001
Adrienne Clarkson   22 February 2005
Felix Monserrate   22 October 1998

Chapter Thirteen
Dennis Mills   5 April 2001
Ezra Levant   17 May 2001

Chapter Fourteen
Jeff Greenfield   22 November 2000
Bart Voorsanger   26 October 2001
Jan Hoffman   26 October 2001

Chapter Fifteen
Lata Pada   21 June 2002
16 March 2005

Chapter Sixteen
Sally Edginton   12 January 2000
Mike Rees   17 November 2005

Chapter Seventeen
Salam Pax   3 September 2003
4 February 2004

Chapter Eighteen
Mike Stevens   23 September 2000
18 November 2003

Chapter Nineteen
Desmond Tutu   23 December 1998

As It Happens Producers 1997 to 2005

Laurie Allan
Jennifer Bakody
Kevin Ball
Jaeny Baik
Jet Belgraver
Leith Bishop
Jon Bricker
Barbara Budd
Affan Chowdhry
Marie Clarke
Bob Coates
Anita Elash
Natasha Fatah
Brooke Forbes
Kathleen Goldhar
Datejie Green
Linda Groen

Kent Hoffman
Chris Howden
George Jamieson
Sinisa Jolic
Adam Killick
Lesley Knight
Anna-Liza Kozma
Tim Lorimer
Reuben Maan
Sarah Martin
Alison Masemann
Dara McLeod
Mark Morrison
Neil Morrison
Lynn Munkley
Max Paris
Leslie Peck

John Perry
Meagan Perry
Tina Pittaway
Catherine Porter
Jamie Purdon
Kevin Robertson
Thomas Rose
Neil Sandell
Harry Schachter
David Shannon
Robin Smythe
Ann Sullivan
Mark Ulster
Carlos Van Leeuwen
Talin Vartanian
Gordon Westmacott

MARY LOU FINLAY has had an illustrious thirty-five-year career in broadcasting in TV and radio for the CBC and CTV. She co-hosted *Live It Up* at CTV (1978–1981), and she helped launch the CBC primetime news programme *The Journal* in 1982. In 1988 she moved into radio to host *Sunday Morning*, and from 1997 to 2005, she co-hosted *As It Happens*. Mary Lou lives in Toronto.